# HYPER EDUCATION

# Hyper Education

## WHY GOOD SCHOOLS, GOOD GRADES, AND GOOD BEHAVIOR ARE NOT ENOUGH

Pawan Dhingra

NEW YORK UNIVERSITY PRESS
*New York*

NEW YORK UNIVERSITY PRESS
New York
www.nyupress.org

References to Internet websites (URLs) were accurate at the time of writing. Neither the author nor New York University Press is responsible for URLs that may have expired or changed since the manuscript was prepared.

Material in chapter 3 appeared in Pawan Dhingra, 2018, "What Asian Americans Really Care about When They Care about Education." *Sociological Quarterly*, 59, 2: 301–19. Material in chapter 5 appeared in Pawan Dhingra, 2019, "Achieving More Than Grades: Morality, Race, and Enrichment Education," *American Journal of Cultural Sociology* 7, 3: 275–98.

ISBN: 9781479831142 (hardback)

For Library of Congress Cataloging-in-Publication data, please contact the Library of Congress.

New York University Press books are printed on acid-free paper, and their binding materials are chosen for strength and durability. We strive to use environmentally responsible suppliers and materials to the greatest extent possible in publishing our books.

Manufactured in the United States of America

10 9 8 7 6 5 4 3 2 1

Also available as an ebook

*I dedicate this book to my family, both nuclear and extended. It is with you that I want to continue to live and grow. Thank you.*

# CONTENTS

# Introduction

## *The Growth of Extracurricular Education*

"Your next word is *zubrowka*," the announcer said to Rita, the thirteen-year-old girl standing on stage at the microphone, in front of now empty rows of chairs where other competitors had sat. This was the spelling bee national championship, with children from all over the country, even from abroad. In previous rounds, this same child had knocked out words. This time, though, her eyes were wide open and she looked lost.

"May I have the part of speech?"

"It's a noun."

"May I have the definition?"

"It is a dry, straw-colored Russian liquor that is distilled from rye."

After a few more questions, Rita held her palms together over her nose and mouth and stared down at the floor. Her father, Sunil, sitting in the audience, also stared at the floor. A friend held Rita's mother, Sharmistha, in her arms as they waited. Rita then started in an almost pleading voice, "Zubrowka. Z-U-B-R-O-W-K-A. Zubrowka."

Confetti showered down! Sunil rushed on stage. Sharmistha stood up from her chair but stayed back. Rather than join her daughter on stage, she wiped tears from her eyes. Rita's spelling coach had an enormous grin and gave Sharmistha a hug. The television crew zoomed in on the champion. She received an oversized check for $10,000.

Rita had beaten other highly competitive spellers, all winners in their own right. To make it to the national competition, spellers had to win or place second in one of the regional spelling bees held across the country, such as in Boston, New York City, Chicago, Orlando, Atlanta, Houston, Phoenix, Los Angeles, San Francisco, Seattle, and elsewhere. Families had flown or driven to the finals, mostly paying their own way. An hour after the victory, a dance party was in full force for all the spellers and their families, who were celebrating making it to the finals and letting off some steam.

Yet this is a competition almost no one knows of. It is not the Scripps National Spelling Bee, held annually in late May in Washington, DC, and broadcast live on ESPN. Rita will not make the news rounds, appear on late-night comedy talk shows, or meet the president of the United States, as the Scripps winner often has. Rita won the 2016 South Asian Spelling Bee in New Jersey, a bee constructed by and for South Asian Americans and composed almost exclusively of Indian American children. One must have a parent or grandparent of South Asian origin in order to participate.

Nor is this the only national spelling bee circuit by and for South Asian Americans per se. The North South Foundation (NSF) offers multiple competitions beyond just spelling bees in cities across the country, including math, geography, and more. In my research for this book, I volunteered as a spelling-bee pronouncer for children in grades four through eight for the NSF Boston regional competition held at a local university outside of the city. (There is a separate competition that day for children in grades one through three.) Parents sat in the back of a classroom while around twenty kids sat at desks up front. Two volunteer judges sat at a table in the front of the room, facing the participants and parents. I stood next to them at a podium and read the competition words. I was terrified. I tried to correctly pronounce words I had never heard of; I had prepared in the backstage volunteer classroom by using a pronunciation app on my phone. Parents could challenge results if they thought a word was mispronounced or judged incorrectly. Luckily, no one felt the need to challenge me, but I wouldn't have blamed anyone if they had.

Some had traveled hours just for this regional competition. Parents even petition for their kindergarteners to be eligible to compete despite rules that restrict entrance to first graders.

Some joke that the Scripps National Spelling Bee is practically an Indian-only event (it is the "Indian Super Bowl," according to comedian Hari Kondabolu). Since 1999, Indian Americans have won all but four Scripps bees, and they have won every one since 2008. This follows champions in 1985 and 1988. In the 2017 Scripps bee, thirteen of the fifteen finalists were Indian American, as was the champion, with Indian American champions again in 2018 and 2019. In fact, in 2014, 2015, and 2016, there have been two co-champions, each of Indian descent. The last time there had been co-champions before 2014 was in 1962. Remarkably, in 2019, there were eight co-champions, seven of whom were Indian American. They are "breaking the bee," to quote the title of a documentary on Indian spelling-bee youths. This is despite the fact that for the 2016 match, Scripps made the final round longer and included more challenging words (already nearly impossible to spell for almost everyone) in order to prevent co-champions.[1]

Indian Americans currently are dominating other academic competitions as well. In 2018, Venkat Ranjan, an eighth grader from California, won the National Geographic Bee, becoming the seventh-straight Indian American to win that competition. The 2019 winner was Nihar Janga, who also co-won the Scripps National Spelling Bee in 2016. As BBC News put it, "From 2005 [to 2016], the winning rate of Indian-origin children in [the Scripps National Spelling Bee and the National Geographic Bee] has been well over 80%."[2]

Indian Americans have become the latest and most prominent version of the Asian American "model minority"—that is, a minority group praised for its achievements (most notably in academics), in contrast to popular opinions on African Americans and Latinxs. Along with children (mostly boys) of well-educated Chinese and Korean immigrants, they also dominate math and science competitions. For instance, MATHCOUNTS is a national competition for sixth, seventh, and eighth graders. The finalists and champions routinely are Asian American boys. In the 2016 finals, the top twelve contestants were Asian American boys except for one white boy. In 2017, 2018, and 2019, the results were largely consistent with this trend. Many more math and science competitions—such as the American Mathematics Competitions, Math Kangaroo, Math Olympiads, International Science and Engineering Fair, Regeneron Science Talent Search, United States of America Mathematical Talent Search, and so on—have comparable results.[3]

Nor is extracurricular education limited to competitions. Private learning centers specializing in math have seen tremendous growth in recent years.[4] Well-known options include Kumon, Russian School of Mathematics, Mathnasium, Kaplan, Sylvan, Huntington, JEI, and others. In middle-class and wealthy suburbs across the country, there are also numerous nonchain businesses. Enrollment costs at private centers vary, but $150 a month is standard. Asian Americans are overrepresented, using academic enrichments at a higher rate than other groups, even as they are not solely responsible for this increased popularity.[5] All types of kids attend these classes once or twice a week, much like children attend gymnastics, soccer, or other extracurricular activities.

Private tutoring in general, including learning centers, is expected to become a $260 billion industry by 2024.[6] Conferences on the business of education bring together hundreds of investors, start-up businesses, major politicians, and after-school education leaders.[7] Kumon alone has an annual revenue of about $40 billion as of 2015.[8] As of 2017, nearly three hundred thousand students were studying in one of the almost 1,500 Kumon centers in the United States.[9] The number of Kumon-franchised centers grew 26 percent since 2007, and enrollment grew 59 percent. Mathnasium has over seven hundred locations and joined with the national nonprofit National PTA to promote math education.[10] A smaller but quickly

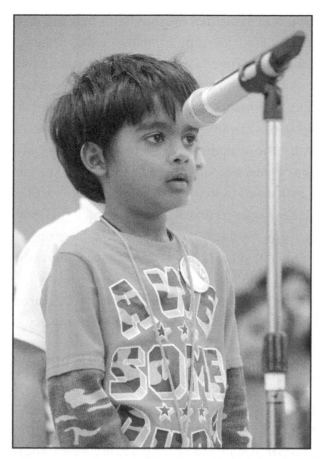

FIGURE I.1. A young speller at the Bay Area's South Asian Spelling Bee regional spelling bee, Milpitas, CA, June 2018. Photo courtesy of Rahul Walia.

growing franchise is the Russian School of Mathematics. Started in Massachusetts in 1997, it has over forty branches across the country, with more than 22,000 students.[11] About 2,500 students attend just one of its locations in an affluent Boston suburb.[12] Online options are growing as well. This is on top of tutoring spaces catering to particular groups, such as Korean Americans' hagwons and Chinese Americans' buxiban spaces.

While it is impossible to know how many children pursue extra-curricular education for academic *enrichment* rather than remedial purposes, it is safe to say that the number is only growing.[13] Kristina, the founder of a math learning franchise, said that her growth plan is to open in neighborhoods with highly ranked schools for families that value education and are willing to pay for more. The Art of Problem Solving, a well-respected online math enrichment center based in San Diego, is expanding its physical footprint to serve more clients. William,[14] the director of a franchised math center in a wealthy Boston suburb where Asian Americans make up the largest minority group, estimated that 30 to 40 percent of his students sought advanced rather than remedial education. Strip malls in cities, suburbs, and exurbs routinely have these learning centers. They even target children not yet in school. For instance, Junior Kumon, which serves three-year-olds, promising to help them learn their numbers and recognize letters, has seen much interest from parents.[15] I saw a child still in diapers getting instruction at a learning center.

## Hyper Education and Its Discontents

With Asian Americans' prominence on the national academic stage and investment in after-school learning, popular media naturally ask why this group achieves so much. Is it because they care about education more than others? Is it because their immigrant parents grew up learning English and/or math so well? Is it because the education system in Asia emphasizes memorization? Is it because of a spelling or math gene? (I will not even entertain this last option.)

Rather than concentrate on why some groups do so well in academic competitions or learning programs, I have a more fundamental question: Why do families pursue enhanced educational options in the first place and with what kinds of implications? Teachers often resent it. Neighboring parents are both impressed and fearful. Children are at the heart of it. And yet we know little about it. This book concentrates on Asian Americans (specifically Indian Americans) to understand those at the cutting edge of this trend and because public media so often associates them with such parenting choices. But these choices are not limited to them and include many white families who also participate. Moreover, the book is oriented toward those interested in this educational and childhood trend more broadly.

These choices by families speak to a new truth in intensive parenting, which I call *hyper education*: the pursuit of enrichment education—whether through academic competitions or learning centers—for very young children, in middle school and often younger, who are already performing at or above their grade or age level and are enrolled in well-resourced schools. I use the term *hyper* education to draw attention to the voluntary nature of this after-school activity meant to make children more academically competitive above and beyond their already strong school curriculums. Participation rarely comes only from the insistence of children themselves.

Other forms of hyper education not studied here are at-home teaching by tutors or parents (not connected to competitions) or online-only classes; I focus on types that take families out of the home, akin to other extracurricular pursuits. While some attention is on ethnic spelling bees, for the most part, the spaces of enrichment education here also are mainstream ones (i.e., franchise math centers and national spelling and math competitions). I do not focus on ethnic after-school programs that cater to immigrant populations.[16]

Importantly, I am not referring to the use of after-school learning intended to help children keep up to grade level or compensate for poorly ranked or underresourced schools. The children in this book attend highly ranked schools, whether public or private. They are doing well in school; none of the children I focus on started extra schooling because they needed help. They are children of highly educated professionals. And they are young, most often in elementary school and age fourteen or younger (and all started these scholastic activities while in elementary school or earlier). There is no immediate credential to attain for the vast majority, such as something to include in their college applications.

So how does paying to spend one's weekends or weeknights to make such children more academically competitive become routine to those involved? How and why do these youths become math and spelling wizards? Despite the growth of extracurricular education, there is generally little information on what families are seeking, much less on enhancement opportunities for such young children.[17]

It is not just out of curiosity that I ask these questions. The growth of these academic pursuits has led to significant pushback. Most other American parents resist these activities, but not because they refuse to invest in their children's activities. Most parents in the United States spend between $100 and $500 a month *per child* on youth sports alone, and about 20 percent spend between $1,000 and over $2,000 a month.[18] Yet even parents who push their children to compete in activities and organize their children's time—a dominant trend in contemporary child-rearing—will often turn away from enrichment education because it rarely fits a child's passion.[19] To them, assigning more academics after school seems authoritarian and indifferent toward children's preferences and fits stereotypes of Asian and Asian American families as using foreign, cultural parenting tactics. Critics cite the reports of Asian American children's stress and their regretting an upbringing of academic intensity as evidence against such choices.[20]

More significant than harming the children engaged in it, hyper education supposedly hurts children not involved as well. Those with the most assets can more easily pay for the classes, tutors, or software for academic competitions on top of their already well-resourced school curriculums. Educational inequality in academic outcomes just worsens between those with more money and those with less.[21]

Even well-off children suffer. Additional education after school by Asian Americans and others raises the bar of what is considered normal in a district, making it harder for other children—mostly whites in these affluent schools—to measure up. The meaning of childhood itself hangs in the balance, with parents who endorse hyper education seemingly ruining it for their own and other children by making them anxious and overly focused on academics.[22] This is over and above the stress that youths already experience in their busy lives.[23] Some middle-class parents actually flee districts with many Asian American professionals.[24] Those who do not flee often begrudgingly enroll their children in math classes, alongside soccer and ballet, in order to keep up with high academic norms, and they blame Asian Americans as a key reason why.[25] Or they launch efforts to "take back childhood" from growing academic intensity in their neighborhoods.[26] Even educators critique hyper education and its "foreign influence" as harmful to children. In an ironic twist, educators deprioritize academics and see school rather than home as a place where youths can be themselves.[27]

Hyper education appears to be a foreign threat not only to families and teachers but to the public-school system more generally. Public schools already are critiqued as failing to adequately teach minorities, rural whites, nonnative English speakers, those with learning disabilities, and undocumented immigrants.[28] Hyper education represents another attack on schools, this time coming from families who should be the most content with their districts, as they are well funded and highly ranked. Instead of being satisfied, these parents seek education outside of the school system. It seems schools please almost no one.

What's more, hyper education arguably erodes the centrality of school in kids' educational lives. Other common extracurricular activities for children are those not commonly taught in elementary school, such as dance, soccer, robotics, chess, and the like. In fact, schools assume youths get exposure to many of these fields outside of school. Kids do not make the middle-school baseball or softball team unless they have played for years in a Little League run by parents. Enrichment education, on the other hand, covers topics central to a school's mission.

## What Is Driving Hyper Education?

Given all that is at stake and the pushback against it, what is driving hyper education? I am not trying to predict who will engage in hyper education and who will not. Instead, I am attempting to understand what is behind the pursuit and its pros and cons. This book concentrates primarily but not exclusively on the academic commitments of many Indian American professionals. It does so with an outward outlook so as to speak to families not involved in hyper education. I am not conflating Indian Americans with other Asian Americans, for meaningful differences exist in terms of histories of immigration, the degree of pan-ethnic identity, religion, and more. But I connect them with other Asian American professionals when applicable, such as in terms of their educational background, parenting practices, and social stereotypes (e.g., the model minority, the forever foreigner, authoritarian parenting style). They are the second-largest foreign-born group in the nation; in 2016, more new immigrants arrived from India than from any other country.[29] While heterogeneous in terms of their socioeconomic class status, educational levels, documentation status, and other factors, many have achieved professionally and academically, ranking among the most highly educated groups in the country.[30]

The best way to understand a key driver of extracurricular education is to concentrate on a group heavily invested in it. Much popular media attention is on Asian American professionals and their children. They are stereotyped as pressuring children for high educational attainment and being overzealous "tiger parents," to use the phrase from the controversial best-selling book *Battle Hymn of the Tiger Mother* by Chinese American author Amy Chua. In addition, the discourse around education has long been racialized, meaning that group members' practices are read as signifying essential racial differences rather than individual choices.[31] In the case of Indian Americans, why they choose after-school education and how others react to this growing trend illuminates how race operates within schools and society at large.

The pursuit of enrichment academics is not limited to Indian Americans or other Asian Americans.[32] I have studied white American families who participate in advanced education so as to broaden the understanding of this trend and reach beyond one ethnic group. With family sizes shrinking in recent decades, parents spend more time and money on their children.[33] Middle- and upper-class parents increasingly are pursuing extracurricular education for their young children as another form of organized activity, along with Girl Scouts, lacrosse, and so on.[34] "Hothousing"—that is, giving preschool children academic and cultural training well before standard exposure—has become a trend among affluent families seeking a competitive edge.[35] Kristina, the founder of a math learning franchise, told me that whites can be the main group engaged in advanced academics in certain locations. Some whites even join Korean or Chinese ethnic cram schools.[36]

*Hyper Education* concerns the overarching issue of how we should make sense of middle- and upper-middle-class families' participation in learning centers and academic competitions for their young children and what the implications are. Three main questions animate this topic: First, what do hyper education and public reactions to it signify in regards to childhood, education, and race? This discussion is based on conversations and time spent with educators inside and outside of the public-school system as well as changes in education policy and rhetoric in recent years. Second, what motivates Indian American and white parents' involvement in hyper education? This discussion is informed by conversations with parents. Lastly, how do children understand their participation and handle the reputation, often stigmatized, of being so academically minded? This is based on being with and talking with children engaged in advanced education to a significant degree.

I have talked with educators (both teachers and administrators) in public schools and private organizations, including admissions officers of highly selective universities, to understand their take on hyper education. (More detail on the research design can be found in the appendix.) In addition, I have talked and spent time both one-on-one and in groups with Indian immigrant parents from South and North India (often those working in the IT industry and arriving through work or family visas) engaged in hyper education. All families had at least one child in the elementary or middle school grades (below grade nine). I also have interviewed and spent time one-on-one with white families raised in the United States who were in professional occupations and had children enrolled in private math centers, a few of whom also participated in math competitions. Whites by far were the most typical group, alongside Asian Americans, who pursued enrichment education in these sites, whereas very few African Americans or Latinxs did so. A few interviews were conducted with African American, Chinese American, and Eastern European / Russian families. I spoke with Indian American and white children as well, including former Scripps spelling bee top-ten finalists and champions (some now adults), and had other informal conversations with youths.

From 2010 to 2017, I attended spelling bee competitions (both South Asian–centric and Scripps, including spending weekends with South Asian American families at finals competitions), a MATHCOUNTS national competition for middle-school students, Boston-area locations of nationally franchised math learning centers, independent math programs, receptions for spelling bee finalists in New York City, community meetings, learning center events, and other related settings. I also spent time in families' homes, observing daily engagements and study practices. Beyond observing, I volunteered at bees, guided children to their competitions, assisted with setup and takedown, and more. I enjoyed breakfasts, lunches, tea, drinks, and dinners with families.

While I studied this topic thoroughly, I am not removed from it personally. When I was waist-deep in this research, I had two children in an elementary school with a fine academic reputation in the Boston area. Like others in my neighborhood, our family struggled with how to balance the boys' free time with their organized time. At different points, they participated in Little League baseball, soccer, basketball, karate, swimming, piano, and drumming. And they took part in extracurricular math at a local learning center even though they were doing just fine in math class. My wife and I—both Indian Americans—enrolled them in the program because it offered a version of math not taught in school. While one of my kids somewhat enjoyed it, the other all but hated it. We pulled both kids out after a short while, satisfied that they had sufficient exposure to the program and not wanting to inadvertently turn them off of math by forcing too much of it. After learning more about South Asian spelling bees, I asked my kids if they wanted to participate in one, since they were ethnically eligible. It was a firm "No!" Needless to say, we never pursued it. I share this to say that I can speak to a motivation to participate in hyper education and a motivation not to. I have heard concerns raised by supporters and critics.

## What's in Store

*Hyper Education* unfolds across three parts, each addressing one of the main questions of the book. Part 1 explains hyper education as an institutional practice—namely, what is at stake for public education with the rise of such trends from the point of view of teachers and administrators and relative to broader trends in education. I first elucidate the reactions, often critical, of on-the-ground educators and white parents to Asian Americans' pursuit of after-school academics, which is thought of as a foreign cultural practice that causes anxiety. The solution of local schools is to have Asian immigrant parents assimilate into American liberal parenting norms, which will supposedly dampen their emphasis on academics and reduce the education arms race. Yet what becomes clear is that local teachers' and parents' investment in white privilege also guides their critiques of Asian Americans' choices. The reactions reveal that the school systems racialize Asian Americans alongside other minority families in defense of a white privilege rather than fully consider their own roles in student problems.

Despite hyper education being read as a culturally foreign practice by teachers and local parents, it is actually in line with current educational norms. Under recent federal reforms, public education has become more rational and rule driven, with greater reliance on standardized assessments and test-taking. It also utilizes the private marketplace more and more. School effectiveness is routinely criticized by politicians, pundits, and nonprofit agencies (e.g., the Bill and Melinda Gates Foundation). Learning centers and academic competitions fit into and are supported by these institutional reforms rather than being a foreign practice. So there is a clear divide between institutional educational trends, which hyper education suits, and local school preferences. Hyper education is an increasingly normal part of the education system despite resistance at the local school level.

Part 2 takes on the perspective of parents, both Indians and white, to understand what motivates their use of extracurricular education. Contrary to popular and academic assumptions, immigrant parents' main interest is not academics per se. Instead, Indian American parents care first and foremost about outcompeting others. Education is deemed by them as the most appropriate avenue through which to stand out, as shaped by their ethnic and racial experiences. The parents demonstrate what I call an "Asian American style of concerted cultivation" to help ensure their children get into college and secure future job prospects. *Concerted cultivation* refers to the commonplace parenting of young children through extracurricular activities, robust conversation, and significant attention in order for children to have fun and develop character traits such as discipline, perseverance, and self-confidence (i.e., develop cultural capital).[37] All kinds of parents believe such development will help kids in their school and future workplaces. Asian Americans go about this in their own way with an emphasis on after-school scholastics. They believe the typical approach to concerted cultivation taken by their white neighbors—of caring about school but finding a child's passion in nonacademic after-school options (e.g., sports, drama)—will not lead to success. So even as hyper education suits contemporary education and parenting norms more generally, parents' motivations are to resist an assimilation into standard pathways for achievement.

Unexpectedly, Indian American parents also articulate moral reasons for hyper education beyond its strategic use. It is part of a cultural package that helps raise "proper" girls and boys who avoid sex, violence, drugs, and complacency. So while educators worry about the negative emotional and social effects of pursuing extra academics, parents often have the opposite point of view. Much more than simply keeping kids too busy to make bad choices, parents believe more education can help prevent their children from assimilating into problematic "American" norms. Ironically, the norms they want to avoid are those of white upper-middle-class professionals—the group that immigrants supposedly feel comfortable, even fortunate, to connect with. Whites are stereotyped in ways akin to African Americans.

Instead of these motivations being unique to Indian immigrants, white parents engaged in hyper education share many of them. As for Indian Americans, often it is a concerted cultivation practice for whites—that is, something children hopefully will enjoy rather than something that is forced on them against their will. Moreover, these white US-born parents see hyper education as a moral choice as well. They happily align with immigrants and against other whites of their same privileged class status through their use of supplemental academics. Racial assumptions inform these families' decisions. In other words, the motivations for hyper education are much deeper and multifaceted than assumed.

The final section, part 3, turns to the children. For those who have followed the public rise of Indian Americans in the spelling bee, it is no surprise to hear that they have been ridiculed in social media. I explain why such attacks can be so meaningful and elaborate on the familial and social dimension for youths who engage in academic competitions, often spelling bees. Their preparation is a family affair. While oftentimes youths find the studying to be a chore, they enjoy the benefits of their labor and make friends with peers engaged in like-minded pursuits. As such, they maintain a motivation to achieve.

This cohesive portrait of youths in academic competitions contrasts sharply with how they are framed in the media. Beyond social media, even mainstream media treats them as novelties to be figured out because of how unique they are. Within their schools, youths receive more support than mockery, but they still can be marked as deviant. Given the contrast between the support and enthusiasm they receive in the private realm and the varied reactions in the public realm, youths can experience an identity conflict of sorts. They handle it in various ways, such as by comparing their "brain sport" of spelling bees to athletic sports, but it is difficult to fully overcome all the challenges they face.

I hope to elaborate on what is at stake with hyper education, both the practice of it and its consequences. Families and educators who are tempted to push back on this trend are better served by understanding the motivations behind it and their own reasons for resenting it so as to create allies in their efforts to curtail its growth. Indian Americans and other families should recognize the unintended consequences of hyper education, even as it often feels necessary, so as to better serve their children, who are the key actors in this dynamic. Educational equity should remain the goal, and hyper education should be understood and evaluated within that mission.

# PART I

# Good Schools

# 1

## "Overprogrammed Families"

A few years ago, I taught elementary health for third graders. I asked them to share three things that cause them
stress. The top things they wrote were "Am I going to get
into a good college, am I going to do well in the SAT, [and]
am I going to do well on [the state standardized test]?"[1]
This is third grade!

Mary is a prevention specialist for a well-ranked suburban Boston
public school district. A tall, slender, middle-aged white woman with
three daughters who graduated from this district, she met me at the
entrance of the high school on a late-spring day in 2016 and escorted
me to her office. I was there to talk to her about the mental and
social well-being of students given the high academic standards in
the school and the enrichment education practiced by families in
the area, as evidenced by four after-school math learning centers
in that town. She has her finger on the pulse of students' problems.
As we walked out of one building and into another toward her office,
a few of the students passing us by said hello. She takes pride in
knowing the students. She serves the whole school district and its
two-thousand-plus student body, which includes a high school, two
middle schools, and six elementary schools. She also leads the district's efforts around healthy decision-making regarding alcohol,
other drugs, food, sex, and risk-prevention practices. But stress
reduction is a main emphasis. No longer reserved for high-school
students, stress reaches down to elementary school. For the fifth
graders in the district, Mary said,

I do mindfulness activities with them. I have two hours with each fifth grade in a school year. We do brain break activities. We do a minute or two of meditation.

Fifth graders apparently require a break from their mental taxation and need to learn self-care tactics.

The fact that she is referring to stress among elementary-school children is indicative of the significant preprofessionalism that permeates upper-middle-class school districts across the country, both academically and in extracurricular activities. The increased pressure contributes to mental health concerns for students well before high school.[2] As quoted in the *New York Times* in 2016,

> "I'm talking about 5-, 6-, 7-year-olds who are coming in with [migraine headaches and ulcers]. We never used to see that," says Lawrence Rosen, a New Jersey pediatrician who works with pediatric associations nationally. "I'm hearing this from my colleagues everywhere."[3]

Similarly, as reported in *Newsweek* back in 2006 in Colorado,

> Some scholars and policymakers see clear downsides to all this pressure. Around third grade, Hultgren [the principal of an elementary school in Boulder County, Colorado] says, some of the most highly pressured learners sometimes "burn out. They began to resist. They didn't want to go along with the program anymore."[4]

Jane, a retired health specialist responsible for health education in the same school district as Mary, lamented,

> I worked mostly at the high school, and kids there are falling apart left and right. The numbers of students with anxiety and anxiety-related disorders—I mean, I don't know if anybody's been keep-

ing track of the numbers, but it's pretty high. I just know from the [number of] students who end up getting hospitalized because of suicidal behaviors or self-harm or substance use have been increasing. . . . It breaks my heart because, as a health teacher, our offices were like a safe space. And when kids were freaking out or breaking down, they'd come to us. And there were so many times kids would show up at the door in tears. "I just can't handle it. I can't cope."

While stressed-out third graders are alarming, the tension ratchets up so much during high school that educators worry their students feel they are in a life-or-death situation.

Stress and self-harm are often linked for middle- and high-school students, and more recently they result from troubles not only with parents, peer pressure, and the like but also from academics.[5] Teens across the country report even higher levels of stress than adults during the school year, with fatigue and skipping meals not uncommon.[6] Hospitalization due to anxiety and depression is increasing.[7] Beyond the psychological effects of so-called helicopter parenting and constant supervision by parents, middle-school students worry about testing and future academic success.[8] In a Boston suburb, one in fourteen middle-school students had tried to commit suicide according to a 2018 self-study. In 2014, another affluent school district in the Boston area experienced three teen suicides, a cluster number recently shared by other high-performing school districts in other parts of the country. In another suburb, 95 percent of high-school students identified as heavily stressed over their academics; 15 percent considered killing themselves in the past year, including 17 percent of Asian Americans.[9] Middle schools in California are treating youths for stress and anxiety by bringing in canines to pet and speak to; they also organize "primal screams" to relieve stress if yelling feels more therapeutic.[10]

## Academic Bullying

"The Asian families are not alone but are more extreme" in their educational practices for their children, Mary said. Her school district is over 30 percent Asian American, mostly children of Chinese, Indian, and Korean immigrants, often professionals. As more and more Asian American children outperform other students, she sees a ripple effect:

> [In] our Asian American community in particular, I have students saying that anything below an A is unacceptable. . . . [This pressure] impacts all the students; it sure does. In a couple of years, Asians are expected to be 40 to 50 percent of the student body. . . . A pressure is expected to keep up with the Asian students. . . . [White and non-white] kids report academic bullying: the idea that if you're not taking [advanced placement] classes or getting As in all your classes, you are not worthy or not going to get into a good college. When you talk with groups of students and you say something like academic bullying, they say that's what it feels like.

As Asian American students excel in certain subjects, they are thought to block other students' opportunities, such as in advanced placement (AP) classes.[11] Given how focused they are on exams and essays, they raise the stress levels of other students. They are a key ingredient in causing the stress epidemic in the school districts in which they reside, according to educators. The result is that other students, mostly white students in these districts, feel outperformed academically and bullied emotionally.

Rachel, an elementary school principal, echoed the concerns at stake with hyper education in her suburban Boston school:

> I would speculate that probably three-quarters of the students who fall into those [Asian American] cultural categories are doing some-

thing [academic] beyond the school day. It's a lot. . . . Teachers have observed groups of Asian students, who are very capable students, who kind of flaunt their academic strengths in front of their classmates. So they make other kids feel bad, because they're brighter, more capable, and they do more, and they can do it faster. I mean, the kids who were particularly nasty to their classmates are a group of boys.

Here, ironically, academic excellence is criticized by an elementary school principal of all people, as it comes with negative emotional consequences for those not achieving as much, with gender differences in how it's articulated. Asian Americans, known to be bullied by peers within schools,[12] are now labeled the aggressors. White students often refer to academic pressure coming from other students, not from their parents, and Asian American students supposedly cause these self-doubts when they are present in large numbers.[13] A math coach who brought a team of excellent students to a MATHCOUNTS competition in Washington, DC, for middle schoolers, said to me that his team, with no Asian Americans, could not effectively compete there. "My job is to reinflate their egos," he sighed. Even high-achieving students get beaten up by Asian Americans, it seems.

I spoke with Melissa, a white elementary school principal in another well-off Boston suburb whose school ranking had been moving upward in the past five years and whose number of Asian American students had similarly grown recently. With that presence has come more debate on student homework, with her sense that Asian Americans wanted more of it. She had a firm belief:

I don't think more homework for elementary-age students makes sense. They need time to play. My own [elementary- and middle-school-age] kids don't want to do homework, and it's a struggle. Some [Asian Americans] are doing more work after school. But we don't want to have more homework from the school.

School principals worry about the effects of Asian Americans on other children's "time to play."

Perceptions of Asian American students hurting others academically and emotionally were not limited to school officials. I first met Sally—a white mother of two children in public elementary and middle school in an affluent Boston suburb—at a community forum on Asian Americans and stress. We later sat in her spacious living room as we discussed her concerns about the school district. She has a self-described "relaxed" attitude toward academics and wants her children to do their best in school and enjoy their childhood, nothing more. Yet her daughter experiences anxiety over not performing well enough in school, one with a sizeable minority of well-educated Asian Americans, despite her parents' laid-back philosophy. Sally believed the culture of extreme high achievement came from "overzealous parenting and an administration that, at the highest level, is getting overly caught up in the 'prestige' of the district's national and international reputation." She and her husband feel that they are "having to swim against a tide that is becoming too difficult to navigate" and that their preferences are in "contrast with the growing norms." What are these growing norms, and who is to blame? She answered,

> High-stakes testing; overzealous parents; overprogrammed families; and an infusion of diverse cultural norms, some of which seemingly place academic excellence, as marked by achievement, above all else.

Sally greatly appreciates the racial and ethnic diversity in her town and believes in public education, but she regrets the increasingly advanced curriculum that attracts "overzealous" parents to her neighborhood schools. She specifically blames the "diverse cultural norms" of immigrant parents who are "overprogrammed" and prioritize academics above all else for causing stress in her own family, as echoed by white parents in other districts with Asian American professionals.[14]

Teachers and parents were more agreeable with participation in learning centers or competitions if it seemed a minor time commitment and clearly enjoyable to those youths. But because academics is rarely fun, extracurricular schooling (beyond remedial purposes) not only does not come to mind to most parents, but such a choice is critiqued as improper relative to opportunities that nurture kids' cultural and physical development.[15] Even parents who push their children to compete in activities and organize their children's time—a dominant trend in contemporary child-rearing—are turned off by enrichment education for similar reasons.[16]

A "white flight" from suburbs with high concentrations of high-achieving Asian Americans results. The *Wall Street Journal* documented this trend in 2005 for districts in Silicon Valley.[17] Sally shared,

> We watch peer after peer elect to remove their children from the [public school] system *not* because it falls short academically but because of concerns that going through the [school system] may ultimately undermine their children's emotional well-being.

Because academics is rarely fun, extracurricular schooling (beyond remedial purposes) not only does not occur to most parents, but such a choice is critiqued as improper relative to opportunities that nurture kids' cultural and physical development.[18] Even parents who push their children to compete in activities and organize their children's time—a dominant trend in contemporary child-rearing— are turned off by enrichment education for similar reasons.[19] Private schools (and possibly homeschooling) become an option for those wanting *less* intense academics than in districts with many Asian Americans.

The other tactic to prevent academic bullying was to keep up academically, often to parents' irritation. Tanya—a white US-born, upper-middle-class mother living in Boston—explained her and her husband's open-minded philosophy of what they would like for their third-grade daughter, Mimi:

> I think that it's totally fine if you really want to be—I don't know what—if you want to be a dog walker in life or whatever, that's fine. . . . I was quite intentional about [enrolling her in the math center]. . . . The reality is, you know, we have competition [here] from Asian countries and . . . different parts of the world that are just stronger in education. [Competition] for colleges, for jobs, for everything. I want my daughter to be prepared to compete in whatever she wants to do. . . . It's a different world to even when I grew up, . . . [where] you go home or you go to the pond or go skating in the afternoons. That's great too. It's just not our reality.

Mimi did not take extra math because she had trouble with the subject. "She's not bad at math, not at all," her mother said. Even parents who are fine with their children growing up to be a proverbial dog walker feel the need to enroll them in after-school learning, and they blame Asian immigration in particular and globalization more generally for their kids not having a relaxed childhood.

## Asian American Children as Victims

Rachel, the elementary-school principal whose school had about a third of Asian American students, expressed her concern for them:

> They're exhausted. They're not finishing homework from school. They are unhappy. They talk about it. They write about it. They have social issues, and then when you probe a little deeper, [you realize that] they're stressed. It's not a large percent [of the whole student body], but it's clearly a minority, so it's centered around the Asian community. They're reacting to this overscheduling, multiactivity life-

style, a sense of one instrument isn't enough; they have to take two, and Chinese school, and Chinese math, and the homework from here. And so they're unhappy. And if you see a seven- or eight- or nine- or ten-year-old who feels that weighted down, that's very disturbing. . . . I think the boys may take it on, not like it, but just do it, for the most part. The girls will complain about it and be stressed by it and wish that they had more opportunities to participate in choosing the activities.

Good schools should be enough for these youths, and the fact that parents sought more academics created social and emotional problems for everyone.

Betty, a third-grade teacher, reflected on Asian American children's mental and physical health as we talked in her classroom one morning:

I see third graders who think they're not good at something when they're perfectly fine at something. And it bothers them. I see kids who have a hard time verbalizing their ideas because they're worried. There's a lot of stress. . . . This is my twentieth year. So there's so much anxiety. And I don't know where it's coming from.

When I asked her for examples of the stress, she stated,

Not talking. Being almost nonverbal. Overreacting to a small problem. A lot of times I hear about it happening at home. So they hold it together in school. And then I hear about not sleeping, things like that. There are always a couple of kids who are always late. Yeah, kids at the end of the day who are dragging. I don't see it as a prevalent problem.

While not prevalent, this exhaustion happened often enough in her classroom to strike her as a new trend after twenty years of teaching. Asian Americans who perform just fine in school doubt their

FIGURE 1.1. Youth take a written test at a North South Foundation regional competition, Barrington, Illinois, March 2016. Courtesy of North South Foundation.

abilities relative to other Asian Americans—known as the Asian American paradox[20]—and this happens before age ten. Betty could read the stress on their bodies.

The negative implications of hyper education afflicted even kindergarteners. A former kindergarten teacher in the same school as Betty, Alexa spoke of stress at length when I asked her if she sees problems among Asian American students compared to others:

> The stress. Kindergarten stress—the crying, constant. I mean, if you have a full-day kinder, then after the full-day kinder, you do swimming, you do math, you do piano—[and] this is like [for] a five-year-old. And then after all that, you have to make time for reading. I think the issue is that we're pushing them above and beyond, and not every child is ready for that.

The sense that Asian Americans carry more anxiety is not simply anecdotal. One cannot deny that many Asian American youths are under significant academic stress and do not often share their emotional states.[21] Asian American college students, for instance, are more likely than white college students to have considered and attempted suicide, even as their suicide rates are lower than the national average.[22] The pressure to live up to parental expectations as well as the model minority stereotype cause anxiety for Asian American youths.[23] Asian Americans in Mary's school district report troubling trends, second only in level of concern to the LGBTQ student body (some of whom are also Asian American). Mary elaborated based on a survey in her school district adapted from the Centers for Disease Control and Prevention Youth Risk Behavior Survey:

> [In general] our most concerning population are students who identify as homosexual or transgender. They are our most vulnerable population. For all that we do to educate and provide awareness, they are the highest in terms of self-reporting [of risky behaviors]. Asian Americans are second when we break it out. [They exhibit] cutting, pills, alcohol [use]. All of our numbers have gone down, but alcohol and marijuana still remain. Depression. Anxiety. Eating disorders have gone down a lot due to health education. Females seem to have a bit more. . . . [The] Youth Risk Behavior Survey shows a correlation between extreme stress and risky behaviors, like alcohol [use], eating disorders, suicidal thoughts. The number one reason kids report for doing drugs went from peer pressure to stress.

Beyond the psychological and physical tolls, educators like Jane worried that youths in extracurricular academics could stop caring about learning in general:

> The thing that breaks my heart—because I'm an educator, I love to learn—is when I talked to high-school students about what do you like about school. [They] respond, "Nothing. I hate it." The only thing they like is the socializing with their friends. They don't see the value to [school]. The other thing that has come out of these conversations is there's a lot of cheating that goes on in order to do well.

Academic training can cause burnout for youths and a lack of interest in school lessons.[24] Also, students can come to treat school as a game to win; cheating makes sense from this lens.[25]

Hyper education causes other pedagogical problems for those enrolled. Michael, a middle-school math teacher in an affluent Boston suburb, believed that such youths benefited less from classroom learning:

> Those who are enrolled in [learning centers] do more posturing in class. Their attitude at first is "I know this." Then I tell them I want you to think about this concept differently. We talk about the context of it, go deeper. I'll tell you, the other students get more out of class.

He had to treat those enrolled in learning centers differently so as to keep up their interest in class while not isolating them from others. Tom, a middle-school math teacher, said,

> As a teacher, our problem [with math after-school centers] is that the kids have gone ahead, but they have gone ahead from a memorization point of view. I'll ask them to use what they have learned to solve a problem, and they'll have no idea what to do. . . . There is so much rote learning, memorizing formulas.

Other educators echoed the point that public-school systems provide deeper, more thoughtful, well-researched means of teaching math, writing, and other subjects than are offered in learning centers.

Franklin, an admissions officer at a prestigious private university, criticized the push toward academic competitions and learning centers from a different angle:

> I see [competitions and learning centers] as a problem when people are using it instrumentally, as something that they think will get

them into college or make them better than it appears. And I see it as problematic both because I think (a), it's emotionally toxic, and (b) it's unlikely to work. [*Laughs*] . . . Authenticity [matters]. I would define authenticity as something strategically nonstrategic, un-self-conscious action, where I would say, "Would you be doing this even if nobody was making you do it? And even if it had no impact on your college chances?"

Children without perceived authenticity are handicapped in the exact professional goals they seek. Jane commented on the costs of not developing adequate thinking and work skills:

A lot of businesses and corporations say they are looking for people who can work collaboratively, people who can think outside of the box, people who have cultural proficiency. So the skills that these [Asian] parents are talking about don't necessarily translate into what people are looking for after college.

Teachers noted their own challenges stemming from having students engaged in hyper education. As Michael suggested,

It is harder on teachers to have kids do extra math [in a learning center]. Students have different abilities. Some have taken the course in advance.

Alexa, now a second-grade teacher, expressed her frustrations through an example from a recent class:

Yesterday we were working with money and time. So there was one group working on just identifying the hour, because they still get confused, you know, with the minutes. And then I had another group doing elapsed time, which is a very hard scale. I had to read it to them three times. And then you had the other ones who just had coins, and they were counting the coins and identifying them. So you try that every single day, and that's what I do. I think if parents come one day, they would go, "Those teachers deserve a medal! How do they do it every day?" And we do.

Teachers felt that by seeking out more academics, parents inadvertently minimized the schools' accomplishments—a reaction far removed from giving them medals.[26]

Rachel tried to be sympathetic toward the use of enrichment education but could not fully get on board with it.

You're going to move [to this suburb] and know that the schools are fine, and I don't mean just fine—I mean great. But there's no guarantee, even with those really wonderful schools, that your child is going to have all the opportunities open to him or her in the future. And given that you've got this extra set of activities that you could avail yourself of, how can you not do that too? [There is a] generalized anxiety. . . . I think we live here in a place where there are so many other wonderful [nonacademic] opportunities for children to participate in after school that I'm not sure I would make academic the focus. . . . If a family asked me, I would say that [after-school education] doesn't make sense to me.

Anxiety among middle-class and even wealthy families makes sense at times of economic uncertainty, such as during the Great Recession starting in 2007.[27] But still, hyper education was a mistake in her eyes.

Regardless of sympathy toward Asian Americans, the effect is the same. Asian American children's and other children's well-being are under threat because of an overemphasis on educational excellence without a clear payoff for college admissions or a commitment to learning.

## Racial Assumptions

Anxiety and workload are the surface concerns of educators and white parents. Embedded in their criticism of hyper education is the reinforcement of a white normativity in the school system—that is, the notion that white students' interests, approach to education, and levels of attainment are normal and should be the standard by which others are held. Immigrants do not mimic whites because, according to educators, immigrants parent in stereotypical and problematic ways. I am not suggesting that reproducing white normalcy is the "real" motivation of educators' critique of hyper education or that they are racist. Their concerns around stress are real and heartfelt. Yet any efforts to address the problems articulated above must recognize that educators rely on stereotypical assumptions of Asian Americans and a sense that white students act in "appropriate" ways. This leads them to downplay schools' culpability in student stress when Asian Americans are present and to possibly misjudge Asian American homes.

Jane, the retired health specialist, referred to Asian Americans as culturally prone to focus on education:

> You have a confluence of things happening in this country, of people coming into the country—some of them for the education specifically—coming with their cultural perspective of what they think is appropriate and how things should be, putting pressure onto school districts.

Teachers often carry racial assumptions about minority groups.[28] Educators do not simply refer to Asian Americans as acting in a particular way (e.g., studying a lot) or as responding to their financial conditions; they assign that behavior to a supposedly ingrained "cultural perspective" that fits long-standing stereotypes of Asian Americans as too focused and competitive.[29]

I spoke with Max, a director of a challenging and respected math center, at length in person a couple of times and on the phone. He gave a few reasons for why Asian Americans are overrepresented in his program:

> And then another part of that story is twenty to twenty-five years of immigration of very high ability people in math and science. And you're talking about people who came here from much poorer countries and were able to come here because they're good at math and science. And obviously, they're going to pass on both genes and culture to their children. One, it's the genetic component. These people [from Asia who are able to immigrate] got through the [immigration law] filter. They married each other and had children. And then the second is cultural. These two [parents] escaped dire poverty because of this thing [education], and that's why we're going to take their kid to a special math program in second grade or third grade and start investing.

While he *credits* Asian Americans for their pursuit of enhanced education, as it is good for business, most others *blame* them.

The fact that educators consider Asian Americans to be culturally, even genetically, prone to care only about education fits racial portrayals of the group in recent decades. This academic priority has been applauded at times. News stories from the 1970s to the 2000s portray Asian Americans as "whiz kids."[30] After explaining the accomplishments of diverse Asian American groups, *Time* magazine's 1987 cover story on Asian American achievement went on to offer explanations as to why:

> One claim is that Asians are simply smarter than other groups. . . . Most researchers are unconvinced by the natural-superiority argument. But, many do believe there is something in Asian culture that

breeds success, perhaps Confucian ideals that stress family values and emphasize education. . . . All this would appear to be another success story for the American dream, an example of the continuing immigrant urge to succeed and of the nation's ability to thrive on the dynamism of its new citizens. . . . The performance of Asian Americans also triggers resentment and tension. "Anti-Asian activity in the form of violence, vandalism, harassment and intimidation continues to occur across the nation," the U.S. Civil Rights Commission declared last year. The situation can be particularly rough in inner-city schools. Young immigrant Asians complain that they are called "Chink" or "Chop Suey" and are constantly threatened.[51]

In this view, Asian Americans—here referred to simply as "Asians"—are either genetically or culturally preconditioned to excel academically, as if coded in their very beings. They stand out as the opposite of negatively stereotyped blacks (i.e., those in "inner-city schools"), for they excel in a system in which educators see blacks as unteachable and as needing discipline.[32] They supposedly affirm what is possible in a meritocratic America. Within this viewpoint, their achievements uphold the popular color-blind ideology that race does not matter in a significant way anymore, and attention to race (e.g., affirmative action) is the real cause of racial divisions.[33]

Yet there is a limit to the applause Asian Americans receive. Fast forward to 2011 and the depictions of Asian American achievement match the concerns raised by educators here. *Time* magazine ran a cover story on Amy Chua and the notion of the "tiger mother." On the cover, the child is no longer smiling and instead holds a violin and nervously faces an overbearing and oversized mother. The article starts by painting a backdrop of a rising Chinese economy and the United States slowly recovering from a major recession. The possibility of Americans being taken over by Asia and, by extension, Asian Americans seems real. These "tiger parents" hail from the aggressive "tiger" countries of Asia. The 2011 article nears its end with a quote from the editor-at-large of *Psychology Today* magazine:

"American parenting, at its best, combines ambitious expectations and a loving environment with a respect for each child's individual differences and a flexibility in parental roles and behavior. You can set high standards in your household and help your children meet them without resorting to the extreme measures Chua writes about." Western parents have their own highly effective strategies for promoting learning, such as free play—something Chua never mentions. On a national scale, the U.S. economy may be taking a hit, but it has far from collapsed. American secondary education may be in crisis, but its higher education is the envy of the world—especially China. We have not stopped inventing and innovating, in Silicon Valley or in Detroit.[34]

This critique of Asian Americans as overly competitive relative to white students (no longer black students) is reminiscent of historical depictions of Asian Americans as threatening white American workers. They were considered unnatural in their work and living arrangements.[35] Immigration quotas were established to limit Asian immigration in order to protect white workers and then relaxed to let in more immigrants when they were useful to support specific industries. Asian American youths are not yet in the labor market, but they do "work" in the school system. Here they encounter the same critique as adults before them (which continues today) as pushing too aggressively. Chua may get strong results, and lessons can be learned from her book, but the lessons are ones that the United States already knows: work hard and expect positive outcomes. According to the article, the United States can return to world economic dominance without Asian cruelty and lack of individuality.

## Asian American Parenting

Tom believed he recognized an Asian parenting style:

> The after-school math center is not fun. Parents are forcing it. Students are bogged down by all their stuff and can't catch up with their other classes. Parents do it because they see their peers doing it, and they need to do it to keep up. Not all kids should pursue the same path.

He was not critical of extracurricular mathematics per se and in fact avidly supported math competitions. Toward the end of our afternoon meeting in his classroom, students filed in. He had a more secluded area in a corner of the room for five advanced students, about half of whom were Asian Americans and most of whom were boys, to work on a separate project. He was happy to teach students at different levels, but he saw the psychological toll that more math classes put on youths who did not eagerly participate.

Jane commented on the perceived effects of the Asian immigrant parenting style:

> A lot of Asian students would talk about how they don't like how their parents are always pushing them to do things. And how anxious it makes them, and how they feel like they're not really enjoying their life. And one of my students I'll always remember, I would say, "Well, say a little bit more about what it is that disturbs you," and he says, "Well, my parents have told me that if I get anything less than an A, I'm going to be going to community college." And the kids joke that a B or a C is an "Asian F."

There appear to be two forms of parenting according to educators: "American" and "Asian." To be American is to be humanist— that is, to raise children within the Western notion of the liberal (and liberated) human, to nurture the personal dignity, autonomy, and passions unique to that individual.[36] "Good parenting" involves helping children grow into themselves and appreciating childhood as a distinct stage of development from adulthood.[37] Kids should "go to the pond or go skating in the afternoons," as Tanya reminisced. To be Asian is to be robotic—that is, to be programmed by an external force (in this case, calculating parents like Chua) and lose the essence of one's individuality. Asian Americans have long been characterized as robotic in their demeanor,[38] and this attitude has shaped educators' judgments of Asian American parents, whom they blamed for Asian American youths' stress, nonverbal communication, and distaste for learning.

Because whites and Asians supposedly parent in fundamentally different ways, educators had divergent narratives about white and Asian American children engaged in extracurricular education. Richard, a white teacher from Colorado whom I met at a national math competition and who worked with gifted and talented students in his school district, said,

> [At math competitions] it is predominately an Asian and Indian crowd: Asian, Indian, I think some Middle Eastern. A lot of those kids have parents who are engineers, who work in the field of mathematics. I don't know if they sort of inspire or motivate or push or just direct their kids that way. So I think that there are two different groups. I think that there are kids who simply gravitate that way because they get math [like my son]. They like math. It excited them. It's something that they can do, and it's something that if the time and place are right, then they'll just run with it. Or the converse is that I think that there are parents who are going to say, "This is the way to an MIT scholarship, so this is what you're going to do."

Richard believes there are "two different groups" even in the same activity: one that is excited by math (normally whites) and the other that just seeks out scholarships (normally Asian Americans).

This same Asian parental top-down pressure was read in other educational venues. Jennifer, a past coordinator of a Boston spelling bee, observed,

> A lot of the Indian community [in the Boston-area bee] was pushing me, like, "Well, my kid can participate [in the bee]," even though their school isn't [registered with the bee]. I'm like, "I'm sorry, it just doesn't work that way." [They] also are a little harder on their kids. A girl won the first year she participated, and then the second year she came in second. And you could see the immediate—when she misspelled her word, or each time she was even unsure, she'd look right at her dad, and he would give her this very intense look and shake his head either, you know, in approval or disapproval. And when she misspelled her word, she just broke into tears. She was reprimanded right on stage by him. You'd speak to him afterward, and it was very, you know, "She was very silly. She was very foolish." It was just a lot more critical of their child. And then a couple of the other students, it wasn't as dramatic, but we felt very much that the student was upset with themselves [when they made a mistake] but much more concerned—[they] would look right over at particularly the dads and be very, you know, sort of nervous. . . . I mean, the most intense, I would say, family commitment has been from the Indian community.

She referred not to a particular school district but to overcritical families, and fathers in particular, involved in the city's regional spelling bee.

I do not doubt the veracity of Jennifer and others' observations. I also witnessed a few Indian American parents over the years tell their kids in a demanding tone to "stay focused" and "take this seriously" as the kids were competing. One child started crying on stage when he misspelled a word at a Boston regional spelling competition. And yet there are a variety of white and nonwhite parents on the sidelines of youth soccer games as well. The few that yell at their kids and referees do not represent all parents there, much less all parents of their ethnic group, and the same conflation should not happen for Asian American parents, the large majority of whom applaud their children's efforts and console them after a loss, as the mother did to the child I saw cry. There are Asian American parents who push math and spelling despite their children's prolonged protests, but such tiger parenting is the exception rather than the rule. Parents repeatedly said that they took their children's preferences into account, discussed later. This does not mean that parents did not place children into certain activities without consulting them, but they were sensitive to kids' likings and stopped if children protested, not uncommon for parents generally.

Heena, a learning director of an international math franchise, observed that most students enjoy rather than resent coming after school:

> There are students who don't want to [come], who don't like math because the first year is the most challenging. Then after that, later on— second, third year—most of the students are coming because they want to come and they love it. Of course, I cannot say all of them. But once they see our approach and that math can be really easy and it's not as scary as it used to be, then they come with more pleasure, actually.

Max said,

> There's definitely some [children] who are forced into it for much longer than you would want them to be. I don't think it happens too terribly often. . . . It's a real thing, but it's not just with Chinese parents. I look at what my [white US-born] friends are doing with their kids, and they're investing in different things. Music, plays, or whatever it is that help the kid get into Harvard. If you're looking at the upper-middle class, yes, the kid is on a traveling soccer team.

Young clientele might come against their will, but most left if they wanted to, signifying that Asian immigrant parents were more open-minded than given credit for.

These nuanced observations by Heena and Max fit with what is known about Asian American parenting. Scholars differentiate between "authoritarian" and "authoritative" parenting styles.[39] The former is a top-down approach to parenting with little warmth or allowance for children's agency—that is, tiger parenting.[40] The latter has a healthy balance of parental guidance in response to children's interests. Based on these two styles, Asian immigrants demonstrate more authoritarian parenting than do whites.[41] Yet rather than a simple contrast of authoritative versus authoritarian, parents borrow from both styles. Chinese American parents use a "training" parenting style that, while similar to authoritarianism, involves more contact and involvement with their children.[42] Korean Americans often parent using a ga-jung-kyo-yuk (family socialization and processes) method that involves an emphasis on family hierarchy and family obligations and an expectation of respect for and use of appropriate etiquette with parents and the elderly.[43] This is coupled with parental reasoning, warmth, and a close parent-child bond. Indian American parents also mix authoritative and authoritarian modes of parenting, especially the longer they live in the United States.[44] They have close family bonds, stern expectations, and respect for children's preferences. Asian American parents also often are more involved in their children's education than are other groups, which provides a major boost to student success.[45] While parents rarely discuss the particulars of classes, they stress the importance of college, assist with homework, and discuss the need to do well for the sake of the family.[46] Such engagement in and encouragement of education contrast with a caricatured approach that privileges results over motivation or process.

Educators and white parents tend to stereotype Asian American parenting as uncaring and pushy and as encoded in their culture or genetics, views echoed in popular media. This leads them to see extreme episodes of authoritarian parenting as representing the race. It then becomes easier to criticize the use of enrichment education in blanket rather than family-specific ways for Asian American students, who are presumed to all be forced into it, unlike whites. Such stereotypes lead educators to generalize Asian American parents as deserving much blame for student stress.

## Selective Concerns

Educators saw Asian American parenting as deviant and, correspondingly, felt white middle class parents and kids set an appropriate standard that others should conform to. For example, when white children outperform minority students, teachers rarely see it as "academic bullying" or express sympathy about minorities' "emotional well-being." Similarly, educators do not create pathological rationales for whites' weaker performance relative to Asian Americans, as happens for minorities relative to whites.[47] Whites are not expected to emulate those who achieve more (i.e., toward Asian Americans), whereas black and Latinx youths are (i.e., toward whites). Also, teachers, predominantly white, reinforce a "hidden curriculum"—that is, informal norms for what constitutes proper behavior, dress, attitudes, and discipline in schools.[48] Racial inequalities arise even in integrated and reasonably resourced schools.[49] Educators make significant efforts to address the learning gaps facing minority youths but do not disrupt the white supremacy embedded in standard practices.[50] The taken-for-granted assumption that white students' practices are "normal" contributes to why Asian Americans' are framed as "deviant" and "a problem."

Similarly, white parents criticize Asian Americans for pushing their kids within the school system but do not question their own comparable efforts. Joanne, a white US-born mother in an affluent Boston-area district with many Asian Americans said,

> We do know [Asian American] parents who are calling the schools and saying, "My kid is more advanced than you realize. And he's going to be advanced, and he's going to be starting this this year." And they find out, or we find out, that they got their private tutors over the summer, and they had them take online classes over the summer.

Yet the facts that students in AP classes are overwhelmingly white and that there is an industry of private tutoring options for affluent families for support in these classes are not similarly questioned.[51] White middle-class parents try to "hoard opportunities" by keeping academic inequalities in place (e.g., tracking, school choice) when their children are on top.[52] They often complain to teachers in order to advocate for their children, and their children advocate for themselves without teacher pushback.[53] So when whites lead academically, other students must be taught to catch up. When Asian Americans achieve more than whites academically, they must be taught to calm down.

Worries about families' pursuit of private support also are selective. Little mention is made of how Asian American children could be at a disadvantage to white youths in sports, the proliferation of club sports for young children, and the stress that comes with trying to measure up to one's peers on the playing field.[54] While white parents may bemoan the rise of private youth leagues, they do not see it as a racial problem as in academics. Nor do they recognize the racial concerns facing Asian Americans in education. As discussed in more depth later, Asian Americans admitted to selective universities might have higher standardized test scores than admitted whites on average, making excelling in academics a necessity for them beyond any parenting preferences.[55]

The fact that white administrators and parents only selectively worry about the well-being of students does not mean that their concerns for Asian Americans are not sincere or based simply on a desire to reproduce the status quo. Mary, Sally, and others want to protect children. Still, educators demonstrate how a white normalcy is at play in the critiques of Asian Americans' hyper education. Asian Americans are a "problem" in part just because they deviate from what is "standard." This white supremacy is easier to overlook when relying on stereotypes of Asian American parents' cultural differences. An unquestioned white privilege can lead to lopsided judgments of both who is to blame and, as seen next, what actions to take.

## Surrogate Parenting

Rachel recalled her own background when she spoke bluntly about hyper education among Asian Americans:

> I think that exposing your child to a wide variety of areas to find that passion or talent and then promoting it is, in my mind, the job of a caring and more grounded parent. I mean, I can give you a personal example. We have two sons. One became an avid woodworker. When he was eleven, I was taking him to Home Depot regularly, and he was building Adirondack chairs. It came from inside him, and he ended up at an Ivy League school. . . . So if your child is phenomenal at the ukulele . . . In my mind, again, [they need] to have something they're passionate about, and I can't believe you're going to find kids who are passionate about long division. I just don't believe it.

For her, Asian American parents were not sufficiently caring or grounded. She speaks as a mother and refers to her own children, just as educators use their personal experiences in their conceptions of students. Because schools place much of the blame of student stress on Asian culture rather than questioning white privilege and school practices, their actions to fix the problem involve trying to assimilate Asian American parents into a "proper" lifestyle—namely, that of white middle-class educators and parents.

Immigrants have an informal contract with the nation to affirm the cultural norms of the country in order to be accepted as equals.[56] Because Asian Americans engaged in hyper education disrupt this contract, the school feels the need to correct them. In the areas of Boston, San Francisco, Princeton, and elsewhere, public forums discuss the psychological stress that students are under and place explicit blame on Asian Americans.[57] For instance, in a movement referred to as "Take Back Childhood," a school district in West Windsor, New Jersey (near Princeton), made headlines when it changed its educational policies to reduce academic pressure on children.[58] Asian American parents expressed chagrin, worried that their children would no longer be sufficiently challenged.[59]

Schools and towns partner to, in effect, reprogram Asian Americans rather than treat them as authority figures and listen to their points of view. I attended a morning-long community event in spring 2014 put on by a Boston suburb. The program focused on the balance of stress and achievement for Asian American students. The public event originated through the town's Asian Mental Health Initiative with support from their Youth and Family Services program and took place in the downtown auditorium meeting center. It included mental health experts, high-school children, and community leaders from the Asian American and white communities. The three-hundred-plus-person audience was composed of predominantly Asian American (mostly Chinese American, Indian American, and Korean American) parents in the town and surrounding area. The theme centered on the stress that Asian American high-school students face due to their parents' priorities and styles. Studies in the school district found that students compare themselves to other students in order to measure their worth. Even if performing well in school, students had low self-esteem because they knew others who were earning higher grades. Attempted suicide, cutting, and drinking are not uncommon among Asian Americans—girls in particular—because of stress. A youth panel of Asian American students elaborated on the pressures of high school. They noted the aforementioned "Asian F." They recited the model minority stereotype that made them feel that they had to live up to unreal expectations. As one said, "I do not want to disappoint my parents and owe it to them to fulfill their goals for immigrating." These US-raised, Asian American youths encountered intergenerational conflict with their immigrant parents, who came across as only focused on academic success and achievement.

A key goal of the session was to teach Asian immigrants how to parent differently. Toward that end, a US-raised Asian American psychologist lectured on the different value systems between Asians and Americans as found in Western psychological research. Asian American parents were told how to create a more loving relationship with their children so that youths felt all right opening up to parents in a more American style, which would limit their fear and anxiety. Specifically, parents were coached to tell their children that they loved them and to not shame them if they did not receive a perfect grade. The psychologist explained how parents should talk to kids: look at your child, have an open posture, physically lean toward the person, and so on. The biopolitics of parenting was on full display, as parents were literally told how to hold their bodies as part of an effort to assimilate them into the Anglo, middle-class culture that is standard in psychological studies. Factors that motivate parents beyond a supposed authoritarian culture, such as concerns over racism or their lack of social networks and cultural capital (e.g., fluency in elite tastes), were not invited for consideration (discussed later).

Asian American parents in the audience did not object to this treatment. Instead, they appeared to acquiesce to the suggestions, as if the panelists were preaching to the choir. One parent stood and said,

> Asian parents push kids too hard. "You should only get As." We always tell kids they can do better next time even if doing well. Makes kids feel can never do enough [sic]. Do things this way, not that way. Don't tell kids we love them.

Non-Asian community members joined in this effort to chastise and assimilate parents into their way of parenting, for they worried about the effects on their own children. The shaming of Asian parents became so accepted that during the question-and-answer period, Sally went on stage and said, in effect, that Asian American parents were hurting her children and needed to change. Her young children were getting stressed about schoolwork as they compared themselves to their Asian American friends, who themselves were stressing out due to their parents. She pleaded to the parents to stop parenting as they do. Speaking to a predominantly Asian American audience, she received not resentment or confrontation but applause. Asian Americans were rhetorically framed as needing to apologize for their parenting preferences and agree to assimilate.

In other venues, parents are explicitly told to raise their children in the same manner as local cultural leaders. Rachel believed she herself would gain little traction in trying to get families to change. This does not mean she did not try. She said,

> [A concern about stress is] what prompted me to bring in [a] psychologist who came and spoke with parents earlier this year. When I talked to her in planning her evening, I said I want to try to help parents think about what the goals are for their children and articulate them

and then move backward to think about, Is what I'm providing for my children now something that's going to get them there, and what are the tradeoffs? . . . You're not constantly trying to add and build their resume but thinking about who they are.

She enlisted an Asian American psychologist trained in American psychology to represent these cultural norms to other Asian Americans because, in her word, parents need to think "about who [their children] are," as if they are not already.

Other educators explicitly insert themselves to students as surrogate parents to youths. Mary relayed an example:

I had a student who was Indian in [my office] every day, anxious about going home and facing his father. Worried about college. Sometimes he would push back, and sometimes it would go well and other times not go well. I saw him over four years; I saw the toll it took on him. To his credit, he made healthy choices. I was on him all the time. "I'm not your mother, but I am your mother." He skipped over pieces of his childhood that no child should have to do. . . . I have the opportunity to get to know kids. I can tell them messages. They ask, "Am I nuts?" And I say, "No, you're not nuts. Everyone else is around here." . . . I know eighth graders who are taking SAT prep classes. I would hear them talking in the car that they couldn't do things on the weekends because they were doing SAT tutoring. I don't keep silent about that. I say, "Who's idea is that?" They say their parents wanted them to take it.

Mary refers to herself as a type of "mother" to the student, trying to give him a version of childhood denied to him by his parents, who are "nuts."

Jane would directly tell Asian immigrant parents that they were making mistakes in their choices:

A lot of times when we're talking about the educational system, we're focused on the end goal of college or university. Well, what happens after that? What happens to some of these kids when they get to college and university? So then I would also say to those parents, "Look, is your child happy? Is your child well adjusted? Does your child have friends? Does your child have time to play?" I mean, as a mother, one of the things I knew from the really early stages was that I wanted to make sure my daughters played and played a lot. . . . I had a student, a Chinese student, who stopped being able to function and had to be hospitalized because he was so overwhelmed. And his parents were beside themselves because they didn't even know or realize that this could happen.

While teachers often struggle in their classrooms with how to talk about black-white race relations, they appear more confident in voicing their criticisms of Asian Americans.[60] In her opinion, Asian parents did not care enough about their children's happiness and so could be ignorant of their feelings. She argues this not as a specialist but "as a mother," something "tiger moms" apparently fail at being. The school sees it as its responsibility to parent the children and parent the parents.

This cultural intervention takes place across age levels. For instance, a preschool director in Connecticut whose school has predominantly white and Asian American children is quoted as saying,

Asian kids are very quiet in the classroom settings. I think their parents are very pushy at home and, also, they have very high expectations from their preschoolers, which I do not think does any good, but we help them to be themselves here.[61]

The director, in effect, argues that the preschool knows the children better than the parents do, for it is a space where the kids can "be themselves." This caricature of Asians as overly intense denies the reality that Asian American parents care about their kids' happiness (discussed later) and that all kinds of middle-class parents invest heavily in their children's activities because they too are concerned about the development of their skills.[62]

Schools' interventions involve not only lectures to parents and children but also their actions during normal business hours. Teachers might modify how much they push kids based on how much work they think kids do at home. As Alexa said,

> There are some kids here that I know that could give me a whole lot more than what they're giving me, but they're already stressing out. So you've got to kind of back up a little, give them a little bit of something, let them be. So you're juggling all of this at the same time.

She adjusts how much material she provides children based on her impressions of how stressed they are outside of school due to after-school education, not based on their cognitive abilities. Ironically, as she downgrades the amount of academic training students receive in school because of youths' external learning, she affirms parents' critiques that the schools do not challenge students enough (discussed later), which then furthers parents' commitment to extracurricular education. And the cycle continues.

Teachers and administrators are trying to support Asian American youths, and the psychological problems they identify are well documented. Because the problems can be serious, it is important to understand what is behind them. Educators put their energies into reprimanding Asian American parents. Asian Americans, like all parents, can learn to parent better. But such an approach downplays both the fact that Asian Americans already parent in a variety of ways and that stress in school stems from multiple factors, including educators' own actions.

## Educators' Roles in Student Stress

William relayed a commonplace impression of his Asian American students at his math center:

> I can't say it's true for every child, but there is a little bit more discipline with the Asian, and I'm including Indians in the Asian students that I see. [They] sit down, [do] the work, and [are] focused, and—you know—[they] don't goof around, don't get up and get snacks all the time or whatever. They sit down, and they just do the work, and also in the way they actually do the work and the way they answer the math problems, they're a little more meticulous.

While it is entirely reasonable that his observations are correct—that he sees Asian American children not getting up as often for snacks and not ostensibly goofing around—he generalizes those observations to all Asian American students even as he says it is not true for every child. The implication is that Asian Americans are inherently more focused, almost robotic in that they can study without food and without walking or standing. In these ways, interpersonal interactions with educators contribute to stereotypes of Asian American children.

All the focus on Asian Americans' presumed authoritarian parenting leads schools to underplay their own culpability in student stress beyond increased testing and standards. Educators like William are often guilty of stereotyping students, whether in positive or negative ways, and then treating students in ways that affirm those stereotypes.[63] Asian Americans experience "stereotype promise"—that is, an expectation that they are high achievers that causes teachers to treat them in a manner that facilitates that achievement.[64] This is the opposite of "stereotype threat," which treats blacks as likely to perform worse than whites.[65] While seemingly positive, the stereotype for Asian Americans creates heightened expectations and anxiety to meet those expectations. It also further demonstrates the connection of Asian Americans to antiblack racism, for that racism facilitates the treatment of many Asian Americans as "better than blacks." In other words, Asian Americans are negatively impacted psychologically by anti-black racism even as they are complimented on the surface. Teachers similarly have been known to complement Latinx students for receiving the same grade on homework or an exam that they would express disappointment to Asian Americans about, playing into the expectation that Asian Americans will perform at a high level and Latinxs will not.[66] The pressure to succeed comes in part from these stereotypes.

Also deemphasized due to racial stereotyping and white normalcy is how schools contribute to the academic anxiety facing all students, beyond just Asian Americans. Local curricular standards can be set higher than state levels as a means to differentiate a school, and students are expected to reach them. High-stakes federal testing similarly causes stress for youths, even in elementary school.[67] A focus on Asian Americans' educational practices and cultural backgrounds downplays these issues. Also, teachers can give students mixed messages about the value of private learning relative to their public education. Jaya, an Indian American elementary-school student, reported that her teacher counted her math center assignments as satisfying her school homework, for they were more advanced than the school curriculum. The relationship of extracurricular learning to school education becomes blurry.[68]

Schools do not always blame parenting or external conditions for student problems. As noted earlier, the needs assessment survey at Mary's school found that LGBTQ students were the "most vulnerable population" in the district, with Asian Americans coming in second. And yet the presumed locus of the problems facing these two groups of students differ. Schools work to make themselves more accepting of queer students, recognizing that bullying in the school is a frequent problem.[69] Mary's school, like so many others, tries to "educate and provide awareness" so as to help such youths. The social-emotional challenges facing queer students are recognized as located at least partly within the school. In other words, it is not inevitable that schools blame the domestic sphere for the problems facing their students, and yet they do so for Asian Americans rather than fully consider their own responsibility in student stress.

## Fitting a Pattern of White Supremacy

Such criticisms of minority families and downplaying of schools' own roles in student problems suit a history of white supremacy in the school system and therefore should not be surprising. The American education system has been used explicitly to assimilate "problematic" ethnic and racial groups and the poor into a culturally narrow and idealized way of life while considering itself a neutral and benign force.[70] For example, Native Americans in the 1800s and onward were "civilized" through classroom instruction.[71] Outside of the settler colonialism of the United States, other colonizing efforts by the United States and other countries routinely relied on the school system to "save" natives from themselves, including by teaching them how to develop relationships between women and men, how to engage in physical activity, and more.[72] The lack of bilingual education is another mechanism to culturally "uplift" seemingly weak immigrant communities and protect the national culture.[73] The goal is to turn parents into "abstract citizens"—that is, general members of the local polity who belong based on their ability to afford a home in an affluent area and their commitment to upholding established norms, including those around parenting and education.[74]

The school operates as an arm of the state, and this relationship helps explain its approach to immigrants. Schools use "soft power" in that they teach the norms and ideas of the dominant class in order to persuade others to agree with them and accept them as legitimate. While soft power is normally conceived as relevant to US interventions abroad, it also pertains to the treatment of immigrants.[75] Schools maintain the ideology of the nation as a liberal enterprise, one committed to protecting the freedoms of individuals to practice the faith they want, to be educated and become what they want, and live how they want.[76] In paradoxical fashion, they use soft power over others (e.g., telling Asian American parents to change their attitudes and actions) in support of the liberal ideals that people have the right to live as they want. Such a contradictory exercise is actually normal within state practice; state power and even violence are used in defense of liberal ideals.[77]

Ironically (or not), this white-washing within schools takes place alongside expressed and sincere commitments to multiculturalism. Educators, including the ones I spoke with, value the cultural diversity that Asian and other immigrant families bring. This "diversity" is recognized within a benign multiculturalism.[78] Educators applaud when children speak their parents' native language, play a traditional instrument, and know ethnic rituals. Cultural differences are celebrated as long as they do not threaten the established way of life.

## Public Health Crisis

Much is at stake with hyper education. On the surface, it appears as a public health problem—a cause of stress and anxiety brought by an authoritarian Asian parenting style that infects their children and spreads to other children through "academic bullying," no matter how inoculated other parents think their children are. There are diagnosed cases, with surveys and anecdotal observations identifying many infected youths. These families' good schools should be enough for parents, critics say.

In response, suburban communities go on a public health education push to inform Asian immigrants that they are carrying the virus and teach them how to eliminate it. Racial stereotypes and a white normativity guide this reaction. This is seen in educators' assumptions around Asian parenting, the responses to Asian Americans when outperforming whites (in contrast to the responses when whites outperform minorities), the efforts to tell Asian Americans how to talk to and stand next to their children, and the like. The critiques of tiger mothers similarly fit a history of schools assimilating minorities and the public targeting of women of color rather than being only a concern over parenting norms.

The fact that racial hierarchies and white normalcy guide the efforts of educators and neighboring parents does not take away from the concerns they raise about mental health well-being or suggest that hyper education does not impart such problems. Authoritarian parenting and undue academic pressures on youths are a problem and are not limited to Asian Americans. But a reliance on Asian stereotypes and a protection of white normalcy leads educators to deemphasize how heightened academic standards, standardized tests, stereotype promise treatment, and more contribute to the problem. Because the mental health concerns can be serious, it is necessary to have a full understanding of such causes. Moreover, it is possible that the racial framings of hyper education obscure how it signifies an *integration* into dominant education and parenting trends rather than a foreign deviation, discussed next.

# 2

# "If the Schools Were Doing Their Job, Then We Wouldn't Need to Exist"

Max is a thoughtful, passionate, middle-aged director of a math center for advanced mathematics students in California. He would tell you that his business exists because of the "failures" of the public school system. Schools are "ruining" and "killing" children's interest in math. In fact, he told me, "If the schools were doing what we are doing, then we wouldn't need to exist." This rhetoric against the school system is commonplace among private educators, pundits, politicians, and those parents invested in hyper education.[1] Hyper education fits within the proposed solutions to these critiques and should be seen as a normal outgrowth of contemporary education reform rather than a foreign practice as earlier framed. If people do not like the trends of hyper education, there are more important forces to blame than Asian American parenting.

There is a long history of considering the American education system as inherently flawed and needing to be rethought, whether for those struggling or excelling in school. A key moment in this history of school reform was the 1983 publication *A Nation at Risk: The Imperative for Educational Reform* by President Reagan's National Commission on Excellence in Education. The report argued that American schools were failing. Concerns revolved around the academic performance of those Americans struggling in school—in particular, minorities and the poor—and of the nation at large relative to other countries.[2] Responses to these ongoing problems have led to the assumption of the private marketplace as offering more effective results than government-run programs and to the culture of high-stakes, quantifiable testing; these developments are all in line with hyper education.[3]

The most impactful school reform response in the past twenty years has been No Child Left Behind (NCLB), which promotes a more rational, bureaucratic system premised on economic and political principles that privilege the private market and individual self-sufficiency in order to increase efficiencies, cost savings, and performance.[4] Market competition supposedly promotes efficiency and creates needed outcomes, including the closing of poorly performing schools.[5]

Private learning centers, along with charter schools and school vouchers, flourished under these conditions.[6] From 2001 to 2015, the law channeled public money to private tutoring outlets for students in underperforming schools, with some promising but uneven results.[7] During that time, Kumon, Sylvan, and other centers grew and received tens of millions of dollars a year.[8]

The law's most well-publicized intervention was to increase student testing as the main measure of progress, a method typical in academic competitions and learning centers.[9] Teachers were considered untrustworthy to gauge student progress.[10] Politicians from New Jersey to Tennessee to Wisconsin to Arizona make the case that schools need to be held more accountable for how much students are actually learning.[11] The standardized test format can contradict the normal assessment procedures of a school, yet districts are forced to reckon with it.[12]

Education reform also has made the school experience more predictable.[13] A standardized curriculum is meant to solve the problem of uneven learning across districts. Assessment procedures are built in and lead to "teaching to the test," giving teachers less latitude to create their own lesson plans.[14] Teaching to the test furthers a rationality: the need to control human behavior, often through nonhuman mechanisms.[15] Federal legislation since NCLB—namely, the Every Student Succeeds Act, its grant program Race to the Top, and the state initiative Common Core—continued these changes.[16] As elaborated upon below, learning centers and academic competitions are premised on these same rational dimensions and the assumption that these can improve student learning.

## Public Schools as Failures

It is not simply policies and politicians whose critiques of schools create the conditions for hyper education to flourish. For many years, conservative pundits and think tanks such as the Heritage Foundation, the Hoover Institution, the Milton and Rose D. Friedman Foundation, and others have criticized public schools and called for their privatization.[17] More mainstream, arguably liberal foundations recently have a similar role. The Bill and Melinda Gates Foundation has had a profound impact on the public-school system. Its premise is that schools are failing and must be revamped, as written in a 2003 press release:

> Nearly one-third of American students aren't graduating from high school. This represents nothing short of a massive failure of America's high schools. . . . The good news is that we can reverse this trend. More students will succeed if communities provide a rich variety of educational options, and effective alternative schools are one such option.[18]

The Bill and Melinda Gates Foundation's first major initiative was to decrease the size of classrooms and promote small schools, with mixed results.[19] Since then, the foundation has turned its attention and money to teacher quality based on the belief that students would perform better if they had better-trained teachers.[20] The rational notion that all people must be measured in order to gauge their worth has even led to devising teaching assessment tools for gym and choir teachers.[21] The foundation's ideas resonated up to the highest levels of government, including then secretary of education Arne Duncan, and it supported organizations that helped initiate the Department of Education's Common Core Standards in 2009.

Critics of these reforms argue that testing is less a way to ensure quality learning than a means to discipline students, teachers, and schools.[22] Teachers' job satisfaction is at its lowest point in decades.[23] This is the same critique made of extracurricular education, of increasing teacher workload, relying on constant quantifiable measurements of learning, and undermining their authority.

As the Bill and Melinda Gates Foundation has impacted schools, other public figures have impacted home learning, again with the premise that students can learn more than they are being taught and that an increased marketplace of educational options can facilitate that outcome. Most notably, in 2006, Salman Khan started the Khan Academy, an online resource dedicated primarily to math education and later expanded into the subjects of science, economics, and the humanities. It has been translated into over twenty languages, and one hundred million people use it every year; it also has expanded into schools with a curriculum that teachers can use.[24] In Khan's book *The One World Schoolhouse: Education Reimagined*, he suggests that his academy can serve as a "free school" to provide youths with the intellectual engagement they need. He critiques the school system, including those in his vicinity of affluent San Francisco suburbs, as creating passive learners, leading to "educational malaise."[25] He claims that schools simply offer "rote memorization and plug-in formulas aimed at nothing more lasting or meaningful than a good grade on the next exam."[26] In his estimation, children are victims of the standard school model that has not been incentivized to improve due to a lack of competition, and the school system should be reimagined.[27] Other visions for revised schooling and teaching exist.[28] Again, the message is the same: the school system does not provide youths with the education they need, much less deserve, so they should look elsewhere while they wait for drastic reforms.

Critiques of the public-school system are ubiquitous. The 2010 award-winning documentary film *Waiting for Superman* praised charter schools in contrast to teacher unions and general public school systems. The popular nonprofit Teach for America places recent college graduates, with only a summer's worth of teacher training, into classrooms.[29] The premise continues to be that teachers and schools are failing and need interventions. The effect is increased public doubt in schools' abilities and the decentering of the public system as the main arbiter of youth education.

## The Problems for High-Performing Students

Even as affluent students tend to outperform poorer ones and compare favorably on international tests, the premise remains that teachers do not effectively meet the needs of these students or others who perform above grade level.[30] As "evidence" of their concerns, parents refer to their youths' workload as too easy.[31] This is especially the case for parents who had exposure to other nations' schools. Kristina, an immigrant from Russia, sharply criticized the American school system:

> The literature classes here are pathetic. No one is reading things that provoke, that make them think. Our kids are treated like stupid dolls. . . . We are lucky to be in this country where anything is possible. In Russia, as Russian Jews, we have to be very smart to earn our money. I cannot afford to produce stupid kids.

An Indian immigrant father in a crowd of other coethnics said,

We also tend to compare [our young kids] with their cousins in India, who are doing three-digit divisions and using different measures altogether. [*Crowd laughs in agreement*]

A US-born, white father referred not to personal knowledge but to the United States' poor rankings in math within international standards as part of his critique of the public school system.

Directors of math centers agree that public schools, even those that are well resourced and highly ranked, do not provide challenging programs to youths. Andrew, the director of a Chinese math center in a Boston suburb, said, "As you may know, for science or math, they really do not learn much during elementary school. They don't learn much here." The "here" he refers to is one of the highest-ranked public-school systems in Massachusetts. Such systems basically "produce stupid dolls," as Kristina believed.

Tom, a middle-school math teacher in a Boston suburb, lamented,

We are doing what the state is telling us to do. . . . State testing means we can't teach the way we think would be best. But it does ensure that everyone gets the minimum. You're teaching to the masses. . . . If it weren't for MCAS, I'd be doing number theory and other things.

Nor is he alone. Educators elsewhere regret when leading students do not receive instruction at their level or cannot be assessed in nuanced ways while more attention is given to those at standard learning levels.[32] Joanne, whose seventh-grade son attended public school, visited a math and science enrichment event at a local private school in the Boston area, where she spoke with the school director:

The conversation led to a point where I was like, "Seriously, though, if we're in the public school, what is your advice?" He said you have to supplement [with private learning centers]. It's as simple as that. [The public school] simply doesn't have enough content in the curriculum.

Even though the test score differences between the United States and other industrialized nations stem in part from the gross class inequalities in the United States, the sense is that higher-performing children receive an inadequate education. This echoes the critiques of schools in public rhetoric.

Academic inequality also takes a gendered form. Girls' performance in mathematics tends to dip during elementary school (discussed later), and teacher expectations for girls are lower than for boys.[33] Boys are overrepresented in math competitions as the competition progresses and becomes more challenging. Carter, the director of a national middle-school math competition, explained,

> Six months go by from the start of the school year until the first competition happens. So for those first six months, we're 55 [percent boys], 45 [percent girls]. It's only once you get into these later levels that you do see this change in the competition of those who advance.

Girls have an interest in math competitions, but they do not thrive in math in school systems. To alleviate this, extracurricular education can make sense, as seen later.

These complaints by parents and even teachers that advanced students remain underserved are not unfounded, for the Department of Education itself seems to downplay such students' needs. At a national math competition, Max lectured to parents in an urgent and free-flowing manner on the deficiencies in American math education, with its emphasis on memorization and nonchallenging curriculum. He then showed the following quote from a Department of Education grant reviewer to illustrate that schools have no intention of changing:

While challenging and improving the mathematical problem-solving skills of high-performing students are surely every-day objectives of those who teach such students, it is not a problem, relatively speaking, of major import in American education.

When I asked him later to expand on that quote, he said,

This is the wall that a lot of parents hit or kids hit when they try to get their school systems to do something special for [advanced] kids. [Schools say to themselves,] we've already served them well. This is the attitude that that quote is an example of. . . . I mean, in my perfect school system, if the teachers can't handle the top kids we'd let the kids out of the school system and let them get their math somewhere else [like his learning center]. Now that's obviously a hard ask. But in a better system, they wouldn't be forced to go at the slower pace that the school is going at just because the teachers can't handle them.

Carter similarly lamented that the Department of Education had little interest in the needs of high-performing students:

The Department of Ed. really is focused on, when it comes to grants and funding or what it seems the bulk of it is . . . targeting students on the lower end of the spectrum and trying to get them to reach the proficiency on standardized tests. For a program like ours, which is extra, that's not something that they're—that's not where they're putting their money.

Parents felt justified in joining enrichment education as a response to school systems that did not seem to prioritize them and "teachers [who] can't handle them."

It should be noted that addressing inequalities in the school system need not come at the expense of excellence.[34] Rather than spend money and time developing standardized tests and teacher assessments, attention could be paid to the lack of available teachers, the funding model of schools, and entrenched social divisions.[35] The property-tax model of funding American public schools pits schools against one another and has created an unequal allocation of resources, for instance. Tracking, AP courses, and other hierarchical processes also contribute to students' disenfranchisement by siphoning resources away from most students.[36] Nor does tracking necessarily assist those students tracked in high levels, who do not always show higher achievement than they would without tracking.[37] Instead, having high standards that all children are held to, with sufficient investment in support for struggling students, is a viable process.[38] Such a perspective moves past the dominant tracking model, with different expectations for different students.[39] Yet with such reforms not yet widespread, parents conform to the educational practices and after-school options surrounding them.

## The Neoliberal Logic of Supplemental Education

Private educators and parents of students performing at or above grade level believe that schools can and should work more effectively and that the one-size-fits-all system and the Department of Education do not serve them. Hyper education follows as a logical response and will become even more embedded in academic life because it furthers the same rationale that both the policies and critics embrace.

At the conceptual level, hyper education fits the current cultural moment of neoliberalism in contrast to an earlier epoch. Under classical liberalism, humans were understood as homo economicus, as those who are identified as workers and so engaged in exchange. Workers distinguished themselves from capitalists and saw themselves as exchanging their labor for pay, which made collective bargaining, workers' rights, upward mobility within a single corporation, and other labor practices core interests.[40] Because a world of work awaited children, childhood had a more relaxed, carefree nature and gradually became more adult through developmental stages.[41] Until the turn of the twentieth century (with the passage of the Fair Labor Standards Act in 1938), childhood was understood as a time to labor. But with the dawn of liberalism and the Progressive era, that perception was considered crude.[42] While today young children across the world still toil in sweatshops, in the domestic realm, in the fields, and the like, we frown on this and work to end it.[43]

Both liberalism and neoliberalism share the notion that economic activity is the basis of a human as a social and political self. A key difference between liberalism and neoliberalism is that under the latter, workers see themselves not in contrast to capitalists but as potential capitalists.[44] Economic inequality is now an accepted part of social life. As such, it is incumbent on individuals to make themselves competitive relative to peers through accumulating human capital (e.g., education, work skills) in order to be able to seize available opportunities or create opportunities.[45] Supplemental education serves that premise by augmenting youths' human capital skills beyond the school curriculum.

Neoliberalism alters the meaning of childhood and parenting. To be prepared for the future work world, kids must be made competitive at a young age, for competition is both inevitable and productive. People should turn to the private marketplace to prepare their children.[46] Under neoliberalism, people choose to use private solutions to public problems: bottled water instead of public drinking water, private delivery services rather than the government post office, and private insurance rather than push for universal, state-run health care.[47] Youth sports similarly now involve private, year-round options on top of town leagues; it has become a multibillion-dollar industry.[48] Private education outlets and competitions for young children, even as young as age three, are just another example. Parents appear lazy if they do not take advantage of such opportunities.[49]

From this perspective, participation in extracurricular activities should be seen as a form of child labor to prepare youths to become homo economicus. (I am not equating hyper education with the severe and often illegal forms of child labor mentioned earlier.) After-school education, sports, arts, and other options have become taken-for-granted avenues toward future work.[50] Unlike traditional work that siphons youths into particular occupations, such as apprenticeships, investments in human and cultural capital (i.e., character skills such as perseverance and ability to focus) provide youths with a flexibility in careers and an entrepreneurial mind-set. These are hallmarks of neoliberal ideology.[51] Capitalism depends on workers supplanting their desires in order to fulfill their duty to employers, much like the critiques of supplemental education that claim it keeps youths from developing their "true" interests.[52] Along with the cultural capital of character development, hyper education provides cognitive, problem-solving skills valued in advanced academics and the workplace.[53]

Families turn to extra academics on their own accord to make themselves fit for the standards of work. Hyper education represents a natural shift from what is known as sovereign power, that of individuals performing tasks because they are made to (e.g., taking standardized tests in school), to disciplinary power, that of individuals seeking out tasks (e.g., learning centers and academic competitions) so as to conform to social expectations—in this case, the expectations of more academic and character development.[54] It makes sense that public school teachers, as state employees, do not feel comfortable with the rise of private, for-profit spaces and their ideologies around child development. At the same time, it makes sense that parents who find standardized testing a necessary, even if unfortunate, experience would gravitate toward enrichment education as an evolved form of that logic. So, far from complaints that parents who engage in hyper education are uncaring, they are just practicing contemporary neoliberal logics as expected of all of us.

## Private Learning Centers

Learning centers, math competitions, and spelling bees specifically fit within the neoliberal response to perceived scholastic problems. Within the for-profit learning center field, there are many types. In the United States, the most common version is known as "shadow education," which refers to academic offerings outside of standard school hours meant to help children advance in their schoolwork and scholastic exams.[55] Tutoring and SAT test preparation are the most frequent.[56]

A growing type of supplemental education, and more the subject of this book, is private learning centers. Common national franchises include Kumon, Kaplan, Mathnasium, Sylvan, Russian School of Mathematics, JEI, and others, along with many regional options. Unlike a strict shadow education, learning centers do not aim to help students progress within the school curricula and standardized tests per se; they do not "shadow" the school, in other words. Instead, they devise their own curricula meant to develop students' engagement with the subject and their long-term study habits.[57] In this way, parents build up their children's human capital from a variety of perspectives, presumably better preparing them for various future workplaces. Centers teach at both the remedial and advanced levels, with some specializing in one type or the other. For instance, Mathnasium and Kumon primarily help students who want to do well at their grade level, according to directors and parents (although parents used them for enhancement purposes also). Other math centers, such as the Russian School of Mathematics and the Art of Problem Solving, focus on more abstract problem solving and were considered to have a more demanding curriculum among parents I spoke to.

As state-sponsored primary and secondary education for all children becomes accepted worldwide, after-school education naturally grows as well.[58] It has become more common in countries where it previously was less so, such as the United States, and has evolved to encompass a larger swath of people in countries where it was already well established, such as Japan and South Korea.[59] Learning centers' offerings reach beyond math and into reading comprehension, study skills, and preschool cognitive development. For instance, Junior Kumon is a preschool program within Kumon that targets children starting at age three to instill in them "a desire and motivation to learn; learning the letters of the alphabet, their shapes and sounds; learning numbers; recognizing patterns of dots."[60] It seems it is never too early to start extra education.

Learning centers' growth suits the contemporary neoliberal era in terms of their raison d'être. Centers gain their worth not by aiding students within a broken school system or fixing that system but by providing private, market-driven alternatives to it.[61] They advertise that they can assist advanced students that school districts presumably neglect.[62] Directors echo the critiques of pundits that the public-school system has not been incentivized to reform and serve a diverse array of students, including those above grade level. Instead, schools adopt a "cookie-cutter approach" because they are a "mass-market product," according to one center director.

Richard agreed. A public school teacher in Colorado who dealt specifically with high-performing students in his school district, he said,

> Very often [advanced] students will raise their hands, they ask questions, and the answer that they'll always get is "Well, you don't need to know that because it's not on the test." Kids hear this nationwide

all the time: "You don't need to know this because it's not on the test." Their answer will be "I *do* need to know this. I don't need to know it because it's on the test, [but] I need to know this. It's not what I need to know. It's what I *want* to. I want to know this." And this is sort of an off-shoot or a side effect of the standardized test culture in which we live.

Richard points to another negative side effect of the education system: the irrationality of rationality. While state-mandated standardized tests are popular, they lead to more homogenized instruction that is less tailored to individual students' interests or abilities. Eva, the director of a rigorous math center in suburban Boston with many Asian Americans, said,

> Classrooms are so big in public or private schools. The [better] teacher/student ratio that we have is one thing. [The] second thing is the curriculum. A differentiated curriculum is something that most schools don't have the advantage of giving to their students, while this is one thing that they get with our school. If the student is [a] beginner-level student and later on during the year things change and then they can move up, then that's what they need. This is one thing that schools, unfortunately, cannot address as well, just because they are not that flexible.

Sylvan Learning Center's online advertisements warn,

> [There is] no one-size-fits-all math program. Your child isn't one-dimensional and learning math shouldn't be either. We offer diverse math programs to make sure your child is learning in the way that works best for him or her.[63]

The company, in effect, insinuates that public school teachers do not know the kids in their classroom but instead treat them in "one-dimensional" ways. Centers also routinely boast of their smaller teacher-to-student ratio or even one-on-one instruction, as trumpeted by the Bill and Melinda Gates Foundation and others.

The media reinforces this critique of schools and the benefits of private centers. As reported in *Forbes,*

> Kumon could probably get lots of traffic even if public schools were excellent; some parents are obsessed with getting every educational edge for their children. But it doesn't hurt that taxpayer-funded schools have lots of distractions these days, such as the federal No Child Left Behind Act. This 2002 law compels school districts to focus on low performing students, leaving less time for high achievers.[64]

The learning centers' supposedly correct flaws in the education system while still abiding by their organizational tenets, such as using quantifiable assessments. Directors take pride in their frequent assessments of children, and most develop their own assessment procedures. Students complete weekly or biweekly worksheets that are immediately graded in the center, they complete homework that is graded and returned after each class, or the like. As franchised operations, the centers use standardized worksheets and curriculum created at a centralized office. This creates a predictable experience for youths even if they change locations. Even the decor of the centers is relatively uniform, with bright-colored or white walls, pictures of smiling children and animals, and so on.

As centers respond to the dysfunctions of the education system, they point to the testimony from youths as a vindication of their approach. William said that his company shares letters from families:

> Kids will write handwritten notes saying thank you. You know, "I love coming to [this learning center]. You make math make sense. I used to hate math. Now I love it." We get those all the time. It's awesome. It's not school math.

Such learning centers, in effect, rely on the schools as a foil. Their narrative differs widely from that of educators, of children being overly stressed and emotionally at-risk.

Kristina commented that her learning center, which has grown into a national franchise, was similar to (but cheaper than) a private school. Even her customers agree:

> One guy said, "You are giving everything to my children. I didn't need private school." It gives them good learning skills and driven families. That's what private school does. Parents look around, see the cars in the parking lot, talk to the families.

Much like private schools' allure stems from the sense of economic privilege among the families, so too can a learning center's. Nice cars indicate not just wealth but also "driven families" (presumably, no pun intended).

Given that centers consider themselves solutions to the public system, it is not surprising that they, like pundits and politicians, speak in backhanded ways about teachers. When I asked Max how to respond to teachers' concerns that students who attend supplemental education exacerbate the uneven classroom dynamics of some students being much more advanced than others, he did not hold back:

> I understand it makes the teacher's life hard, but at the same time, are we going to retard our kids' intellectual growth because the teachers can't—but oh, I shouldn't say "the teachers" because it's not just the teachers here—because the school system can't or won't [properly serve them]? . . . Somehow, we solved this problem with the basketball team. Somehow, we solved this problem for the band.

The school system presumably "can't handle" its higher-performing students. In his ideal world, schools would not even teach the subject but instead outsource it to private organizations like his.

Roger, an admissions officer at an elite university in the Boston area, castigated teachers:

> I'm professionally sympathetic to the fact that teachers have require-
> ments and they have standards. But if you're looking at the broader
> system of education as a whole, I have extremely low patience or sym-
> pathy for the idea that the correct answer when a student is advanc-
> ing and learning more is like, "Tsk, tsk. You should be proceeding at
> a slower pace." . . . I personally know the frustration of being the stu-
> dent who is reading at age eighteen when you're a ten-year-old. If you
> don't have that kind of sympathy [from a teacher] or that kind of ac-
> cess or the support of teachers who are like, "Yeah. You do you," then
> it's, like, very damaging and frustrating. It can be hard for teachers
> that don't know what to do when they have a standard curriculum and
> state requirements and things like that, but you've got to figure it out.
> You have to be more creative.

Schools are not flexible institutions like the private sphere.

Beyond their logic and internal organization, the learning centers' business model also suits neoliberal business principles. Their organizational growth is based on franchising, of individuals building out a company's brand. The franchisee takes on the risk and debt of the physical property and pays fees and dues to the company and in return receives the company's product guidelines, marketing, brand recognition, training, and assistance. Starting a Kumon franchise, for instance, can cost between $65,000 and $140,000 depending on one's geography and specific building location, plus fees, advertising commitments, and more.[65] The franchisee has to pay for the construction of the physical space when applicable. William commented on the start-up costs of his suburban Boston franchise:

> It's a lot. It's a lot. I mean, for me it was a lot more than I expected it to
> be, but every center's going to be a little bit different. In the Northeast

the commercial real estate market is such that you're going to pay a lot more than in most other places, and the landlords are less likely to kick in to the build-out. So the build-out was very expensive. Literally it was just concrete. It was nothing. It was a new construction, and I had to pay for the whole thing, so that was a lot.

Franchising as a business model suits the current economic era, for individuals work with private companies in some ways as employees, since they must follow the company's directives, but they take on great financial risk and have no guarantees of compensation.[66] At the same time, franchisees have large upward earning potential. For-profit education ventures that fill a niche supportive of school districts perform better than those that compete directly with schools.[67]

As a for-profit business, the learning centers are most interested in a return on investment. Learning centers frequently serve those with higher economic means. This is not simply because those with more money can afford private options to address public school problems. Such people are actively targeted, thereby reinforcing educational inequality. William explained that he is able to filter by income level in his vicinity in terms of who receives his advertising:

> The lower the income level, the more people there are, and so the bigger the mailing. I've done a 75 [thousand dollar annual income] and higher, I've done 100 and higher, and I've done 125 and higher. But doing 75 and higher is triple the size of 125 and higher. More people who are 125 and higher are going to be interested in spending a portion of their salary, so it makes more sense for me to focus my postcards on that, just because I have such a limited marketing budget. . . . A lot [of the customers] seem to be working in the universities, but I have some that work in financial institutions. I have some that are lawyers. . . . They're, by and large, mostly professionals.

Kristina said that her company's business model is to grow in areas with well-ranked school districts. This way she was targeting affluent families already prone to care about educational performance. Of less monetary interest were families in underserved communities needing to compensate for embedded educational inequalities.

For franchising, the emphasis is placed not on pedagogical expertise as much as on business sensibility. For instance, teachers or former teachers rarely are recruited to become directors, according to one franchisee. Another director had a career in IT management but wanted a more fulfilling career. His only pedagogical experience prior to starting the franchise center had been helping tutor his nieces. With well-respected nonprofit organizations such as Teach for America contending that people with hardly any teaching or training can effectively lead a classroom, such a business model is not surprising.

Learning centers also utilize a questionable pedagogy. William elaborated on the incentive structure for students to complete their work:

> We have this reward system where they get a stamp every time they finish a page. They get two stamps if they get the whole page right. They get three stamps if they bring in an A from a test in school. And then we have a reward cabinet here that they can exchange their cards for, so once they have a completed stamp card, they can exchange it for something. So the idea is that they have a little bit of incentive to work hard and stay focused and get their stamps.
>
> Q: That works well?
>
> For some kids, yes; for some kids, no. The older kids tend to care less, but once we added the Amazon and iTunes cards, they got a little more interested.

Encouraging academic achievement through external rewards may help encourage performance in the short run but gradually loses effectiveness over time and requires nicer and nicer rewards to maintain a commitment. Such a strategy does not ultimately serve parents or youths, but it helps the businesses show immediate results.

## Math Competitions

Math competitions such as MATHCOUNTS, Math Kangaroo, and Math Olympiad offer advanced elementary- and middle-school children opportunities to test their skills. The competitions aim to encourage all students interested in math even while they are geared toward those already highly competent in it. While these and other math competitions vary in their procedures, they generally begin their testing at the school level, and winners can move on to the state and then national levels. Subjects include number theory, ratios and proportions, properties of integers, probability and statistics, and much more. About 350,000 seventh and eighth graders participate in MATHCOUNTS annually, with many more in Math Olympiad, which spans fourth to eighth grades (not including competitions for high-school students).

MATHCOUNTS receives support and sponsorship from private and public entities, including NASA, the National Society of Professional Engineers, and most notably Raytheon (the competition is formally called the Raytheon MATHCOUNTS National Competition). The private-public partnerships for these competitions represent the broader trend of the increasingly blurry line between public education and private funding that suits neoliberal ideology. Supplemental education has become a big business. According to the *Washington Post*, "For-profit education [which includes supplemental education] is one of the largest U.S. investment markets, currently topping $1.3 trillion in value."[68] Investment firms and venture capitalists are moving into the for-profit education field.

Math competitions, like math centers, aim to serve students who need more than the school system offers. When I asked Carter if his

FIGURE 2.1. Siyona Mishra poses with her Florida MATHCOUNTS trophy. Photo by Basanta Mishra.

organization's math competition had value because the school curriculum did not adequately serve students, he replied,

> Yeah, I think that's a fair statement. . . . I think you've said it right. . . . When we think about what makes us special, it's that kids who only have one type of experience with math and that's going to class, doing worksheets that are too easy for them because these are kids who are really good at math, there's no challenge to it, and it bores them to tears. While on the flip side, kids who freeze up when they see that worksheet of fifteen problems, they don't know where to start. It's not a fun experience for either side. People would rather take out the trash than do it. And we hear this all the time from kids who do these programs, like, "I've never had fun doing math before."

Nor did most public-school math curriculums prepare students for advanced classes in high school or college, according to center directors.

Math competitions have seen considerable growth. In Massachu-setts from 2014 to 2015, for example, there was a 16 percent increase in the number of students participating in MATHCOUNTS and a 14 percent increase in the number of schools participating.[69] Diversity remains a challenge for math competitions, for they draw over-whelmingly from boys and typically from whites and Asian Ameri-cans. Efforts to diversify are under way, with mixed results.[70]

## The Spelling Bees as Edutainment

The Scripps National Spelling Bee and spelling bees in general have a slightly different relationship with public education than do pri-vate learning centers and math competitions. They take place in schools and do not compete with school curriculums as do learn-ing centers. But like those other types of academic opportunities, the bee represents not a deviation from neoliberal, privatized prin-ciples and rational norms of the education system but an alignment with them.

In 2019, 562 youths participated in the Scripps National Spelling Bee (of the over eleven million who participate in qualifying spell-ing bees in schools across the country). This is far and above the nine youths selected for the first official national spelling bee in Washington, DC, in 1925.[71] Before there was a national spelling bee, there were local spelling bees.[72] The earliest recorded spelling com-petitions in the United States were in New England in the mid-1700s. In 1766, in Newport, Rhode Island, teachers held "trials in spelling" at schools.[73] At that time, students had to not only spell words but explain why the words were spelled as they were.[74]

The civic dimension of the bees was part of their allure. Com-munity matches took place at schools in the evening, bringing champions from various districts to compete, as documented in Connecticut in the early 1800s.[75] They were festive occasions, with children dressing up and attending from over a mile away to compete or watch. In fact, the term "spelling *bee*" referred to community gatherings, such as cornhusking bees and the like, where people gathered to complete a task together, and even with recommendations of music being played during the bees so as to break up what could be a "somber affair."[76]

The civic dimension of the bee dissipated as it gradually became more market- and privately driven in terms of both its organization and its competitors. While there are various national-level spelling bees, the largest and longest-running one is the Scripps National Spelling Bee, which is now synonymous with the national bee.[77] The E. W. Scripps Howard Company took over the bee in 1941 after years of waxing and waning interest.[78] As a for-profit company traded today on the New York Stock Exchange, Scripps naturally looks for ways to heighten its mass appeal while maintaining its academic core mission. The company owns the largest share of independent TV stations in the nation (thirty-three) as well as radio stations and journalism outlets.[79] Scripps has positioned the bee within brighter media spotlights. In 1946, the national finals aired live on NBC television. After moving between different television outlets, the finals have been broadcast live on ESPN in primetime since 2011.[80] More and more countries are now participating in this ostensibly "American" tradition.[81]

Despite its mass media profile, the community element of the bee remains part of its allure.[82] The spelling bee does not just represent America; it helps construct it. The bee contributes to the idea of diverse people coming together within an American multiculturalism, not one of simply Anglo conformity. For example, finalists represent a wide swath of the country, both girls and boys, from large cities and small towns, and from the children of immigrants to those settled for generations.[83] Even the word lists are multicultural. In 1983, the winning word was Purim, a Jewish festival. Muslim holy words are now used. News profiles of the spelling bee—in particular of Indian Americans at the bee—embrace the notion of youths' cultural background influencing their learning and interest.[84] All of this suggests an America that welcomes diverse cultures as part of its identity. To participate in the bee is to help assimilate into the nation—that is, to take part in an American tradition while affirming the idea that the nation is equally open to all.[85]

Yet the meritocratic and community empowering elements of the spelling bee today are more in doubt than ever. Families' socioeconomic status has a clear impact on students' ability to excel in and even participate in the bee. Among other requirements, those who make it to the National Spelling Bee must have won a classroom bee and a school-wide bee (or home-school consortium), then a district- or county-level bee, and then possibly a regional or state-level bee city and/or regional-area bee (with other possible pathways).[86] While this process seems meritocratic, it depends in part on the financial status of families and their neighborhoods. The speller's school must be enrolled with the Scripps National Spelling Bee during the fall before the bee.[87] Fees to register range from $160 to $235 (as of 2019) depending on how early schools register. While this might seem like a little money, it often comes from parent-teacher association fundraising, and so it relies on parents having the financial means to contribute to the district.[88]

Scripps created a new route to the bee, starting in 2018, that directly benefits families with financial means. The RSVBee program allows into the Washington, DC–area finals a certain number of spellers who win their school bee and meet the eligibility requirements but who did not make it into the finals. In 2019, there were 294 RSVBee spellers (up from 241 in 2018), making those who paid their own way a larger share of the total contestants than those who won their regional competitions.[89] The 2019 bee had a record-breaking 565 spellers thanks to the RSVBee program, topping the 519 from the previous year, which had been the previous record.[90] The new program is meant to compensate for geographic areas that either lack corporate sponsorship or have multiple highly competitive spellers. But the costs are high. In 2018, RSVBee families had to pay a $750 participation fee, which doubled for the 2019 bee.[91] RSVBee families are responsible for transportation costs and incidental expenses as well.[92] The 2018 bee champion, Karthik Nemmani, was an RSVBee program participant.[93]

Just as Scripps has changed its entry rules in ways that privilege those with socioeconomic means, so has preparation for the bee become more hierarchical and market driven in contrast to its folk roots. At the bees' inception, students simply studied spelling in their schools or at home, and bees provided a community atmosphere to compete. Even up to the mid-1980s, there was little formality to the official preparation put forward by Scripps. Neeru, a former speller, said of her participation in the mid-1980s,

> I didn't know that formal spelling lists existed until I studied the nominal list provided for the district spelling bee. . . . I wrote out my own pronunciation guides and learned diacritical marks and some etymology in doing so.

Today, as fitting the rise of the privatized market in education, for-profit supplements have become popular for competitive spellers. The Scripps' Paideia (now called Spell It!) list (comprising around three thousand words), which has the official word list of state and lower-level bees, and its Consolidated Word List (comprising almost twenty-five thousand words) give students a predictable set of words to memorize. Spellers also use the Scripps/Merriam-Webster Spell it! website (*Merriam-Webster Unabridged Dictionary* is the official competition dictionary). But entrepreneurial youths develop their own pronunciation guides and language-origin training, and/or they purchase such guides online. Scott Remer's *Words of Wisdom* is a popular choice, currently in its fifth edition. Families of serious spellers purchase spelling software and lists of commonly used etymologies. They use dictionaries with only prefixes and suffixes. They also turn to spelling coaches. Some coaches offer their lessons for free online.[94] More and more, however, previous spellers—often still in high school—have turned their knowledge and skills into entrepreneurial opportunities, charging between $50 and $100 an hour. The software company Brainsy started offering spelling coaching with past champions and finalists as staff, charging up to $200 an hour to current contestants.[95] Beyond providing personally curated word lists, coaches offer tactics, such as spelling tips and words, so competitors have less to worry about.

It is not simply past spellers who monetize their skills. Parents of past Scripps contestants create and sell their own word lists, including words' part of speech, origin, definition, and more. There are even spelling academies—that is, for-profit businesses dedicated solely to preparing students for academic competitions. GeoSpell, for instance, was started by the father of a competitive speller. It is a tutoring business in the Dallas/ Fort Worth area to prepare students for spelling and geography competitions. While open to all students, he and his wife cater to fellow Indian Americans inside and outside of Texas. Weekly tutoring costs $120 per month. He took pride in helping 2018 champion Karthik Nemmani. In 2019, he and his wife helped three of the co-champions. GeoSpell, like other tutoring organizations, sells products (e.g., Greek-origin word lists) and courses, now expanding to standardized test preparation.[96] It hosts its own competitions as well. Another family, the Dasaris, with two former Scripps finalists, started SpellPundit based on their own teaching methods. The largest company selling products for the bee is Hexco, which specializes in materials for extracurricular pursuits (e.g., history, spelling, and geography bees). For instance, it offers word lists meant to help children get past the written round of the Scripps bee.[97] Families have paid over $2,000 for eight one-hour spelling coaching sessions or $3,450 for sixteen sessions.[98] They invest similar amounts of money for study materials.

According to the Hexco website, "94% of those who advanced to the finals on ESPN were Hexco customers, and 31% of the finalists were [privately] coached [by Hexco]" as of the 2019 finals.[99] As Anita, a young speller at a South Asian Spelling Bee, said, "Most people, they have lists, like they study from Hexco lists or stuff like that." Comparable consumer options exist for math and other competitions.[100] Not surprisingly, youths who make it to major competitions tend not to be in struggling financial conditions.[101]

The disconnect between the clear advantages that wealthier families have and the meritocratic image of the bee is often overlooked. I spoke with a spelling coach at an ethnic bee who was there to urge on his student. A former competitive speller, he enjoyed the fact that the bee represented a meritocracy, that anyone could win. When I asked him how he reconciled that perspective with the fact that coaches like himself benefit those families with financial resources, he recognized the contradiction for the first time and couldn't reconcile it, ultimately acquiescing that it was something he would think more about. So while the spelling bee prides itself on being a meritocracy, in this neoliberal age clearly private businesses play an oversized role.

Indian Americans, mostly of professional backgrounds, also participate in two bee circuits designed by and for South Asian Americans. As Paige Kimble said in the documentary *Breaking the Bee*, Indian American spelling bee options help explain their dominance at Scripps: "Kids who participate in more spelling bees probably are going to enjoy more success in spelling bees; it's as simple as that." The two major circuits are the North South Foundation (NSF) and the South Asian Spelling Bee. Ratnam Chitturi, a retired engineer in Chicago, started NSF as an educational charity to serve the poor in India in 1989. In 1993, as NSF began to look for ways to support Indian Americans, it decided to concern itself with the lower scores by Indian American youths on the verbal SAT section relative to their scores on the math section, so it started a spelling bee. He explained why Indian Americans would gravitate toward academic competitions:

> Two reasons. They care about education. And they want to measure excellence. This is why the spelling bee is tied to the Scripps standards. The math is tied to Singapore textbooks. The geography bee is tied to the National Geographic. You have to establish a standard. And Indians are very competitive.

His instincts proved correct. NSF has grown to over ninety chapters across the country.[102] Registration for each bee typically costs $35. Parents asked for math competitions, which began in 1994, followed by geography and then public speaking. NSF has enabled youths to achieve not only at the Scripps bee but also at MATHCOUNTS, the National Geographic Bee, the National Science Bowl, and the National History Bee. It even offers a "confidence-building program" that encourages public speaking. Chitturi refers to it as a "mini university" that has served over 4,000 students as of 2018. At the 2018 finals in Houston, about 1,250 youths participated and relied on over four hundred volunteers.[103] Remarkably, this is all volunteer driven, and the money raised from participation fees and the like in part goes to NSF's charity in India. Corporate donations bring in assets as well. Having volunteered at the Boston regional bee for three years as a spelling bee pronouncer, I can attest to the time and planning that parents put in behind the scenes. Volunteers find the venue, run the logistics, send out media alerts, secure other volunteers, administer and grade the tests, mobilize the parents, attend to the children, give out awards, and more. Alumni sometimes return to assist as well.

Despite its altruistic purpose and structure, NSF recognizes that it benefits by tapping into the current neoliberal moment, of parents' instrumental goal of making their children more competitive for college admissions and their distrust in the public school system.

The NSF website embraces the competitive dimension of college entry:

> As middle school and high school is becoming more competitive, students are striving to find ways they can stand out. Simply put, just excelling in academics isn't enough; instead, it's becoming much more about how effectively students can communicate and how confident they come across.[104]

Its other benefits include "building self-confidence," "setting goals and meeting them," and "developing discipline" and other character traits (i.e., cultural capital) that celebrate personal qualities meant to overcome obstacles.[105]

Beyond helping Indian American children achieve academically, NSF believes it can serve as a model for the school system at large. Santosh, a leader within the organization, commented,

> People [have been] concerned about education for the past thirty years. We haven't come up with a low-cost model. Increasing pay for teachers hasn't worked. Changing the syllabus hasn't worked. This model works.

NSF gets its salience by advocating for its role as a needed fix to the school system without "increasing pay for teachers."

The South Asian Spelling Bee (SASB) has a more recent history, although it too has become an institution within South Asian American communities since its inception in 2008. It offers only spelling. Like NSF, it has regional chapters that culminate in a final spelling competition held at or near Rutgers University in New Brunswick, New Jersey, in August of each year.[106] SASB is a venture of its parent company, Touchdown Media, run by the founder, Rahul Walia. The spelling bee started as a tool to support his advertising company, to show corporate advertisers that he could connect with the Indian

American client base. The bee was a product that would attract the Indian American audience and thereby attract advertisers to his parent business:

> If you know you want to connect with this audience, let's do a spelling bee for them. For every South Asian child that is being represented on the national stage [at Scripps], I'm sure there are hundreds that are wanting to emulate [and are looking for a competition].[107]

SASB can boast of having a well-run and highly competitive bee. Even South Asian American Scripps champions rarely end up winning it, instead placing among the finalists (and Scripps champion Ansun Sujoe could not make it past the regional round of the SASB one year). SASB's spelling list differs from that of Scripps, and Walia obtains it through various sources well versed in spelling bees generally. Some families fly across the country to participate in regional bees that they imagine will be less competitive than those in their own region.

Like the Scripps bee, corporate sponsors make the SASB competition possible.[108] While NSF depends on hundreds of volunteers, SASB runs on just a few staff because it has variously received financial support from Metropolitan Life Insurance, Air India, C2 Education, Sony Television, and more. As in traditional sports, private corporations team up with SASB to offer awards to winners and contestants. The prize money varies by how much the major sponsor is willing to give. In 2013, for instance, the winner earned $10,000, sponsored by Metropolitan Life Insurance. In 2018, the winner, Sohum Sukhatankar, earned $3,000. That is not the only kind of prize: Air India has given two round-trip airline tickets to India to contestants who had long been attending the SASB finals.[109]

SASB does not just chase corporate sponsors; corporations also chase spellers in the same way that sports celebrities are coveted by major advertisers and become lucrative "products" for the advertisers.[110] For instance, on June 11, 2013, Touchdown Media hosted a reception in a New York City Indian restaurant in honor of the recent Scripps champion Arvind Mahankali, an SASB alum. Representatives of SASB corporate sponsors were the main guests; along with past judges and family and friends, they were there to congratulate Mahankali and have videos and pictures taken with him, and the event was to be aired online and on Sony Television. At this event, corporate sponsors told me that they want to target the lucrative Indian American audience, stereotyped as wealthy, education focused, and family oriented, which fit their brands. This mixing of education and the private sphere is what parents seek out in order to advance their children. Children in spelling also often do these other types of after-school educational activities—they are all related.

## The Real Cultural Tug of War

If the stress facing Asian American youths in schools is akin to a public health crisis, it is important to realize that the so-called virus is not a foreign agent introduced into the educational ecosystem by Asian immigrant parents. The crisis is part and parcel of that ecosystem already created by government policies, nonprofit agencies, and public rhetoric. All of these entities have contended that good schools are hard to find and alternatives to the system are useful. Stereotypes against Asian Americans and an investment in a white normalcy prevent people from properly recognizing this overlap.

There is a cultural tug-of-war going on, but not between Asian culture and American culture. On the one hand is an increased rationality within the school systems represented by the neoliberal ethos of increased competition, privatization, and personal responsibility for families. On the other hand is a longing humanism represented by on-the-ground educators and parents who want to "take childhood back." The disease assigned to the foreign, polluted agent of

Asian Americans actually starts from the public critiques of and federal changes to the education system that have made schooling less humanistic. Private learning centers and corporate-sponsored academic competitions fit within this neoliberal turn in education. As such, hyper education is not going away, even if efforts to assimilate individual Asian immigrants prove successful. If parents want to push back against the growing academic stress on and "bullying" of children, they should realize that they have a much bigger battle ahead than originally realized.

# PART II

# Good Grades

# 3

## "You've Got to Survive in This World"

We parents are first generation [immigrants from India]. We compare [our kids' school] to our education in India. We had to really study to get into college. Here, everyone gets an A. Everyone from ninety-nine to ninety-one gets an A. In India, do you know how many people there are between scores ninety-nine and ninety-one? That single mark makes a huge difference. . . . I wish the teachers would push a bit more. They say [my daughter is] doing well and is an A student. I know she's doing well, but how do I get her to an A+? . . . Life, as they get older, is not going to be that easy.

I sat with Kavita, a mother of three children, all in middle school and younger, in the banquet room of a 2015 SASB finals competition weekend in Piscataway Township, New Jersey, while children talked and played together before receiving instructions for the next day's competition. Differentiating between an A and A+, she echoed a commonly held sentiment among parents I spoke to, that standing out among peers was essential in life. Good grades were not enough for her.

Later that evening, as I stood in the back of the banquet room, families had just finished dinner and were mingling. Deepak and his family had flown in from the Houston area. He and his wife had two children, one middle-school girl and an elementary school boy competing there for the second year in a row. He drove home a similar point:

If you're going to get anything [in India], you have got to get at least two marks above the other kids—if you want to get the right engineering degree that you want, you got to get ten marks more than the other people, otherwise that tells them that you're not interested. [Otherwise,] there's no place and your kid is completely lost. Once you [get higher marks], then you immediately see the benefits. So somehow it's ingrained in my mind that you have to . . . differentiate yourself. And if you do differentiate, then a lot of opportunities suddenly open up for you.

The message is clear: life is a competition, and one must stand out to get ahead.

## Safety versus Risk

Hasan, a father in his forties, explained to me at the 2014 SASB finals,

Every resource in India is scarce. You have to be cream of the crop to get anything into it. OK, so museum trips [for example]. I come from a very suburban school [in India]. Twenty kids from school are chosen to go on the museum trip, so you've got to be good at something [to be chosen]. And this scarcity mentality is everywhere. If you go to airports, right, people are rushing toward the gate. You don't see non-Indians do that. We have this scarcity mentality built in that we need to be there first to get some resource. Otherwise, it'll be gone. So we have the competitive thing built into us, so we are pushing our kids to it.

These parents grew up middle class in India. Some attended private schools. Their own parents were educators, business owners, engineers, farmers, and more. Still, they dwelled not on middle-class privilege but instead on the all-encompassing competitive environment in which they grew up, defined by a "scarcity mentality."

The sense that they must compete across all aspects of life shaped their parenting inside and outside of school. A father said in a group conversation in regards to various types of pursuits,

> I think we as Indians, from what I can see, we like our children to succeed in academic competitions. But when there's time for, let's say, the school basketball team selection, we want them to practice, practice, practice and sort of make it to that too. When there's a music competition, we expect the same thing. It's just that I think, because our strength in [academics], we sort of tend to excel here, and the chances of excelling in sports and music are less compared to this.

Parents emphasized less the inherent enjoyment or fun of competitive activities.

At a 2016 national math competition, Mahipal, an Indian American parent of a seventh grader, echoed what I had heard at spelling bees:

> You've got to survive in this world. Asians and Indians do this because they want to differentiate themselves from the competition. Not everyone is doing this, but many are. In my country, everyone did it. If you don't do it, if you don't become a doctor or engineer; you have to do it. There are no options. It's a supercompetitive environment. We should have started [extracurricular math] in second or third grade.

Indian American parents operated on a binary of safety versus risk. Hyper education was not just about getting into one's top school; it was about the need "to survive in this world," for which education, preferably started at a young age, set the foundation. This was necessary so that children would not become "completely lost," and it prevented a "life of nothingness," as another parent told me. At the heart of Indian Americans' commitment to education,

FIGURE 3.1. Shobha and Shourav Dasari celebrate her victory at the 2013 Houston Public Media Spelling Bee. Photo by Usha Chava.

including enrichment education, was an emphasis not on academics per se but on the need to outcompete their peers in order to secure economic, family, and personal opportunities. If their child did not succeed, someone else's child would.

Parents even lobby competitions to have their underage children participate. For instance, NSF starts in first grade, but some parents petition for their kindergarten students to enter. During an NSF Boston regional competition in March 2013, a child as young as age six was announced as a contestant; parents applauded in encouragement of someone so young already participating.

Parents also worried that ethnic stereotypes could lead their children to misjudge their abilities so that they would not push themselves academically. As one mother said during a group conversation with parents at the same NSF competition,

[This competition] is like a reality check for them. Especially when my son was young, he was the only Indian in the whole school. So everyone was already like, "All Indians are good at math"; that's what they used to tell him. And then he thinks that he doesn't even have to work hard, that everything will just come naturally to him. [*Crowd laughs*] So this was a reality check for him, and realized that I'm compared to so many other people [outside of my school.]

Parents enroll in learning centers with the same motivations. According to William, parents come to his franchise math center because they want their kids to excel over others. The parents, in his opinion, believe,

"Sure, [the children are] caught up with everybody else at school, but I don't want them caught up with everyone else. I want them to be ahead. I want them to have the best chances. I want them to be able to get to the top schools, you know. I want them to get over seven hundred on their math SAT, you know, whatever." So I think [parents] recognize that, to a certain extent, they want them to be ahead.

I sat in the modest living room of a mother, Heena, who ran another franchised math center. Over chai, she noted that in India, one had to be highly competitive and that immigrants needed their kids to be ahead, especially if they returned to India but also so as to boost their US college-entrance chances:

In India, Asia, you have to be the best of the best to get a job. So much competition for spots. Why did we come from India to here? To get a better life. Since you came here for a better life, you want to give your kid a better opportunity. God forbid if I have to go back to India; I need to make sure the kid won't fall behind. Many Indians who come to my center are on H-1B visas and might have to go back. . . . That's the whole point. Do more now so [you] stay good in math, get into [a] gifted program, get AP classes, get good SATs. It's all geared toward that.

To her point, the likelihood of entrance into the university system in India has gotten so low that students find themselves rejected from elite universities there but accepted into US Ivy League universities.[1] The Indian Institutes of Technology, the most prestigious university system in the country, has "an acceptance rate of less than 2 percent—and that is only from a pool of roughly 500,000 who qualify to take the entrance exam, a feat that requires two years of specialized coaching after school."[2]

Parents do not simply carry over their mentality to the United States without a sense of context. Here too, they see competition for selective institutions, SAT scores, AP classes, and the like, as Heena said. As Andrew, the director of a Chinese math center in an affluent Boston suburb, said,

If [students] started to enhance math in middle schools, it's too late. Because you want to be in [the] top tier, get into a good college. Because middle school [already has] top-level [students], if you don't do anything in elementary school, it's too late. You never get to [a] good college.

For one to stand out in high-school academics, it is necessary to be high-performing before high school. Parents imagined their children competing globally for jobs. As Aashadar, a father of two young teenage girls involved in math and spelling, said,

If they have to go to some other country eventually in search of their careers, that's fine. So I guess there is this mind-set that they'll probably be competing against a national or an international student body at some point. So the notion is to try to expose them to that sort of competition at this age, so that means with respect to words and math, which are kind of foundational, so for words, you have the spelling bee, and for math, you have the AMC [American Mathematics Competitions], MATHCOUNTS, that whole track.

For these parents, it is not just that academics is competitive; life itself is competitive. All the things one wants in life, one must outcompete others for. This includes field trips to the museum, a good job, and more. As one father said in a group conversation,

> Getting married to a good girl and everything depends on the position you have, the education you have done. . . . That's expected in a society, in a family.

With so much at stake, parents felt the safest route was to make their kids highly competitive for any future opportunity. "Otherwise, it'll be gone," as Hasan worried.

## From Competition to Education

Indian Americans are obviously not the only parents worried about their children standing out relative to others. US-born, middle-class parents generally worry about their children being outcompeted by their peers in activities such as academics, sports, music, and more. This leads them to a concerted cultivation of their parenting style of emphasizing extracurricular training and intentional pursuits at an early age (e.g., helicopter parenting, or constantly monitoring and coaching one's child).[3] The activities are meant to be fun but also help children develop social relations and boost their cultural capital, such as a sense of teamwork, a competitive edge, and the like.[4] Even elementary-age youths benefit from participation.[5] Parents who want their children to excel in sports join private club teams rather than just town leagues.[6] Second graders take part in competitive swimming rather than just enjoying the town pool. Robotics and other STEM courses fill up rather than youths just playing with LEGO or Erector sets.

So if immigrant parents are motivated by a fear of competition rather than education per se, like other parents are (albeit some in a more intense way), why do we not see them prioritize more common extracurricular options instead of focus on academics? Asian Americans' pursuit of education typically has been framed as due to their unique cultural background, where education was pushed onto them; due to their fear of discrimination in the United States, which is best overcome through extreme academics; or both.[7] But once we realize that Asian Americans are driven not by a commitment to education but instead by a need to outcompete others, the question is no longer why they pursue education but what mechanisms lead these parents to turn to academics as their safe means to stand out, unlike other middle-class families who also invest in children's competitive edge through sports, the arts, or the like.

Three reasons emerge for their choice of academic enrichment: a sense that other popular pursuits (e.g., sports) are not viable for them, a need to build up human capital given their lack of social capital and possible race-based hurdles in college admissions, and parents' own familiarity with extracurricular education based on their upbringing. The result is an investment in education as an after-school activity and having more of, although not a complete, say in children's pursuits. This is an *Asian American style of concerted cultivation*, one that resists assimilation into the mobility strategies of their American peers, which they fear will not serve them as they do others.

## To Sport or Not to Sport

According to the US Census, sports is the most common after-school option for children in the United States, more so than music, technology, language, or other kinds of lessons and more so than Boy and Girl Scouts, religious-based clubs, 4-H, and the like.[8] Sports is read as a vehicle for mobility and opportunity.[9] Some Indian American youths take sports very seriously as players and/or spectators. But they often dedicate less family time and fewer resources to sports than to other options. Why are they not pursuing what is widely assumed to be a promising tactic toward college admissions? Some Indian Americans wondered the same. As a father asked in a group discussion,

> Why educational? Why not in sports? Why no physical activity? Somehow we don't as parents focus [on] or permit sports as a priority. We only stay indoors, making sure our kids are safe and learn math, English, science.

Nicholas, a college admissions officer at a highly selective university, similarly wondered:

> If you're the sort of student who does a little bit of a herd mentality of "These are the things that everyone else is doing. And these are the things that I must achieve because that's what you do to get into college," then you're actually not differentiating yourself from the pack. And you're miserable. And you're burning out. And it's probably not going to make [a] marginal difference in the case anyway. And the much better strategy to follow in high school and earlier than high school is to sort of do the things that you want to do. Do them as well as you can do them. Trust in that. Trust in that.

Asian American parents may not be doing their children a favor by stressing the same academic path as their peers do. This is all the more reason why they should be distinguishing themselves in other venues, such as athletics.

Yet few Indian or other Asian American families considered athletics, especially team sports, to be a venue for their kids to outcompete others, even as many kids participated recreationally and on competitive teams. Here are some of the most famous Indian Americans that probably no other Indian Americans have heard of: Mohini Bhardwaj, Stephen Raj Bhavsar, Brandon Chillar, and Dalip Singh Rana. This list consists of two US Olympic medal winners, a Super Bowl champion, and a wrestler celebrated for his huge size and strength, respectively. Still, they and many others engaged in sports are not mentioned when talking about famous Indian Americans. They don't fit the image of a "typical" Indian American.

An Indian American former professional athlete in a popular American sport said to me,

> I remember, and this happened on many occasions, when I come out of my locker room, I have my Indian family there, and they are dressed in Indian clothes. Everybody else's family is white or black, and my family looks different. People didn't know I was Indian.

Even this professional athlete's teammates, not to mention the fans, did not recognize him as an Indian American. He persevered in sports, but he is more the exception than the rule.

Saroj, a father of youths involved in spelling, gave a frequently echoed and racially problematic argument for why Indian Americans cannot excel in sports and why other races do:

> We are not sporting people. . . . Everyone wants to be an athlete, but you can't. You can practice hard; you can do what you want. But if you don't have the genes for it, you are not going to excel, no matter how hard. . . . African Americans have an advantage in sports. Because that's their gene [*sic*].

A father similarly explained in a group conversation at the 2016 SASB Boston regional,

We will take them to the sports field, but you have to be realistic in
what your child wants to pursue. There is a certain number of years
that, you know, you have to dedicate before they excel.

Sports was useful to make one well rounded, possibly even to make
one's junior varsity or varsity team later in high school, but it was
not a place to really stand out, since it would take too many hours of
training to compensate for a supposed lack of genetic disposition.
Highly problematic racial stereotypes guided their judgments of
groups. Asian families typically do not think youths are genetically
predisposed to excel in one field or another, except when it comes
to sports.[10] Hyper education is not a natural choice for immigrant
professionals but instead is one they choose as the most practical
way to differentiate their children.

Parents' lack of confidence in sports stems in part from their
own upbringing within a postcolonial nation. Imperial Britain maintained its rule over India partly by constructing Indian men as failing
in sports and inherently subservient in contrast to the able-bodied,
masculine British men.[11] This legacy of empire intersects with the
US treatment of Asian Americans as the effeminate model minority. Contemporary portrayals of Asian Americans as the extremely
studious and submissive model minority are played off against the
athlete and jock. Such images suggest to Asian Americans not only
that they are unfamiliar with sports but also that they should not
bother focusing on them.[12] When they do engage in sports, it is in
precision-oriented fields like ice skating, diving, and gymnastics
and other solo sports as opposed to popular group sports.

The parents I spoke to are the type of Indian immigrants most
likely to conform to a "model minority body." As explained in the
appendix, they frequently are immigrant professionals who arrived through work or education visas, often in the IT industry, or
are spouses of those who arrived as such. Both wives and husbands

typically went through grueling exam schedules in India in order to attain sufficient education levels and earn one of the limited opportunities to emigrate to the United States.[13] The competition to immigrate has become stiffer over the years since 1965, when Indian professionals started migrating in large numbers. The hours they spent studying left them little time to dedicate to sports beyond as an extracurricular diversion. The limited infrastructure for sports within India and the general lack of encouragement of sports for girls also lessen these immigrants' development of a sports ethos when younger.

This is not to say that parents did not participate in sports when growing up. Kavita played basketball in India, and another mother played competitive table tennis. Other parents enjoyed cricket, soccer, tennis, and other games. They liked their kids playing sports as an additional but not a primary activity, at least not one that took time away from more learning. In general, these immigrants developed a particular "body schema" from such an upbringing—that is, a group's "relation to the body at its deepest and most unconscious level."[14] This body schema has less familiarity with sports than do many US-born, able-bodied Americans. When a person highly involved in Indian spelling bees says "we are not a sporting people," he is referring to these immigrants' body schemas relative to the stereotypes of black and white boys and girls.

Indian immigrant parents pass on their "model minority bodies" to their children, whose main access to a sports upbringing comes from organized activities such as Little League but less so from parents and other relatives themselves. Such a brain-versus-brawn binary is not real, for kids can excel in both.[15] Nor did youths necessarily feel removed from sports as fans (discussed later). Youths participated in all kinds of sports, including softball, baseball, basketball, soccer, volleyball, tennis, and golf. But the time dedicated to sports decreased as children entered middle school and high school. Not only was focusing on sports not profitable; it could lead to problems. Fathers in particular weighed in on the pros and cons. As one said during a Boston-area group conversation in 2013,

> I mean, think of the probability. We all want our kids to be successful. We want them to be like a Bill Gates or probably like, I don't know, Shaquille O'Neal. But if you tried to be Bill Gates and you're not successful, there are a million financial analyst jobs that you can get in. Whereas if you're not a Shaquille O'Neal because of the genetics or the interest in some of the sports, if you fail there, you become, in India terms, a clerk or whatever. So the chances of your success are in the education area, [more] than you trying to go into a sport at this point.

Another father said during the same conversation,

> Some of my [Indian American] friends with whom I spoke said, well, our kids cannot compete with the other kids in swimming; they get tired out very easily. Something like basketball—the kids are not tall enough to compete with the regular kids. So I mean, those are physical aspects, and also other issues come into play, but that's why you scale down at sports and start [to] look at other activities which bring you to the top.

In general, all parents choose the extracurriculars that most suit their personal experiences and budget and that seem the most viable for their children's enjoyment and success. Dedicating significant time and resources to the wrong activity not only was considered a waste of money but could jeopardize a child's future, for the family was not helping the child find a venue through which to outcompete others.[16]

In fact, having *too* muscular and coordinated a body could suggest that one did not take academics seriously enough. For instance, during a dialogue session about geography bees at the 2013 NSF finals, a mother asked a set of middle-school youths who had done well in the competitions how they balanced preparation for the bees with other extracurricular activities. A tall, lanky teenage boy with glasses responded that he spent so much time studying for the geography bee that he dropped out of his school's soccer team, which was deemed much less important.[17] Parents nodded their heads with approval.[18]

While fathers spoke more openly about sports relative to their parenting choices, mothers also believed in the worth of sports and facilitated their child's participation.[19] Some played sports competitively, as mentioned earlier. Most others drove their kids to practices and games, registered for teams and kept track of the schedules, cleaned and folded uniforms, and the like. Girls and boys both participated in sports. To the extent that girls participated in sports less, none suggested it was because of parental pressure but instead cited it as a personal choice.

Contrary to popular and academic assumptions, parents could imagine spending considerable time on sports if the child showed significant talent in it—that is, if the child could safely stand out through sports. Their goal was to find the venue in which to out-compete others and secure a safe future, a that venue need not be education. As Rakesh said to me at a math competition,

> If my son was going to do swimming since second grade, and [be] good at it, that would help him stand out. They don't need to be competitive at math. But [they] must be competitive at something.

Jasmin, a mother of a middle-school student, said while at an Indian spelling bee,

> We would like to prepare our kids for what comes naturally to us. We can't tell our kids, "You should do soccer, and you will become a world player, and I'll coach you." We can't do that. This [spelling bee] comes naturally.

To pursue sports as intensely as academics, parents would have to believe that the child had the potential to "become a world player." They respected top-tier athletes and those families whose children were highly competitive in something. The father of a spelling bee champion similarly commented that he would have been happy with his son playing basketball rather than spelling if "he could make it into the NBA."

In fact, it would be naïve not to follow a nonacademic pathway if there was a good reason to believe a child could excel at it. Rishi, a father well known in the spelling bee community, made the following comment at the end of a group interview at the 2015 South Asian Spelling Bee finals:

> What we are good at, we are going to pass that on. That is the underlying thing. If Sachin Tendulkar [an Indian cricket star] had a kid, he's going to give him cricket. All the Kapoor people [a famous Bollywood family] are good actors. [Spelling] is something no other community embraces the way we embrace. We do it because when we were growing up, we were told, "Study hard and you will have a good life." Those are the values that NRIs [nonresident Indians] here are passing onto their children. If any of these parents' kids were good at something else, they would encourage the kid to do that. It's like any other sport.

The crowd of parents nodded their heads in agreement. Because these parents had excelled in academics, particularly math and science, this was the pathway in which they could give their children an advantage over others. Similarly, Asian immigrant youths and the second generation may not pursue leadership opportunities in school due to cultural, linguistic, and racial exclusions, leading them to emphasize academics.[20] Families see those who have excelled in professional sports, the arts, and public leadership as exceptions, often based on parental expertise.

## It's Not Who You Know; It's What You Know

Binita, who had a second-grade son enrolled in an after-school math class, said,

> My problem really is, you can be successful only if you do [academics]. Because that's how I saw people and, even growing up, how they got successful. And so, I don't know if I can take a chance [on letting my son specialize in other interests] and figure out later that that's not the recipe for success. . . . [The people who pursue creative or athletic extracurriculars] might have a lot of connections, so even if you take a bad decision, or take a risk, and it doesn't work out, he has something else to fall back on. For us, we don't have anything to fall back on. For us, education is the only thing to fall back on.

Like all other sufficiently cynical adults, Indian American parents realized that in the work world, it's not what you know but who you know that matters.[21] But if you do not "have a lot of connections," your reputation depends on what you know—and you better know more than others in order to be recognized. One needed more than just good grades. Compensating for a lack of social and cultural capital with high human capital is the second mechanism leading to a commitment toward hyper education and academics more generally.

Without a social and cultural grounding in the United States, immigrants felt handicapped in the workplace. Jigishu, a motel owner in Ohio, relayed how lacking networks to decision makers can block opportunities:

> If you're class of '80 from Ohio State, you're on the board. But you know, I am not a class of '80; I graduated in Mumbai. I am not from Ohio State. I [have] never been from Ohio State, so I'm never going to make the secret handshake; I cannot.

Even US-born and -raised children of immigrants do not feel deeply familiar with the cultural norms of their peers and worry about their prospects for mobility.[22]

Parents I spoke with recognized the importance of cultural and social capital. But as immigrant minorities, they lacked both. Their cultural references and tastes are bicultural, but they are not necessarily fluent in American ways. Their networks stem from their kin and local religious or caste networks.[23] These connections may be influential within certain industries, such as the Gujuratis within the hospitality sector or South Indians in the IT industry.[24] But they do not span a spectrum of fields or geographies. Parents lack the assets that come from membership in fraternities or sororities or from their parents' connections, for instance. In other words, since children will be more reliant on human capital, given their deficiencies elsewhere, they better have a lot of it.

Chun, a Chinese American mother, similarly worried about hurdles to advancement despite having a white-collar career as an engineer in an affluent suburb of Boston. An anxiety shaped her parenting:

> We don't have the education here, so we probably cannot understand the way things are supposed to be. Also, when we were here for our first job, it is difficult. You don't have the visa status. If your English is not good, even if you have good grades, it takes [a] much longer time to get a job. The immigrant parents have experienced that, so they push their kids a little bit harder.

Thaman explained the role of "career capital" as he thought of how to raise his two Indian American boys:

> Do you know of [Academy and Grammy award winner] A. R. Rahman, the composer? Now his son is about the same age as my younger son. We've heard that kid play the piano. And he played really well, but

hearing that, we immediately knew my son was actually significantly better. But if you went to bet on which of these two kids is to make a name for himself in music, you'd probably bet A. R. Rahman's kid. I know nobody in the music industry; I don't know how that industry works. I know my son has a tremendous music sense, but I really hesitate to encourage music as a career. Because I don't have the career capital, I cannot advise him. I'm advising my son to learn math because there I can really advise him. It helps some kids to kind of leverage the parent's career capital. And so that's one of the reasons why all these scientists or Indian doctors are sending the kids to math centers.

The children could take advantage of the parents' networks if they stayed in that same industry, as is popular in India, which in turn made certain educational fields—namely, STEM—the most relevant.

Because parents cared first and foremost about providing their children with a competitive edge, they did not privilege STEM careers per se. Binita said of herself and her generation,

We're first generation here. We're still—as much as we've lived here fifteen years—we're still in that mind-set. "You shall become something." "You shall become an engineer." And that's not been the case with the American families. I'm not judging it. But honestly, I would be scared that if, if [my son] picked something that is not practical. What are the odds of succeeding as an actor, right? So those odds scare me. Which possibly wouldn't be the case with the Americans. Some of the American families [are not scared] because they've been all successful, like clearly they do well in every field.

Q: *You cannot guide them in other fields?*

That's true, yes. That is absolutely true, yeah. The security has to be good.

Most parents worry if their children want to pursue acting or some other career with low odds for success. Rather than look down on those who endorsed non-STEM careers, these Indian American parents were somewhat envious, for those others had more connections or less fear of risk.

Along with lacking networks, informants lacked assets, which put more pressure on children to choose career tracks that parents could assist with. As Jignesh, a father who immigrated on an H-1B visa, said of himself and his fellow immigrants, "They don't have extensive landholdings and so on that can be passed onto their kids." As immigrants without networks or wealth, it was imperative to raise their children in a down-to-earth manner geared toward white-collar employment.[25]

Some parents saw such a plan pay off early. A mother shared with me and others at the 2014 SASB finals that after her middle-school son was broadcast saying at the Scripps National Spelling Bee in 2013 that he wanted to grow up to become a doctor, a medical school contacted him and invited him to the campus. The family visited the campus, and the son is happy to be considering attending after he starts and finishes high school and then starts and finishes college. Here, how much the child knows compensates for lacking social capital in the medical profession, just as his parents had hoped.

When asked about racism or possible blocked mobility as impacting their own lives or as concerns for their children, parents downplayed the likelihood. Nor did anyone bring up explicit racism as a concern, in contrast to an earlier generation of arguments on Asian American parenting.[26] An Indian American college student, Taj, referred to her upbringing in the United States:

So the Asian drive or the Asian parent drive to put you in a bunch of extracurriculars, at least with my parents, was not driven by this idea that I would have to face extra hurdles [due to race].

Racism is real and afflicts Asian Americans in meaningful ways, ranging from hate crimes to a glass ceiling to microaggressions.[27] Yet contrary to common assumptions, parents did not guide their children to STEM careers out of a fear of discrimination in other "less objective" fields like the arts.

Yet this does not mean parents did not recognize that race mattered. While at a South Asian Spelling Bee finals, a father, Murali, explained why his daughter pursued math and spelling, citing a specific set of points relating to the SAT:

> One reason is that it's a very competitive world. You need to be better than the best. Particularly in our Asian community, math is so pronounced. The college admission system [in the United States] is that we need to be one step up. From what I've read, we have to have 130 points above others. That is how admissions are determined. [The] spelling bee will help with the SAT.

According to one report, Asian Americans who attended highly selective private institutions had, on average, higher standardized test scores than any other racial group, with 140 points above whites on the SAT, on average, in 1997.[28] Race creates a double standard that Asian Americans must live up to and that furthers the intensive academic commitments that white Americans witness as over-the-top. Hyper education was partly a response to that. Simplistic caricatures of Asian Americans as "tiger parents" culturally committed to increased human capital overlook how this commitment is a response to racial dynamics, with Asian Americans being compared to one another in college admissions.[29]

A lawsuit against Harvard University by some Chinese Americans, known as Students for Fair Admissions and led by Edward Blum, a conservative anti–affirmative action activist, picks up on these worries.[30] The lawsuit, which was successfully contested by Harvard in

2019, claims that Asian Americans are penalized for having less impressive "personality" scores and are not admitted in sufficient numbers despite having some of the highest grades, test scores, and extracurricular activity lists among applicants.[31] The premise behind this possible treatment of Asian American applicants is the fear of college campuses being "overrun" by Asian Americans, who are perceived as not being "well-rounded."[32] While Harvard won the case, possible prejudice against Asian Americans was not ruled as unfounded.[33] Prejudiced nicknames for elite universities illustrate this fear: MIT stands not for Massachusetts Institute of Technology but instead for Made in Taiwan. UCLA stands not for University of California, Los Angeles, but for University of Caucasians Lost among Asians.[34] Standing out in terms of education among Asian Americans becomes all the more necessary, since they must compensate for possible negative evaluations in other dimensions.[35] Still, many Asian Americans resist the lawsuit against Harvard, for it aims to eradicate affirmative action, and it diverts attention from the real barrier to Asian American admissions, which is spots set aside for privileged whites (e.g., legacy applicants and athletes in sports dominated by well-off whites).[36]

In fact, some considered race-based preferences to support whites over Asian Americans. As Max, a white male and a leading educator for mathematics competitions, said,

> The filter that the Chinese kids have to get through to get into Harvard is much finer than the rest of the kids. There's no question. To me, there's absolutely no question the Chinese have to do much better in order to get into MIT, in order to get into Harvard, Princeton. There's definitely—there's some affirmative action [for white children] that's working against Asians.

He is referring not to the program that assists underprivileged minorities but instead to the possible lower expectations for whites that, in effect, work as an implicit form of affirmative action for them relative to Asian Americans.[37]

College admissions officers deny that there is a higher standard for Asian Americans. But that does not mean that they do not admit that Asian Americans can face a higher hurdle than others. Franklin, a college admissions officer at a highly prestigious university in the Northeast, revealed how his school considers applications:

> The way that we think about our admissions process is, What has the student done with the resources that they've had? So we're going to expect more achievement from a student with PhD parents in Bergen County, New Jersey, High-Tech High School than from a student who is the child of a tailor at a laundromat and a seamstress in San Francisco in a public school, neither parent completed high school. And I use both of those archetypes because those are two Asian immigrant archetypes that we often see. Now, usually hearing that explanation doesn't make people in the high-powered communities happy. Because they feel like they're being held to a higher standard because they did well, which to a certain extent they are. Also, because it raises up the competitiveness a little bit even more. That's the danger.

Asian American students can end up competing against one another in the admissions process. Franklin admits that this process, while striving for equality across applicants, exacerbates a competitive dynamic for parents already sensitive to such problems. Raj, a father in the San Francisco area, told me at the 2015 NSF finals,

> In coming from the Bay Area, [hyper education] is one of those things that helps you get along with the community. They are all doing it.

Another parent in the Boston area, Jignesh, commented, "The competition in high school is really with all the Asian families." Students must achieve more than their coethnic peers with similar resources. This is partly why cram schools with names like "Little Harvard" and "Ivy League School" are so popular and advertised in Chinese American newspapers and why Korean American hagwons can be found across the country and the world. Moving from an A to an A+, as Kavita wants for her daughter, makes sense under these conditions. Parents engage in hyper education in order to keep up with peers who are known to also invest in it.

Asian Americans believed that they fell into a catch-22 scenario. They stress education because they lack networks, wealth, or alternative ways to stand out relative to whites (e.g., sports). But the commitment to academics paints them as comparable to other Asian Americans, whom they must then outcompete so as to differentiate themselves. Yet by focusing on academics, they fit an Asian stereotype that limits their ability to appear well rounded to college admissions officers. They could be nervous to approach schoolteachers with their concerns about their children because they might lack English-language fluency or might be stereotyped as overly anxious Asian parents, so sticking with private learning opportunities makes more sense.

So we see that immigrant parents' emphasis on education for their children stems from their sense of what it takes to make it and what resources they bring (and do not bring) to the table. They feel excluded from sports and other extracurriculars that are read as predominantly white and/or black spaces. They feel compelled to stress rational pursuits for their children, since they do not have the luxury of guiding them in diverse careers, knowing all too well that networks and "career capital" matter. Possible racial hurdles within the college admissions process make doing well in these pursuits all the more important. They may not feel comfortable approaching teachers with their concerns, so they must stand out through their academic performance and use after-school spaces for that.

## How We Were Raised

I used to do math every day, and so for me, for [my son] not doing math, I can't handle that.

For Jignesh and so many other parents, it felt natural to participate in enhanced academics. Immigrants from India and East Asia often—not always—are the cream of the academic crop, not only more educated than the average American, but even more so relative to the average person in their homeland.[38] Their commitment to academics for their kids resonates with their own upbringing and is familiar to them and is the third mechanism driving their decision-making. One father, Karunanidhi, recalled his upbringing in India to me and a group of three other parents at the NSF finals in 2013. We had been discussing the possibility of his and other Indian American children getting burned out on academics. He had little sympathy for such rhetoric:

> When I was [a] student, there was no concept of burnout. [*Others laugh*] Why? Because when you were a kid, you wanted to go out and play, but your parents said, no, study. Right? [*Others nod*] Study. I remember lights used to go out, we would start the kerosene lamp, [our] eyes would burn like crazy, but you were doing your job. That was burnt out! [*Others laugh*]

Binita lamented that in her upbringing, education after school was a normal part of life.[39] She recalled, "School was never enough. You always had to supplement." Parents teach this lesson to their children, and children hear it echoed within their ethnic community.[40]

Rather than simply reproducing what they experienced as children, parents have a love/hate relationship with their youths. Another father, Nityanand, explained,

If my father, who was a professor in university, would have told me that you study when you want to study, I don't think I would have ever studied. When I came over here [to the United States, someone asked me,] how did you become good? I said it was very simple, you have to go look in my closet, the shape of the hangers will tell you why [I] am where I am. Because if those were not used on me, I would have never studied! It's basically the culture. Over here we believe in giving kids the chance, giving kids the environment, and let them grow. And in India who had the time? Who had the time to do that?

These parents might be dramatizing their upbringing, and they are exaggerating a hands-off approach by white middle-class parents, who also push and punish their children for their work ethic. The point, though, is that there clearly was not a love of education per se for these parents. With so much at stake, if one did not attain a sufficient level of education, having parents literally beat you to study was forgivable in his mind. One repaid one's parents' sacrifices by succeeding in school and improving the family's well-being. Their upbringing shaped their outlook, but they can still regret aspects and speak of it in mixed tones.

## Parent-Driven, Child-Centered Concerted Cultivation

This Asian American style of concerted cultivation emphasizes education and involves significant parental guidance but still is responsive to children's preferences, as for parents generally. An interaction with a mother at a South Asian Spelling Bee perfectly sums up this balance of academics and child interest. I told her that my son, in first grade at the time, had shown interest in US history. She was delighted to hear this and encouraged me to enroll him in a history bee. She did not privilege spelling per se and considered the history competition equally valuable. If that was my child's interest, I should pursue that. When I said that he loved baseball and asked if I should emphasize that, she demurred and said an academic focus was the better choice. In that interaction, she affirmed both the rational priority of academics over anything else and a humanistic sensitivity to my son's interests in deciding which academics to prioritize.

While parents were open to various kinds of academic pursuits, they all considered math a necessary tool for the future. As one mother explained, growing up in India, there were only three options open to them: "commerce, science, or arts." The parents I spoke with typically chose science, leading to engineering or medical careers.[41] The liberal arts are much less valued, and majoring in English signaled an intent to get married after graduation.[42] Parents I met were educated mostly in STEM fields in India, as fits the national profile of Indian women and men.[43] Not only had math proved essential to parents; they also saw it as essential for their children's future. Parents believed they were responding to the current and future job market by stressing math.[44] Math also made sense because youths needed to keep up with coethnic peers who were also pursuing it.

As noted earlier, parents criticized the quality of math in American versus Indian schools. Ironically, despite often moving to the United States for better career and educational opportunities for themselves and their children, they uniformly criticized the lower standing of the American educational system relative to other nations. They are not alone. According to a 2016 national survey of Asian Americans, 45 percent rated the poor quality of their children's schools as "very serious" and another 16 percent as "fairly serious."[45] Academic competitions and learning centers were means to instill in children math's priority.

Given that math was essential to a prosperous life, parents needed to make sure that children were well trained. They enrolled children in math classes even if the children did not express interest. However, they also cared that it was enjoyable. If a child did not like his or her after-school class, a parent would switch to a different one. If the children's protests continued for quite a while, that was a sign to find another means of imparting the subject. Parents also devised creative math games in order to educate their children. A mother at a spelling bee instructed me to insert math when playing catch with my first-grade son in our backyard: before throwing the baseball to my son, I should ask him to answer a math question. Like practically all the parents at spelling bees, she cared not just about spelling but about academics generally.

Indian immigrants did not believe that their children were "just not math kids" (in contrast to not being athletic kids).[46] Instead, they felt that people could learn to enjoy or at least achieve in a variety of activities if exposed to them and encouraged to excel. Some pushed math onto their children despite protests. In this respect, they also were following a cultural norm within India of parents playing leadership roles in children's educational and career choices. Mahipal compared Indian and American parenting styles:

American kids are driven by passion. They find something and pursue it. Indian culture says that [they] should do what parents say. . . . In my country, everyone did math. If you don't [want to] do it, if you don't [want to] become a doctor or engineer, you [still] have to do it. Here, there are too many options, so you don't have to do math if you don't want to. That's a problem. That fear [of math] comes early in life. Parents too are brought up in the same environment. They also fear math.

Parents were not as strict as the maniacal "tiger mom" stereotype implies. Still, they did enforce their will when deeply passionate about something, as is common for parents generally.

In a group interview, when I asked a few dozen parents how many of them had pushed their kids into a competition and unless they had pushed, their child would not have participated, about three-quarters raised their hands. When I then asked how many felt their children had an interest in this activity and they as parents were responding to their children's interest, again about three-quarters raised their hands. When I said that those answers seemed contradictory to me, a mother explained,

> I took [my two children] to a rollerblading place a couple weeks ago. And the first time, they kept falling. I told them, "Give it a shot; if you like it, we can come back again. So it's up to you; see how you like it." So this is the first time I'm doing NSF, and I told the kids, "Understand the question and do it. If you don't understand it, just leave it." The way I prepare them, I said twenty minutes a day they have to sit with me. Think of it as going to any other sport or activity that you're trying out for the first time. If you like it, we'll come back again. We'll do it for a couple years, if you like the energy and things like that, we'll continue. Otherwise, we'll figure out something else. So they are not resentful, [and] they're not very happy; they're just, like, OK.

Having the children be "very happy" was not a top priority if it meant losing out on worthwhile learning. This does not mean that parents did not care if children were not happy. Parents did not ram academics down their children's throats while they cried themselves to sleep as commonly assumed. Parents considered themselves as responding to their children's preferences, as is expected within a concerted cultivation style, if their children at least partially enjoyed the activities the parents initiated.

How did parents pick spelling for their children if practically any academic competition would do? One mother, Jahnavi, insisted that they did not force spelling onto their daughter but instead realized her love of reading and then learned about the NSF as a venue:

> It's not that we want [it]—since she was a younger child, we saw . . . that she was doing good in reading, so we encourage[d] her. And then we

came across that NSF contest, and we thought, "OK, let's go there and try." And she did pretty good there, so that's why we wanted her to compete. So it's not that we are pushing her. And because she likes it, she is interested in [it], so we want her to continue.

Parents often refer to emails or notices within ethnic circles about NSF and the SASB as sparking an interest and creating accessibility.

I asked Govind at an SASB competition why his daughter's passion for reading would lead him toward spelling competitions rather than book clubs, creative writing classes, and the like. He replied that bees provided more of a "competitive advantage" than a book club ever could:

> [The] spelling bee is not about spelling, right? It's an expression of a state of mind or a passion or an energy that could have be[en] channeled into anything. . . . I think we need to incorporate some kind of foundational—you know, complement the school curriculum with something else. Right? It could be tutoring; it could be any means of writing—you know, some kind of focused drive there. Because you want them to excel and have a competitive advantage over their peers, right?

Most of the children—in particular, the ones who did well in the regional rounds—read for fun. It was their most favorite activity. Other factors included a love of languages and a desire to learn English as well as one could.

The national spotlight on Indian American spelling also has created a baseline of interest. When Nupur Lala won the Scripps National Spelling Bee in 1999 and was profiled in the Oscar-nominated film *Spellbound*, she became a household name among families. Champions have come to serve as role models for others. At the 2011 NSF finals, the 2010 Scripps champion, Kavya Shivashankar, and her father spoke to a lecture hall crowded with parents and children about their spelling trajectory and offered advice for competitive spellers. At the end, parents and children lined up to shake the father's and daughter's hands and pose for pictures with them. Even adults without children posed for photos with teenage Shivashankar. She was a hero (and her sister Vanya would later become a future Scripps co-champion). Seeing Indians succeed in a venue encouraged others to follow. Once a community becomes known for an arena of achievement, it leads members to see themselves as suiting that image, and it becomes more difficult to imagine oneself as successful in opposite scenarios.[47] When I asked a mother why more families did not pursue chess as an extracurricular option, she said to just wait until the first Indian American chess champion prevails, and then I would see a flood of people interested in it.

Not all parents found spelling bees equally worthwhile. I started a conversation with a father at an SASB regional competition. I asked him what interested him about spelling bees. He replied,

> I think [spelling bees started as] more of my wife's interest than my kid's interest, initially. I don't think [my daughter] will become passionate about it. But I think she'll enjoy where it takes her.

Again, parents are driven by the need to help their children compete or otherwise face "a lower grade in life," as a parent said. Spelling bees were one such venue. In this way, spelling bees serve both the child's short-term interests (an interest in words) and parents' long-term interests (being academically competitive).

The bee also affirmed their belonging to the nation. In a National Public Radio news story, Srinivas Mahankali, father of the 2013 spelling champion Arvind Mahankali, said, "The immigrants want to prove that they belong to the mainstream." They are very eager to show that they have "mastered the cornerstone of the culture here—the language."[48] So even though parents do not refer to racism as a driving concern, they on occasion indicated how race and cultural nationalism filter down to parenting decisions.

Spelling bees also made sense since families believed they could win at them, in part because of cultural traits from their upbringing in India's middle class. Those reasons ranged from parents' fluency in English, often being polyglots; the education system in India; Vedic culture; and more. The most salient reasons, however, were the hours they were willing to spend and the use of family support and supplemental materials, as will be explained later.

## Asian American Style of Concerted Cultivation

Immigrant parents perform an Asian American style of concerted cultivation, similar to middle-class parents generally. Driven by a fear of competition, their goal is to make their children safe by helping them stand out among others while still attending to children's feelings, as many parents do. Education per se is not their main concern. Rather than a simple top-down approach to parenting, Indian Americans pick activities that they think will resonate with their children and provide them a secure future. Even if they insist on math, they look for ways to make academics enjoyable. And so the academic and public discourse on Asian American parenting, that these are "overprogrammed families" who do not sufficiently care about their children and must assimilate, obscures the larger point: immigrant parents have much in common with the middle-class American parents.

Even with this overlap across groups, there is not an equivalency. Concerted cultivation practices are not uniform across ethnic and racial groups of the same class background, as has been assumed, and instead, minority parents raise children with particular skills so as to avoid barriers.[49] White upper-middle-class parents reminisce about a slower and easier way of life, of going "skating in the afternoons" (as Tanya said earlier), unlike the anxious times of today. Indian Americans' concerns, on the other hand, were neither new nor hypothetical ones regarding their children's future. They believed that all of their children's life chances would be defined by competition, as it was for them. Just having good grades would not suffice to help kids stand out and succeed. Their immigrant and racial background impacts their views on other supplemental options, on the need for advanced human capital, and on college admissions. They have a love/hate relationship with hyper education. Their pursuit puts them in a catch-22 situation of appearing like other Asian Americans even as they want to distinguish themselves. But they continue it anyway as they assess their children's opportunities and constraints.

The sociological story to date has been that immigrant professionals presumably do not mind integrating into their local educational and social institutions, even as they want their children to keep their ethnic culture and norms (e.g., food, customs, family traditions).[50] This is especially assumed to be true for those minorities seen as more similar to whites than to blacks and Latinxs, like many affluent Asian Americans are.[51] However, parents here avoid assimilating into the standard strategies of how to achieve success.[52] They do not trust that popular concerted cultivation practices of sports or the arts will prepare their children to stand out in college admissions given the impact of immigration and race. Their children must stand out in different ways and with different tactics—namely, through extra academics. They do not completely disavow their white peers' tactics for upward mobility but instead adapt them to their circumstances and community norms.[53] Such concern over local parenting styles is more often found among immigrants whose surrounding neighbors are thought to rarely achieve economically.[54] But it is unexpected and highly noteworthy in this context of immigrant professionals in well-resourced school districts with affluent white-collar neighbors. Ironically, to provide this distinctive cultivation of their children, Indian Americans turn not simply to ethnic institutions but also to the most American of leisure activities—the national spelling bee—and to ubiquitous, franchised learning centers. What's more, hyper education turns out to signify a resistance by parents to more than just the standard pathways of mobility, as seen next.

# 4

## "Hyper Education Does Something for You on Moral Grounds"

You will have people who are academically inclined and come from "broken" families. But overall, it's not a coincidence that those academically minded also have other good values. It's all about practicality. You are not going to win the lottery. Academics is practical. Practical people will say it's not a good idea to alienate your elders. For us, it's common sense. We are trying to provide the straight and narrow for our kids.

Aadashini and Gaurav, both working IT professionals living in the Boston area, sat together at their dining table as Aadashini shared her impressions and their rationale for why they enrolled their nine-year-old son in a math program. Separately, at a South Asian Spelling Bee, Divya said about her children's involvement with spelling,

> It's not only about [getting a professional job], that kind of stuff. It does something for you on moral grounds.

Parents' investment in hyper education concerned a binary of safety versus risk, as noted earlier. But beyond college entry and a well-paying job, safety also meant becoming a moral person, someone who avoided unwanted behavior and complacency. Parents infused extracurricular academics with a deep cultural meaning that helped make kids *good* people, not just more qualified people, and helped avoid perceived dangers within white upper-middle-class neighborhoods and schools.

## Sex, Drugs, and Education

When I asked Indian American parents what they hoped to get out of their participation in educational activities, they explained a commitment to education, wanting a venue for children to stand out, and the other points noted earlier. But when I asked them what they worried would happen if they did *not* pursue more education, parents articulated a deeper concern, beyond academic mediocrity. Deepak, a father of a middle-school daughter, and I had been talking about how parent-approved dating is more common in American than Indian culture broadly defined. He said,

> Right. I keep emphasizing that you can start having fun any time, but if you can delay having fun one year, it multiplies by ten times. . . . So keeping that busy, I think she doesn't need to worry about texting somebody in the middle of the night about some boy problems. They might get into some kind of issues, some of the bad things that happen around [them]. That would essentially expose [them] to the bad elements within the society much sooner than we want them to know. That's the downside. They get to talk about something, somebody selling drugs or something, [or] drinking. . . . Like 60 percent [of her school] is immigrants—Chinese and Indians probably predominant. She will find enough friends within that where they still have these values that are respected, and she doesn't have the same peer pressure hopefully.

Parents did not simply refer to having their children stay busy in order to avoid unhealthy choices, although that was part of their thinking. They referred specifically to committing oneself to a mission that would reap benefits in the long run even as it denies fun in the short term. Deepak believed that being engaged in academic progress meant that his middle-school daughter would keep a future-oriented mind-set rather than becoming complacent and prioritizing "bad things that happen around" her. He felt a kinship with other Asian Americans in this regard, whom he believed promoted "values that are respected."

Jagdeep contrasted Indians with white Americans:

> So we have the competitive thing built into us, so we are pushing our kids to it. [Also,] we are not satisfied with [the] status quo. [Whites] are comfortable with their skin. They are comfortable with what kids are doing. They are comfortable with kids reading comics, playing games, doing all of those things. They are comfortable with their fifteen-year-olds making out with a boyfriend, whereas we are not.

These parents are not saying that being in a spelling bee or a math center will keep children safe from making the wrong choices, such as wasting their free time with comic books and, more seriously, having premarital sex. But making their children academically competitive orients them toward the kind of upbringing their parents want for them, an upbringing they identify as not American. Whites "comfortable with their skin" have privileges and prerogatives these parents do not share. Instilling such values for girls was all the more necessary because parents saw their affluent neighborhoods and school cultures as consisting of ever-present dangers such as sex and drugs. And to their point, mainstream American popular culture routinely demonstrates parent-approved dating and premarital sex for teenagers. If one was complacent about the future, those "dangers" would creep in.

As an Indian American parent said within a group of peers, "We are not the kind of families who have this problem [of teen pregnancy]." Whereas white American parents worry about the sexual interests of minority teenagers, here the concern is with the white middle and upper-middle class.[1] Part of what being Indian American means for these parents is having a conservative lifestyle, presumably unlike other groups. Such model minority rhetoric ignores problematic trends within the diaspora, such as the high rate of domestic violence within Indian America.[2] Nor is it uncommon for a minority group to circumscribe women's behavior in order to affirm moral superiority.[3] That circumscription involves prescribing dictionaries and math worksheets as well.

Whereas girls can become pregnant, boys can become violent criminals. When I asked Thaman and Kapila, as I sat in their living room, what they thought would happen if their two boys—both in elementary school—did not participate in spelling bees, I expected to hear them say that the boys might not be able to excel in their schoolwork or would have too much screen time. Instead, the parents shared an anecdote of their visit to a neighborhood park. They said boys there were running around playing with sticks as if they were guns, pretending to shoot each other. They did not want their boys engaging in such risky behavior found in their neighborhood. This anecdote is noteworthy because of its banality, of kids running in a park with sticks as pretend guns. Yet to the parents, such behavior represented a lack of ethics within a society known for heavy gun ownership and gun-related fatalities.

We know surprisingly little about the adaptation preferences and strategies of middle-class, professional immigrants. They supposedly like to keep some ethnic culture, such as language, religion, and customs, but otherwise integrate into their affluent surroundings and achieve in school as a result.[4] Here we see their unease with multiple aspects of the white upper-middle class, and education proved an antidote. There was more at stake with hyper education than good grades.

## Bad Kids Come from Bad Parents

Banita and Jignesh had one son, Naresh, in third grade at an affluent public school in a Boston suburb. Banita was in marketing, and
Jignesh was a software engineer, both educated in India and living
in the United States for about twelve years. Naresh, wearing wire-
rim glasses, shorts, and a T-shirt, was throwing a football in the air
and diving onto the couch to catch it, when I arrived. I had met the
family before at a school function and brought my younger son with
me to play with Naresh, thinking the parents and I could talk more
easily if the kids were engaging themselves. So the two boys went
into a side room to toss the football and play with LEGOs. Over a cup
of chai, Banita and Jignesh and I spent the next hour-plus talking at
their kitchen peninsula about their hopes and fears regarding
Naresh. What struck me was the connection between hyper education and their fears.

> Jignesh: You cannot just trust your kid's education to someone else. That
> is exactly what I don't like about American culture, about not focusing
> too much on education. It is left entirely up to the kid whether they
> want to succeed in life or not, right? But again, it's too much of a risk for
> us. Because if your kid is struggling with math or some basic core sub-
> jects that are needed for college, then it will demotivate him to such a
> point that he might just drop off, or take other drastic steps, which we
> don't want. He might get into probably depression or something, right?
> Q: By something, do you mean dropping out of school?
> Jignesh: Mmm-hmm.
> Banita: Trouble. They might . . . they might get into other . . . other bad
> habits.
> Jignesh: Drugs.
> Q: So those are the other reasons you do extra math, besides him learn-
> ing more content?
> Banita: Yeah.

Jignesh did not make a point to bash American culture. But he could not understand those who did not actively monitor their kids' educational ambition, whether through supplemental learning or otherwise. Obviously, no parents are so complacent as to leave it up to their children as to whether they will "succeed in life or not," even if they are not actively engaged in their children's education. Yet education was so paramount to Banita and Jignesh's sense of duty to Naresh that to not prioritize it was to, in effect, leave his future up in the air and invite social problems such as drugs. Only irresponsible parents would do such a thing.

With so much at stake with after-school education, some parents had even harsher impressions of those who did not enroll their children. When I asked Jai, a father at the 2016 SASB finals, why he thought other Americans did not participate in academic competitions as much as Indian Americans did, he gestured as if drinking an alcoholic beverage and said, "Americans are busy doing this."

Parents saw the American culture of their affluent neighborhoods condoning—at times, even encouraging—problematic behaviors. They believed that if they did not invest in academics, they would be setting their children up for possible social problems, which they felt other parents should also recognize. Extra academics served as an antiassimilation tactic, for it ensured that families provided children with the right priorities and the tools to meet them.

This idea that more scholastics can stave off social problems is the opposite of that expressed by educators. As seen earlier, Asian American youths at an affluent Boston-area school district experienced mental health problems at a higher rate than whites as they matured into high school. Educators blamed this on Asian American parent-driven academic pressure, including hyper education. As Mary, the prevention specialist of a suburban Boston school district, said,

Asian Americans . . . [exhibit] cutting, pills, alcohol. . . . The number one reason kids report for doing drugs went from peer pressure to stress.

Parents and educators take opposing points of view. For parents, hyper education helps prevent the exact social problems that educators like Mary blame it for. While Mary focuses on the social and emotional problems of stress from extreme academics, the parents consider the social and emotional risks in the environment as a whole.

## Practically Speaking

I shared with Banita and Jignesh the comment from Rachel, the elementary school principal, that youths like Naresh should not be doing math after school and instead should be engaged in wood-working or some other activity that interested them. Banita said,

> Going back to your earlier question, where you said, "What would you say to someone who would do the woodwork thing for their kid, right?" I guess my question is, What is the success rate for people like that versus the success rate for people like us who kind of try to make sure the kid has a path to follow?

Jignesh jumped in: "We take the safe path, right?" "Yep," replied Banita. Jignesh continued:

> We're not going to get superhigh rewards, but we're not going to have big failures. But in the other cases, it could be either sky-high president of the United States, right? And they could go all the way up to that level versus a homeless person, right? So it's all the way down. So at least you will not find any of [the] Indians in the homeless category.

Hyper education signified a practical pathway to follow, one that protected against the threats of downward cultural assimilation. Practicality was a virtue. The explicit or implicit implication is that other parents, even if thoughtful in their parenting, were impractical and therefore borderline irresponsible in their choices.

The vast majority of parents would not refer to the bulk of American families as possible drunks by any means. Hemraj, the father of a Scripps champion, believed his white peers valued education sufficiently:

> They value [academics] a lot. But maybe the [level of] competition is increasing, that's all. I feel like a lot of mainstream Americans are also there in the spelling bee, you know? So they want to do well in spelling. So it's just the [level of] competition is quite a lot [and so they cannot win.]

Still, parents questioned how intentional most parents were in the values they wanted to instill. Aadashini said while we sat in her home with her husband,

> We think we are doing the better choice. Education is always the better choice. You can be more into sports and still do well in academics. But [you] still need great academics. We think horseback riding and hockey are fun. But we have to get down to reality, and this is what you need to do to be successful. Those other things are formalizing fun.

Most parents were careful not to chastise others as bad parents but instead spoke of "cultural differences." But the families I spoke with could not help but note that their way of life seemed to involve "better choices" than those of whites. Similarly, they referred to themselves as grounded in "reality" with their choices, suggesting that parents who prioritized horseback riding or hockey over academics were unrealistic, setting up their kids for dangerous outcomes.

As Gaurav said earlier, another key form of practicality was respecting elders, with the presumption that doing so led to wise choices. The parents connected being academically minded, respecting elders, and not "formalizing fun," for all coexisted as a cultural package of practicality.

Divya went on to draw a crude line based on class, connecting academic excellence and job status with a higher moral lifestyle:

> When you are out, talking to colleagues, it's a status thing. My husband is a doctor. I have seen a trend among American doctors; they have less divorces. That comes with education. You cannot expect the same thing among handyman families. We feel that if our kids will be better educated, they will have better friends in life. They will enjoy a calm feeling that surrounds you. Plus, you get all the resources. You won't have to worry about paying the electric bill.

Stable careers and stable marriages went hand in hand. To attain the former, it was necessary to be pragmatic. Parents who did not invest themselves in their children's education would have no one to blame later but themselves from this perspective.

When I asked Krishna at the SASB 2014 finals why, on average, fewer other Americans seemed to be engaged in hyper education, he replied,

> The reason Americans may not do it is that they let their kids learn the process on their own. We spend our time bringing our children over here [to ethnic bees]. [White] parents don't push so much because they think the kids will learn by trial and error, learn on their own. The priority is sports. [But] frankly speaking, if you want to get into sports, you have to be really good at it. If you want to be at the

top—if you're not, then everything is gone, all your efforts are gone. At
least in education you have a wider window open. Even if you do 80 or
70 percent of what is possible, you will do well.

It seemed absurd to him for parents to prioritize sports when the
practical option was education. Parents believed that their predominantly white peers had a different mind-set when it came to raising
children and were fine letting their children learn without much
parental intervention. Of course, few parents prioritize just sports
or leave kids to learn "on their own," but Indian parents judged their
peers as irresponsible enough to do so.

Education was not the only activity that could lead children down
a moral path. As Raju, a previous competitive speller now in his
twenties, said, focusing on sports could be fine depending on how
one did it:

> Caring about something is what matters; practicing, doing extra work
> is key. Sports [is the] same as academics. [You] must be committed to
> something. That should be their focus. You should put the blinders on.
> If you are doing athletics, then you should be fully into that.

For Raju, putting "the blinders on" meant turning away from
entertaining distractions. One had to do the "extra work" beyond
the comfort of fun on a pathway to a professional career. Such a
dedicated focus would not only lead to a lucrative profession (one
imagines) but also indicate one's commitment to excellence rather
than complacency and provide the basis for familial security over
drugs and divorce. Such a commitment would entail more sacrifice than that normally undertaken by young athletes. Otherwise, it
would be considered merely an impractical case of "formalizing fun."

## An Immigrant Perspective

Nityanand relayed a romantic image of his child and his immigrant peers:

> The other kids that come [to academic competitions] also place the higher value on studying to compete than on, say, playing video games. We also play video games, but that's not our high valuation for them [compared to] studies. Between studies and video games, they would choose the studies, because they value completing this event. And then they would play the video games. And so that's a value system where they value certain activities more than other activities. . . . So it's not Indian or just other Asians; that's Eastern Europeans [too] maybe.

He mentions a point I heard time and again: that immigrants (not just Indians) have a more pragmatic mind-set to adhere to proper values, not just outcompete others. While hyper education might be an "Indian way of thinking," as one parent put it, most people I spoke to understood it as a non-American practice and, as such, one that connected them to other immigrants. This is an ironic twist regarding immigrants and values relative to earlier in American history. Asians and Eastern Europeans were exactly the immigrants most targeted with exclusion laws and immigration barriers with the Immigration Act of 1924, which severely limited the number of Southern and Eastern Europeans allowed to enter the United States and barred Asians entirely. These groups, once deemed dangerous to the cultural fabric of the nation, are now praised for having a better "value system."

A Russian immigrant mother criticized the perceived emphasis within American culture on personal fulfillment rather than on duty and effort:

If [the American] way of life is right, more adults would be very happy as adults. My [Russian immigrant] women friends are very happy. Our parents told us life is not going to be fun, easy, fair. Life will be what you make of it. To make something of it, you must be prepared.

To not prioritize a safe future for one's child therefore signified improper parenting.

In some people's opinion, this "immigrant attitude" has been lost among contemporary American professionals. Deepak relayed an anecdote a white colleague at his Houston energy company shared with him of how his colleague's father, born and raised in the United States, would work long hours every day in the 1960s and 1970s but never complain when at home:

The immigrants that came forty years ago, they were essentially competing with the people who were here who were also equally hardworking [like his colleague's father]. But I think the immigrants that are coming [now], they're still so hardworking, but I think the hardworking American community has dropped. . . . If you grow up in an environment where you're almost guaranteed a base minimum [salary and job status], then you probably let your guard down a little bit.

According to this thinking, complacency has set in among American professionals, and this loss of a work ethic among the middle class signifies a moral decay in the United States. Contemporary white professionals therefore cannot be trusted to have internalized the right values or to pass them on to their children.

It is important to note that families were not worried about contact with their Americanized environment, did not want to preserve a "timeless" ethnic culture, and did not lack respect for the United States. They found much to praise about American culture. In fact, when I asked Jignesh what he liked about American culture, he initiated his response with "Where do I start?" He appreciated the openness of people and the freedom to pursue what you liked. Families knew many Americans of different races who promoted their kids' education in various ways. They also knew that India was full of people who did not do the same. Nor did they think that one definitively had to do extracurricular academics in order to be moral parents. Still, they believed that American culture at large or even their neighbors did not all prioritize education enough or the pursuit of excellence through sacrifice. The surrounding culture also carried moral dangers, and these two facts were connected, for complacency in academic (or some other form of) excellence could allow temptations to seep in. Parents who relied only on the school to take care of their children's education might be all right and raise decent children, or they could be a corrupting force with impractical priorities that created undue risk.

## Building Character

"You don't quit anything. If you quit, you're a failure." While this sounds like something an intense football coach would say to his players at half time, instead it was Bala, an Indian American mother, who said this to me and a few other adults at an Indian-only spelling bee finals. When I asked her later that day what she meant by not letting her child quit, she elaborated:

> When I said we don't quit, what I mean by that is, in life things will not always go your way. So just because I didn't win, doesn't mean, "Oh I won't do this anymore." You know, if you are capable, if you like that thing, you will figure out a way to get you better if you're willing to put [in] the work. That's what I meant by not quitting.

Separate from but related to moral choices, parents found that enrichment education also helped instill desired cultural traits (i.e., cultural capital), such as perseverance and bouncing back from defeat, as is common within concerted cultivation practices.[5] Such socialization would guide children toward safe choices by giving them the inner strength to overcome challenges—all the more necessary for immigrant minorities, who might encounter more obstacles to mobility.[6] In other words, much more than grades is at stake, even for such instrumental choices as advanced academics.

Lavanya had this to say about why she wanted her daughter in spelling bees:

> The culture is very important. I mean, it will be an advantage for them. They will feel the pressure probably for some time, but after a while, they will know. The process [of spelling] is very intense, right? Just like, you know, sports like tennis. Not everybody is built to endure. So you have to have that endurance here also. You know you will fail sometimes, and then you have to know how to get up, and you have to love that thing for you to get back and [say] let's go again.

Other parents echoed this point: humility provides a sense of insecurity considered necessary to motivate excellence. One cannot teach humility; it has to be experienced.

In fact, academics provided a purer, more fruitful forum for competition than most sports. A couple of parents explained as I chatted with them at the NSF 2013 finals:

> FATHER: You are not competing with these persons; you are competing with these words. And that's such an accomplishment that comes.
> MOTHER: I think that helps them with maturity.

Families compared spelling bees to golf, for in both, one competes against oneself rather than an opponent. At issue, then, is how well you have mastered your stroke, the golf course, German root words, prefixes, and so on.

Math centers also stressed the intangible, character-building benefits they offered beyond simply the academics. Li, a director of a franchise center in a Boston suburb, said,

> One of the long-lasting benefits of [this learning center] is the discipline it teaches students that they use later in life.

Like many franchise businesses, learning centers grow in value and customers by expanding their services beyond core subjects to include test-taking skills, studying skills, and the like.[7] Discipline was a commonly cited trait within extracurricular academics (and extracurricular pursuits more broadly).

A mother explained in a group conversation how preparation for academic competitions taught other life skills:

> It, like, teaches the kids good rules, I think—how they can activate the bigger goals by doing this one. You set a goal, you spend some time, and at certain times, I might study some words, so it actually makes the time management of the goal settings work, which is really good.

There were ancillary benefits as well of being engaged in spelling bees. Parents claimed that standing on stage helped their children get over stage fright and that no one was too young to learn this. The solitary nature of spelling was juxtaposed with the very public performance of the competition.

Youths themselves came to appreciate these skills. Navan, a participant at the 2016 SASB finals, wanted to grow up to be an astronaut, and when asked how spelling bees could help him toward that goal, he replied that the studying taught him "time management." While scholars have considered cultural capital gains for youths from child-centered activities such as sports and the arts, they have analyzed academic pursuits as presumably providing only human capital. Here, we see that academics carries the same cultural benefits that motivate families to pursue other extracurriculars.

The praise of such traits should not go unquestioned. Unfortunately, the public has become very accustomed to conceiving of these cultural skills as normal for youths to internalize and perform. Such traits have become popular within public discourse on child-rearing. The *New York Times* best seller *How Children Succeed: Grit, Curiosity, and the Hidden Power of Character* is just one example of the dictates parents encounter that resonate with them. It is important to recognize why such character traits matter. Cultural capital refers not merely to personal attributes but to skills recognized as capital within certain institutions. Grit, time management, perseverance, and so on are rewarded in the competitive race for college admissions and for white-collar employment or entrepreneurship. Parents feel they have no choice but to purposefully instill them in children at a young age. As explained earlier, building up children's capital should be seen as a form of child labor, since it is meant to provide them the skills needed for the workplace, such as discipline and ability to focus (on top of language and math skills). In this manner, neoliberalism becomes not just a government strategy but also a parenting strategy to create a particular kind of individual who should be able to weather life's storms alone.[8] To not cultivate this kind of self, filled with desired character skills, is to create too much uncertainty in the child's future.

## Schools Should Prioritize Education

Given that parents prioritized academics, it would be logical that they would see school as a safe space relative to the moral dangers outside of it. And yet it was often the opposite. Deepak, whose son was a middle schooler, observed,

Schools put so much emphasis on the sports. So I walk into many high schools because I take my son to various competitions on Saturdays for tennis. Imagine what is there on the left and right, as we enter into every high school—all the trophies of sports. So if I'm a high-school kid, what are you trying to tell me? Here, the most important thing is the sports. So then the other thing was, we were asking the school to invest in math. So then I went to one of the board meetings and said, "I hear that [our town] is spending about thirty million dollars for a football stadium, and you raised the bonds to pay for your thing. But your principal also told me that your school district doesn't have three hundred dollars to pay for the MATHCOUNTS [competition]. So can somebody explain it to me? You're instituting a culture."

Football is "your thing," he said to the board, while math is "our Indian thing" by implication. He did not draw a simplistic binary of academics as good and sports as bad. The only reason he visited high schools was because his son played a sport. But it was the seeming misplaced priorities of schools that frustrated him, as reflected in the financial priorities of even "good" school districts for sports over math competitions. Even though he understood that sports brought in revenue, such investments promoted the wrong culture, which the school advertised with its prominently displayed sports-trophy cases.

The problem is not just how *well* schools teach reading, writing, and arithmetic but even their *desire* to do so. Deepak's was not merely a critique of possible drugs or misbehavior within the schools; nor was it the previous critique of the American education system's weak standings internationally, as articulated by politicians, pundits, parents, and others. The schools' moral failing was in not even caring to push children enough in academics so that they would recognize its priority over other pursuits. The fears of complacency in their neighborhoods and surrounding culture are echoed inside the schools. As such, it was not merely a failing of educational quality but also a cultural failing; parents thought schools had misplaced priorities. Rather than being sites that protected children from assimilation into troubling aspects of the American lifestyle, they accelerated that assimilation into complacency and the associated dangerous, impractical life choices.

Parents did not believe they made up such concerns about the schools. Other parents I spoke with protested that school newsletters trumpeted athletic achievements more than academic ones. For instance, a parent complained to me that his daughter's school would not include a story about her victory at an Indian-only spelling bee, not accepting the school's reason that because the bee took place outside of school, it would not be included in such a newsletter no matter the content.

The concern that schools did not sufficiently prioritize academics did not rest at the symbolic level of trophy cases or newsletters. As a mother said in a group conversation,

> Everyone has similar frustrations with the school system. [In] the school system here, there is a culture shock that we get [from India]. Everyone says the same thing: in the elementary school there isn't much.

Parents frequently expressed dismay that homework was brief, too easy, and did little to help high-performing children, in line with math directors' earlier critiques of the Department of Education.

Schools' deficiencies were seen as embedded in their organization and curriculum. The real problem was not that their children would not do well in elementary and middle school but that they would do very well without having to put in great effort, and therefore they would not learn the values of hard work and practical decision-making necessary to avoid moral dangers. Not only did schools rarely have a sufficiently demanding curriculum; they did not even want to have one, according to parents. Despite moving to the United States in part for its educational possibilities and living in some of the best school districts in the nation, parents believed schools had misplaced priorities. As a father said in a group conversation,

> Part of the problem also that I see in American education over long periods is that it is not really competent. So everybody is equal; nobody is lagging behind. There's a lack of competition that is there; suddenly it comes up that we all rise up at the same time. And I feel like it doesn't prepare the kids very well for the time, and competition is suddenly forced upon them, and [it is] said [that] now you have to succeed. Not everybody gets into Harvard or MIT. I think we tend to propel our kids toward the competition early on.

The sense of academic competition within school was missing here because of how schools understood their mission. A father said in a group conversation,

> Here [in the United States], you see there is an emphasis [in schools] to get every kid to the next level. And that is a very big cultural mind shift, which is different from India versus here.

Kavita believed that education was too important to be left up to her children's suburban Houston schools, even as she referred to the schools as strong, for they did not push children enough:

> Everybody [here] gets a participation trophy, so there is no motivation for them to actually achieve, to go over and beyond. The schools are not doing enough.

American schools appear incompetent given how they are organized. To let one's children assimilate into such a "cultural mind shift" would not ensure their security. Complacency would set in; it is the enemy of the character-building traits parents want to instill. Children would not only miss out on top-quality universities but also lack an internal drive to "go over and beyond" in life, leading to all the dangers they articulated.

Report cards and state aptitude tests—the means by which schools assess children—were also not trustworthy to parents. Given that the schools' mission appeared to be moving kids along rather than challenging them, good grades did not seem meaningful. In the mind of Asian immigrant parents, a B on a report card is akin to an F not because they are so strict on grades but because the criteria for an A are already deemed too low. If one cannot muster the competence to receive an A, one must be weak academically.

Similarly, one mother at an Indian spelling bee finals in 2017 complained in a group conversation that the state exam in California for her twelve-year-old son was too easy and therefore of little use in gauging his academic skills. Bringing him to a spelling competition with fellow South Asian Americans compensated for that. Another parent elaborated at a Boston regional NSF group conversation,

> The American philosophy is not about pushing hard or pushing less. It's basically figuring out how the kids should or can be pushed. And at that level, they're basically trying to not paint the picture or tell a kid that you are not good enough or [that] you are very good. Right? So I think what's happening to people coming from India, we always want to figure out, Where are we, where are we, where are we? So we always are in the mode of unit tests, finding out, Where am I ranking in the class? In the lower levels here, in about second grade or so, we don't have the [state standardized tests] or anything like that.

In Massachusetts, the first state standardized test takes place in third grade, which is too late according to this parent and her peers. While there is a parental movement pushing back against standardized testing in American schools, these families do not share that concern.[9] On the contrary, they want more such testing and a system committed to differentiating students (e.g., distinguishing between levels of As and how to move students to an A+). They felt that the American school system would not implement more testing, especially rigorous testing meant to challenge kids rather than ensure basic comprehension. Instead, the system wanted to make sure all children felt supported by their school and equally respected. A less demanding school system gave youths the time to "formalize fun" rather than push themselves.

Notwithstanding these parents' perspectives, the American school system does rank students, such as with tracking, limited access to AP classes, honor roles, and the like. Yet such differentiations happen later in the secondary school process and are relatively crude measures, and parents wanted more precise assessments of their young children's standings. In reality, the American school system has no investment in all children receiving a proper education. Instead, it is premised on unequal access to resources that disadvantage minorities and the poor more generally.[10] From the perspectives of immigrants in affluent suburbs, however, the situation looks much different.

Complaining to teachers for a more rigorous curriculum would be of little use. Parents believed they were working against their local communities' cultures if they pushed for higher standards in their school system, for there seemed to be a reciprocal relationship between the school and the local community. And to a large extent, that point is true, as when school districts conform their student expectations to white parents' preferences and admonish Asian American parents as culturally misguided, as explained earlier. Gaurav said,

> A family [I know] whose kids are in high school, he was saying that his kids just do sports and that's it. The kids are doing fine in high

school, not the best in academics but hanging through. Another parent said, "As long as my kid gets through school and doesn't do drugs, they will be successful." But personally, I'm looking for something more. Those families don't have as high expectations for their kids, that's what I feel.

In these parents' minds, schools were not motivated to change because of white parents who were happy with mediocrity, even though that is hardly the case. Indian immigrants believed that local parents and schools did not care if their children were pushed academically, that they were indeed OK if their kids made it through school with decent grades and without a drug problem. Immigrant parents felt surrounded by a threatening culture of questionable values and low expectations, which influenced the schools' priorities.

## Hyper Education as the Answer

As families spoke about their turn toward hyper education and concerns about their schools, it reminded me of how I understood my decision to enroll my children in Little League baseball. Little League makes sense because there is no other way for children to properly learn how to play baseball. Schools are not designed to serve this function; recess is not a substitute. Little League also teaches kids how to be good winners and good losers. We also approached it as a family, attending games together and asking each of our kids to support one another. When I asked parents if that analogy applied to why they pursued supplemental academics, they agreed. One cannot rely on school to teach a child sufficient math or analytical skills (used in spelling), so one enrolls the child in a privately organized extracurricular option. Rather than letting children enjoy having less work now, parents see this as a problem that must be solved so that children not only become competitive but develop the right values. Hyper education provided an anchor for families to hold onto amid the cultural challenges surrounding them. It re-created a condition in the diaspora that parents experienced in the homeland, of schools pushing children to excel so as to become both adept students and good people.

According to Santosh, a leader within Indian American academic competitions, a broken school system cannot be fixed with money or curricular changes:

> This model [of extracurricular education] works. And it can be replicated. We did it in the Indian American community. The Indian parents know the value of education; they get involved. They get empowered. We tell parents, don't expect to give your child a book and tell them to study. That's doing them a disservice. You should sit there with them. [You] don't have to help them in their work. That tells the kid how important you feel this is. Indian parents do this more. But this model can be replicated elsewhere.

So while he agreed with the critiques made by the Bill and Melinda Gates Foundation, Salman Khan, and general public rhetoric that the school system fails to engage students and that teachers do not teach effectively, the solution was cultural rather than through policy or technology. For him, the Indian family and ethnic educational spaces were a cure-all to the ills of the school system. Different values needed to be instilled.[11] Other groups should follow the cultural patterns set by Asian Americans rather than those set by the American school system in order to ensure that their children learned the "value of education" and grew up "empowered."

Parents agreed that their participation in ethnic competitions instilled the right approach to education in their children, which schools had failed to do. Rachna said at a Boston regional competition,

My daughter thought she was good in school. She was way ahead of the kids in her school. She comes here and realizes it's a very competitive experience. [It's a] humbling experience, which is a good thing.

Parents, in effect, hoped their children would lose so that they would be sure to study hard, a key to a sound upbringing focused on self-improvement rather than complacency. Being told one is good at math creates a stereotype promise that one will be treated more generously because of one's race. Parents had to work against that racial framing to ensure that their children pushed themselves with a sense of humility.

Indian American families follow this pattern even outside of formal spaces like NSF and SASB or a math center. Kavita helped found a local group of Indian families in her Houston area that comes together to teach children on various subjects for competitions:

We have too many groups going on! [*Laughs*] All the parents are volunteering. We have a huge group for GeoBee. One does spelling; one does math. The groups help makes the kids want to do it. It's like homeschooling. On our Friday group, we have forty kids, from first grade to fifth grade. We occupy an office space that one friend lets us use. First grade and second grade is one group, and third, fourth, [and] fifth is a separate group.

Since the school could not be trusted, families organized their own extracurricular educational spaces. While Kavita probably wants her kids to outscore others in the group, it is still beneficial to study together, for that helps keep the kids interested and reinforces the significance of academics more than the school curriculum does.

This emphasis on educational practice and excellence for young children already doing well in school might appear extreme, and even Kavita acknowledges that there are "too many" groups.

And such intensity around academics appears to fit the caricature of Asian Americans as "tiger parents" who push their kids into education just as educators and counselors fear. And yet parents read useful values in that caricature that are missing in their neighborhoods. A mother commented in a group conversation,

> When I read this book *Tiger Mother*, she learned how to make her kids work hard. Especially if you are good at something, you [still] have to work hard. If they are smarter, they still have to work intensely. And the results are excellent, so they love it. I loved the book. There were many good things to learn from the book.

Valuing hard work did not appear to be a priority elsewhere, according to parents.

## A Non-American Space

Most families disagreed that after-school learning was a uniquely Indian practice, for they knew that many non-Indian families did the same. As noted earlier, they complimented various immigrants as practicing favorable traits. But they viewed hyper education as *non-American* in the sense that it did not fit expected American norms, given that their white peers presumably could rely on their networks and assets to get ahead. One mother spoke of how NSF provided opportunities for assessing children's education:

> I think that's the reason why something like NSF gives a great forum where like-minded people come together, and they're all working hard. So it makes everybody work at least as hard.

As Frederick Barth (1998), the famous anthropologist of ethnic relations, argues, we learn more about a group's way of life by attending not to their traditional cultural traits (e.g., food preferences, rituals) but more to how they maintain differences from other groups. Groups can distinguish themselves from others through a variety of behaviors, clothing, rituals, and so on. Indian American parents highlighted their commitment to more learning as a boundary among "like-minded people"—that is, a mental or social difference between themselves and others.

Coethnic bees felt like ethnic spaces even though they conducted American English spelling contests or public speaking in English. Vijay, a father of a middle-school daughter, spoke at an NSF finals:

> You have a [spelling bee] platform, and when you're in a community, it's as if everybody in your family is a doctor, [so] you want to become one, right? So I think [the effect of other Indians] is more than just consultation. It is a communal effect, a social effect, depending on what environment you're in. Other kids are doing [it], [so] you'll do it.

Engaging in ethnic academic competitions had a "communal effect" akin to going to a temple or speaking an ethnic language, again signaling more than grades or test scores.[12] Similarly, a Chinese American parent of an elementary-age boy engaged in enrichment math referred to the Chinese math class as akin to attending his Chinese American church, for both provided positive outcomes within a tight-knit, ethnic setting. Hagwons serve this purpose for Korean Americans as well. Parents sometimes worried that their children did not have enough exposure to coethnic peers to make friends with and share their background. Ethnic academic spaces provided a useful way to accomplish that.

When education spaces had a significant number of Asian Americans, it became more of an ethnic or pan-ethnic space, even if it was a franchised, mainstream center. Parents sought out such "Asian" spaces. Kajal, a mother, said of her son,

We want to make sure that he—and I don't know if I can generalize that way—but he takes on the perseverance and the hardworking quality that I feel is prevailing in the Asian culture. I'm sure there are tons of Americans who are really hardworking, but that's probably one of the things that we would really want him to take from our culture. . . . That is one of the benefits of putting him in [the math center], that it instills the kind of values.

Despite the worth of competing with coethnics, parents cared most about having their children with academically committed peers regardless of ethnicity. It is important to stress that this was not a simple Asian/American binary of Asians as academically strong and white Americans as academically weak. Parents complimented white families whom they thought prioritized education as well. Even if those families were not engaged in hyper education, they still could be actively involved in their children's schooling. Parents placed Indians and white Americans in different cultural categories but were quick to cite exceptions to those generalizations.

## Fearing Downward Assimilation

When asked why they pursued hyper education, families provided the answers explained earlier of increasing human capital so as to outcompete others in the chase for college admissions. But when probed as to what they thought would happen if they did not pursue hyper education and what they thought of those families who did not do it, parents unveiled deeper concerns. Even highly rational, skill-building pursuits such as math lessons are driven partly by cultural considerations.[13] A competitive approach to school progress suggests to parents a moral boundary that prevents too much assimilation into American culture, with gender differences in how those fears manifest. Hyper education also provides cultural capital, an outcome normally associated with nonacademic extracurricular activities. Education can carry more than an instrumental value, for families impute their personal wants and values onto it.[14]

Ironically, Indian Americans affirm cultural boundaries partly through mainstream organizations, such as franchised suburban math centers, national math competitions, and American English spelling bees. They make sure children learn to appreciate hard work rather than risk a complacency that comes with easy As. In other words, any site can become an ethnic site if treated in that manner.

This fear of assimilation into American culture by professional immigrants is not expected. According to the popular segmented assimilation framework, working-class or poor immigrants try to avoid a "downward assimilation" into the culture of their poor minority or white neighbors.[15] They worry about their children adopting social problems stereotypically assumed to be within the inner city, even as these social problems are greatly exaggerated and apply to all kinds of groups.[16] Ethnic boundaries help uplift children from such cultures, which are presumed to be negative (but that in reality are much more complex).[17] For middle-class immigrants, however, the presumption has been that they want to pass on aspects of their culture to their children, such as language, food, rituals, marital preferences, and the like.[18] But they supposedly are fine with a selective assimilation in which youths become relatively assimilated into their local middle-class, white (or nonwhite) environment.[19] It is surprising how little scholarship has investigated the attitudes and practices of immigrant professionals.

For sure, practically all parents interviewed appreciated aspects of American culture, and they wanted their children to feel at home in the United States. But they demonstrated much more caution and concern around American culture than previously recognized. They appeared more like the working class and poor immigrants in their fears that their children would adopt the views toward education prominent among local peers. Only a few informants actively castigated whites as drunkards or the like. Still, many believed whites overinvested in impractical activities at the expense of sufficiently attending to children's competitive focus on education, leading to social problems of divorce, drugs, guns, premature sex, and complacency. African Americans in the middle class or lower-middle class adopt cultural practices that help them avoid the presumed (not necessarily real) dangers of inner-city lifestyles.[20] It is unexpected for Asian Americans in upper-middle-class neighborhoods populated by white college-educated professionals to adopt a similar outlook. And yet that is what is happening.

In effect, Indian Americans are treating their white professional peers in ways comparable—not identical—to how working-class immigrants treat inner-city African Americans. Mainstream American culture is maligned in a manner reminiscent of stereotyped inner-city culture, with whites substituting for blacks. In essence, American culture generally has become almost synonymous with the presumed (but again not demonstrated) "oppositional culture" of African Americans and Latinxs, defined here as complacency and with dangerous temptations that youths must be protected from through strong ethnic boundaries.[21]

Indian Americans did not refer to blacks as they talked about their educational choices. But the model minority rhetoric they use relative to white peers is premised on Asian Americans' separation from and superiority over stereotyped blacks, and their critiques of their white peers echo antiblack stereotypes. Even the way the immigrants complemented whites is reminiscent of how whites complement African Americans and diversity overall, furthering the symbolic connection between white peers and poor minorities. Banita, who worried about drugs and other influences if Naresh did not have a strong-enough ethnic boundary, was thankful that his best friend was a white boy in the neighborhood:

His best friend is not an Indian; he's a [white] American. It's really good for my son. I feel like [his friend is] great at sports; he is every-

thing that our son is not and vice versa. That diversity and inclusive-
ness in America is nice. You will get better through interactions. We
are glad that he has non-Indian friends and is learning so much from
them. And vice versa. I'll hear from his best-friend's mom that her son
loved learning this math thing with [our son].

Parents did not draw a simple binary that they wanted to instill a traditional culture and avoid Americans, who are by no means all read
as sinful and polluting. Hyper education keeps her son wholesome,
but he benefits from being around others. Such diversity makes
her child "well rounded." But this framing of the benefits of white
peers matches how whites generally appreciate when their children
are friends with people of color or kids from other countries or of
different economic levels: as broadening their children's understanding of the world.[22] This is also the rhetoric, for instance, of how
affirmative action benefits white students.[23] So racial assumptions
are at play in parents' references to mobility and education.

Overall, a moral concern drives Indian Americans' commitment
to hyper education, as they are fearful of a downward assimilation
into the culture of their white peers. It would be easy to read these
responses as those of immigrants committed to their more conservative culture and overreacting to American norms. Yet while they
are informed by their immigrant backgrounds, their critique of
their white neighbors was not as intense or explicit as expressed by
another group: fellow whites engaged in hyper education.

# 5

## "Whites Are Lazy; Asians Are Crazy"

I think that [Asian Americans] prioritize education as
something that is critical in child development, whereas
white people prioritize fun as a critical component of a
child's development. If it's not fun, [if] the child doesn't
enjoy it, then it's not really good [according to white par-
ents]. [But] sometimes you have to do something and
learn something so that you can actually take what you
know and do something you really want to do. . . . [The
math class] and going to synagogue—there's different
ways to get to the same place. I don't want [my son] to
be an American in the sense that he melts and becomes
nothing. I want him to be a contributor. . . . Whites are lazy.

Ed is a white US-born and -raised American. His elementary-aged
son attended a private math class. I met Ed and his son at a June 2017
community event held by the math center for its area franchises.
It took place in a suburban high school. There were awards given
out (e.g., for achieving in Math Olympiads), logic-based math games,
outdoor games (e.g., a bouncy house, miniature bowling), and treats.
Kids from elementary to high-school age moved between the indoor
math games held in the school cafeteria (where they received tickets to use outdoors) and the outdoor options. I estimated that about
a thousand people were in attendance, coming and going over a few
hours, and was later told by a staff member that attendance was
likely twice that. It was a lively scene, with parents and kids trying
their hands at math questions that were at different table stations in

the cafeteria. Families were about 50 percent Asian American (East Asian and South Asian background), about 40 percent white (including immigrants from Europe), and the rest other races.

Kids seemed to be having fun with the mix of mathematics and outdoor games. But for the most part, mathematics is not considered enjoyable, and most parents will not push their children toward hyper education as a result. Ed found this deeply problematic. He wants his son, who is enrolled in the public school, to avoid assimilating into an "American," which for him is coterminous with "lazy." Hyper education and the synagogue serve similar functions: they are anti-assimilation spaces that make his son a "contributor" with a work ethic and competitive spirit. All kinds of parents who pursue concerted cultivation parenting want their children to be productive rather than idle.[1] Here, though, the extracurricular represents not only a specific set of skills or cultural capital but also a "proper" approach to life.

Such a statement is all the more surprising because whites' approach to after-school options is thought to be quite different than what Ed articulates and from Asian Americans. From the widely held concerted cultivation perspective, parents guide children's activities but respond to their interests. Children are still in the drivers' seat even when strapped into their car seats in the back. As noted earlier, Rachel the elementary school principal said, "In my mind, again, [it is important] to have something they're passionate about, and I can't believe you're going to find kids who are passionate about long division. I just don't believe it." Most parents don't believe it either. While there is little research on why families pursue enrichment education (not after school for remedial purposes),[2] a main reason seems to be to keep up with external pressures from their Asian American neighbors rather than parents' and children's own volition.[3] Or parents regret the poor instruction their children receive in public schools, and learning centers serve as a proxy for private schools.[4] In other words, if it were not for these external pressures, parents would not pursue hyper education. Rather than a sign of better morals, parents are reported to even regret their decision to push academics, for they feel it puts too much pressure on children.[5] Families also worry about raising spoiled, entitled children through the overuse of extracurricular activities and unnecessary privileges.[6] I find these trends as well for US-born white parents, who approach extra academics with some reservations, as explained next. And yet such perspectives would suggest that Indian Americans are unique in treating supplemental education as an act of pride and a way to instill cultural values rather than as an annoyance or shame. Ed shows this ethnic exceptionalism not to be the case.

## External Pressures to Be Good at Math

While multiple white parents shared the moral motivations articulated by Ed, the reasons they first offered for advanced education involved more pragmatic concerns—namely, external pressures that drove them to it. I met Charles at an upscale café for lunch in Cambridge, Massachusetts. Soft-spoken, he was the father of three children, ages eleven, eight, and five. He chose his words carefully, taking long pauses when responding to questions. He echoed a commonly voiced sentiment when he said,

> The stratification between the top students and the lower students [in our public school] was so extreme that it was difficult for [teachers] to do differentiated learning in any kind of meaningful way. There really isn't much provision at all for maybe even the top 30 percent, maybe even 40 percent [of students].

As was the case for Indian immigrants, white parents mostly liked their school system but believed that schools should challenge and teach their children more thoroughly, leaving them worried about the quality of their math education.[7] Parents complained that their children's homework was much too easy and could be done "in about thirty seconds, standing up blindfolded," as another mother quipped in reference to her second grader. As seen earlier, leaders of private centers and competitions agreed with this critique, blaming the Department of Education and its pedagogical philosophy. This is despite schools tracking students and offering AP courses and other programs to maintain distinctions that benefit high-performing (and typically white) students.[8] For these parents, their children often were in elementary school, and the tactics to differentiate students typically start later.

The more Joanne, a mother of two boys in elementary and middle schools, learned about her public school, the more she wanted enhanced learning:

> I do read the curriculum that's being covered in [my son's sixth-grade public school math] class ahead of time. I go on the math school website. I download that, and I review it. I borrowed the textbook for seventh grade and reviewed it. I saw what he had already mastered previously, and that was part of the decision of you need to stay at [the math center]. You're already so far ahead of it. You're not going to be challenged in this particular math class.

The reasoning was that if schools had a stronger curriculum, parents would not seek additional lessons as often. But schools will not change, parents thought, and complaining to teachers would be of little use. After-school math centers served as an alternative to private school.

Parents who had international exposure, such as having lived abroad, or who knew immigrants well, were quick to cite the fact that the American school system lagged behind other industrialized countries in terms of education. Donald, a father of a third-grade boy, had done some research and stated,

> Math is weak in the school curriculum. I don't feel that way about reading and writing, but math isn't as advanced as it should be in this country.

Julie, a stay-at-home mother of three children (the oldest of whom was twelve years old), said,

> I majored in biology in college, and I took all the upper-level math. I was a science major, and you had to do all the track for mathematics and physics. It's important for me that [my daughter] is good in math and she feels confident in math.
>
> Q: Is the fact that you have a background with mathematics and science also partly why you're drawn to having your kids do well in math? Probably. My father was an engineer. My brother's an engineer. You know, my husband is a mathematician at heart, so I think that's really important for us.

Parents with STEM backgrounds were overrepresented among the people I spoke to, and given their own experiences and interests, they were more likely to be concerned about a math curriculum and kids' confidence in math. They wanted their kids to be above average in school generally and in math in particular. Without a demanding elementary- and middle-school math curriculum, parents worried that once mathematics became more difficult in high school or college, their children would be unprepared, lose confidence, and no longer push themselves in this core subject. To preempt this, parents stressed advanced math early. Parents enrolled children in the classes regardless of their children's expressed interest; math was just that important.

When I asked Sylvia if she trusted the school in her coveted sub-urb to give her sixth-grade son a sufficient math education, she responded,

> I guess not. It's always about the teacher, right? So the curriculum may not be lacking, right? I looked at the workbook. They had a parents' breakfast, that this is our new math program and this is what we'll teach, and this is how we'll do it. I think it's [the] implementation, the teacher['s] implementation [that matters]. You don't know what you're getting year to year. I remember when I was in public school, all my teachers hated math, all of them.

To compensate for such volatile teachers, parents took academics into their own hands.

Even strong schools and teachers cannot prevent all the challenges youths will face. Parents of daughters, particularly mothers, noted that confidence in math is harder to sustain in girls. Tanya, a single mother with three master's degrees and an eight-year-old daughter, referenced an infamous comment by the then-president of Harvard University that women may lack the same "innate ability" and "natural ability" as men for science, contributing to their underrepresentation in the field:[9]

> I mean, you just have to listen to Larry Summers, you know, this ste-reotype about women and science and math.

Charlotte, a mother of twin "overscheduled" boys in elementary school and a girl in middle school, elaborated:

> There's the gender dynamic, and I talk to [my daughter] explicitly about it. I'll give you examples. There was a recent study—this was about maybe two months ago—where they have taken a double-blind

test. They take math exams filled out by a class, and they give it to a teacher to grade. When the teacher grades it when there's no names, the girls actually did better than the boys, but when the teacher grades it with names, the boys do better than the girls. It's astounding, and I had [my daughter] read this article with me.

Elizabeth pleaded,

I just want [my daughter] to be confident. That's all. I want her to be confident, and I want her to be comfortable, and I'd like her to have choices. It's the whole point of choices. She'll have a lot of choices. She'll have the option to go into science if she wants to. She'll have the option to build things. She'll have the option to design dresses if she wants. She'll have all those options. That's all.

According to this thinking, schools take away girls' confidence, so parents had to compensate. It was unfair if girls, in particular, lacked options because they had self-doubts about their abilities. This was about creating the possibility of various futures.

The sense that other families were engaging in extra education also surfaced as a rationale to attend private learning centers, even if one's kids lacked interest. Tanya commented,

I look at MIT, and I look at Harvard, and I look at, you know, how many people are coming from, you know, largely Asian countries, it appears, who really want to go there. . . . So I feel like we've got to keep our kids at least . . . competitive.

Asian immigrant families are disproportionately represented at the centers and universities in these families' neighborhoods, and that did not go unnoticed. Working at math is a rational response to a sense of global competition beyond instilling confidence in math or compensating for a questionable school curriculum.

Middle- and upper-class Americans often reflect that their youths were a more relaxed and less competitive time. Today they worry about their economic security and that of their children, especially within a time of increased immigration and globalization, rising class inequality, and uncertainty in the labor market.[10] When living under a global capitalism marked by gross inequalities between "winners" and "losers," it feels essential to provide one's children with as many competitive advantages as possible, even if they would rather spend their time going skating or to the local pond. So families were concerned about their children's—in particular, their daughters'—abilities to stay confident and competitive in math as the curriculum grew more challenging and as highly qualified immigrants arrived. Given the structure and quality of traditional schools, parents saw private learning centers as a tool to ensure their children learned enough and worked hard on this subject.

The results kept parents invested in the programs even if kids were less enthused. Charles said that another parent, whose child did not attend enrichment math, noticed a difference between Charles's son and his own son in their homework abilities:

> So David noticed this and said, your son "sure races through that homework" [compared to David's son]. It came out that my son did go to [a private center], and that, as a result, the homework in school is not very hard.

Charlotte remarked,

> So we started [our daughter] in [a math learning center], and it was a big success. She went up the curve very quickly in terms of where her math was compared to when she started. We just kind of kept her in the program because it was working, she liked it, and I started to feel like I could see the difference between what she was learning

there from what she was bringing home from school in terms of math homework. It seemed like the public-school math program just wasn't anywhere near stretching her capability to do math.

Evidence of the effects of supplemental education on academic outcomes is mixed.[11] Still, practically every parent believed that their use of a learning center enhanced their children's abilities, as evidenced by their improved grades in school, ease of homework, or comments from other parents or teachers.

## A Well-Rounded Kid Who Likes Math

Joanne said that her son "loves math" but that she had other motivations too when enrolling him in a private math learning center:

> He just really enjoys math. It depends on the child. If he's not doing the homework or procrastinating about it, then your child is telling you something, but that's not happening. . . . My interest is having a child who can be challenged and fail and go back and try it again, and if we're so focused on achievement, students will do the minimum to get the achievements, and then stop. I don't want that.

While less pronounced than the aforementioned perspective, about a quarter of the parents I spoke to had mostly a humanistic motivation to offer the child an enrichment that made him or her happy. Like other parents, they appreciated the fact that their children would learn more math, but they came to the centers based more on what they thought their children would appreciate doing and less from a concern about their scholastics. As is typical with concerted cultivation parenting, this mother also hopes to instill cultural capital—namely, the ability to bounce back from failure—in an activity the child enjoys.[12] Her other son does not do more math but instead likes to learn about and repair cars. In her mind, attending car shows has "the same value" as math classes—the children are being thoughtful while doing something that they consider fun.

Antoinette, a mother with an adopted Chinese American daughter, commented that she had not even known there were math centers until her daughter asked to attend:

A lot of [joining the extracurricular math] is just because she wanted to learn it, and she wasn't thrilled with the way math was being taught [at her school]. . . . If she never mentioned [the math enrichment class], I might not have ever known about it. She brings home As [on her report card]. I'm not sure I would have thought it out to say, "Hey, I think you should do something even more so," but I thought it was a great idea. . . . A lot of her Chinese friends were also going to [math class].

Similarly, Wendy, who homeschooled her children, said,

When I pulled out books to go through, it was as if he already knew all of it, and so we began going through very quickly, and he really enjoyed math. When he was younger, we didn't introduce the math competition–style problems until pretty much sixth grade, and he didn't really want to put too much work into it, which was fine with me. So then when he was in eighth, he did the local math competition, and then he decided he wanted to work on it for the next year.

A few parents had a child gifted in math, and their investment in additional education stemmed from their child's interests and abilities, not from themselves. For example, Judy explained how if left to her own devices, she would not have enrolled her son in such activities:

I never did any extracurricular academic things. I never did any kind of competitions. So I was an average student. I got into the University of Illinois, my state school, and was very successful. And I became a teacher and I was—so I kind of feel average is good too. I mean, average still can get you a happy life and a successful job, so I wouldn't push him that way. And where I grew up, I never knew anybody who did this. . . . I'll tell you my best friend is back in the suburbs of Chicago, an affluent suburb, and her kids are completely average. She's got a daughter who's eleven, totally average. She would never put her daughter in an academic class for school or camp or a summer program. So her daughter will probably go to a state college. She'll probably go to Illinois State or the University of Illinois and study whatever she chooses to study, and she'll do well.

She was one of the very few parents who did not consider more academics as a worthy pursuit in its own right, but like many parents of a gifted child, she felt a responsibility to nurture her child's interests and abilities.

These parents ended up in learning centers the same way others ended up on the sidelines of youth soccer games, based on what interested their child. When spending time at a math learning center in suburban Boston, two US-born, white mothers shared why they enrolled their children in private math. One said, "One of my kids is into sports and the other isn't, so is here," to which the other mother sympathetically replied, "Oh yeah, I understand." Today's parents—in particular, middle-class professionals—are called "out of control" with how much they orient their lives and finances around their children's social, emotional, and cultural growth.[13] Such activities have become so normal that to not engage in them makes one a "bad" parent.[14]

I spoke to Matthew at length as we sat in the study of his suburban Boston home. His third-grade son was enrolled in sports, guitar lessons, and a math center. He said,

FIGURE 5.1. The regional awards ceremony and math fair for the Russian School of Mathematics, a national math center, Wellesley, Massachusetts, June 2015. Photo by Pawan Dhingra.

> He's actually quite good at [all the activities], like he's just learning pretty well. [Adding math was] truly more of a, "Hey, this would be a good way to be a well-rounded kid, hope that you enjoy it."

These children may not have asked for more math, but the parents sensed that it would suit them. Most parents believed that their children would enjoy math, or at least not mind it, and that it was a worthwhile skill to develop, so it made sense to enroll them even if the children had not initiated it.

Practically all parents mingled their rational motivations to build up their kids' academics with their humanistic desire for their children to be happy and "well-rounded." Learning center directors hoped to make math fun so that parents seeking well-rounded children would not be scared off by it. As Kristina, founder of a math franchise, said,

> You want your child to have fun with this kind of work. A lot of families tell me they want their kids to have fun doing this. It's what we do.

## Hardworking Rather Than Lazy

Building human capital at a young age was important not only for children's math skills but also so that children could develop desired *cultural values*: to be hardworking, respectful, and not spoiled or lazy. Even more than the Indian immigrant parents I spoke to, these white parents chastised fellow white professionals and American culture more generally as moral threats to their children. They wanted their children to mimic Asian Americans in terms of their work ethic and educational commitment rather than their white upper-middle-class peers, as Ed indicated earlier. William, the director of a private math center in an affluent Boston suburb, was careful not to criticize any group. But like Ed, he slowly confided that he saw a difference in how Asian Americans approach academics relative to whites. He explained that Asian immigrant clients were exposed to higher-level math in Asia than their children are in the United States and "value or prioritize education":

> So I think that there is that kind of history. And there is also, I think, a cultural element of focus on education that some communities in the US have and some don't. I mean, I don't want to get in trouble by singling out anyone, but there is a difference in how people value or prioritize education.

I spoke to Anthony at a franchised math center in the Boston area while his son was in his session. He sounded exasperated when it came to his fellow white Americans' priorities:

Who's spending money to educate their kids? I think that's the interesting thing. And basically the weaknesses, you know, the white Caucasian is not doing enough.

White professionals who resist hyper education and choose sports or the arts instead believe they are serving their children's long-term development by making them well rounded.[15] Anthony disagreed. While normally the middle or upper class critiques the working class and minorities for their presumed disinterest in education,[16] here the ire was targeted to affluent white peers.

Helen compared her son's math class to the Greek weekend program he also attended:

> I do think we're putting that priority [on education]. His dad worked really hard. That's why I have him in Greek school too. It's like, "You can have your American friends, but remember that you are Greek, and your grandparents are Greek, and you go to Greece every summer, and that's part of you too." So it's kind of like the same as [the math center]. It's like you can have your American friends and play, but let's remember that math is important in this family, you know? In this family, we really value education. It's funny.

Affluent families engage in various tactics to not raise spoiled children, such as at times denying toys and activities despite being able to afford them.[17] The math class here goes much further. As seen for Indian American parents, extracurricular academics are akin to an ethnic-religious commitment in that both are cultural—not just academic—activities that prevent too much assimilation. Parents who did not pursue extra education were not simply making a calculated mistake for their children's future opportunities but, moreover, were motivated by corrupt moral principles. These internalized, generic ways of valuing education and being appreciative cannot be reduced to cultural capital—that is, cultural skills one uses within particular settings (e.g., asserting oneself to authority figures).

Jack, a father with a grown child from a previous marriage and a nine-year-old with his current wife, dismissively critiqued his neighbors:

> These [neighbors'] kids were out smoking weed all the time, and the parents didn't have an idea what their kids were doing. I think the parents are disconnected, and they don't understand that the kids need a lot more than just school basically. . . . To tell you the truth, if that's any kind of gauge as to how American parents see their kids, it's a scary thing for American culture in general.

While it is not surprising for parents to see children's school involvement as a panacea to "smoking weed," here it is the lack of advanced education for already well-educated children that troubles Jack, echoing the concerns of Indian immigrants. Other parents in well-to-do suburbs are idle and "disconnected." His use of a learning center for his child helped provide a symbolic boundary (where there was no other boundary) to prevent his full assimilation into the white upper-middle-class parenting norms of his neighbors.

For some, an emphasis on sports signified misplaced values for how to raise children. Rebecca, a mother with a ten-year-old girl and a seven-year-old son, spoke regretfully about the differences between her family and her peers:

> I think that there's a different paradigm [from our white neighbors], and I hate to say it. Sometimes when we're joking around, we call [our children] the token white kids [among the immigrant families in their extracurricular activities]. But I think that among, you know, a lot of the people who grew up here, you know, we prioritize different things. . . . Sports is fantastic, and you can spend a lot of time focusing

on sports if you feel entitled to your parents paying for your college someday. Then maybe you don't have to worry about school so much, and you can go and play sports. That's great, but that's not the game that we're playing in our house.

Like the other parents, she differentiates herself from "entitled" whites around her, aligning herself as a token white person alongside down-to-earth immigrants.

Carter, who worked for a math competition for middle-school students and was heavily involved in after-school math activities said,

I can tell you from my personal experience in my neighborhood, it was the Asian families that were really starting a math club [for their kids]. I mean, there's a reason that high-school football [is popular] in Texas. That is the community in Texas. And culturally, they said, "We value this," and people who do well in this are revered. So when you have the Asian cultures saying, "We really value this [math]," and we think this is a big deal—their kids see that, absorb that. Our American culture, kids are more concerned about YouTube views maybe than they are about grades in some cases. . . . And I think our society puts too much emphasis on these physical team, organized activities. And I think if you flip-flop that, then probably that's the way it should be. It shouldn't be zero for physical and 100 percent for academic, but I think you want the majority competing in some academic competition. In the long term, our society will benefit from having kids with sharper mental skills.

Here again is the assumed binary of youth interests and talents, of athletics versus academics. Asian Americans are positioned as culturally prone toward the latter and incongruent with the former. This is despite their interest and participation in sports. Similarly, Asian Americans are major users of YouTube and other forms of social entertainment.[18] Yet in this narrative, Asian Americans have the right values, unlike Americans who should "flip-flop" their priorities.

Sports and education were framed as a zero-sum proposition: engaging in sports symbolized families' deemphasis on academics, for each interest stems from a distinct cultural background (Asia versus Texas). This binary felt all the truer to parents because doing well in a sport meant having to spend considerable time on it due to its increased competition and privatized options—"too much" time in their eyes. Sports were important for making children well rounded, they thought, but those highly committed to sports either were misguided in hoping their children might earn sports scholarships or were too relaxed about education.

Wishing for a "flip-flop" in priorities was not an ungrounded want but instead a realistic expectation given the example that immigrants appeared to set. Parents felt legitimized in criticizing their peers when they cited immigrants—in particular, Asian Americans—as embodying shared educational beliefs. When I asked Helen how she felt about Asian Americans' reported high achievements, she replied,

> See, for me that's almost a positive, because it's just raising the bar. And I think my son will be up there too. So I don't consider it, like, a threat or the stress is a bad thing. I think that's good. It's raising the bar. . . . Isn't that amazing that the whole immigrant family thing is so, like—that it's such a clear delineation between families, for the most part? The American families put more focus on free time. I'm amazed.

For her and the other parents, a difference in achievement between most Americans and certain immigrants was due to mind-set and effort; Asian Americans represented a model, hardworking group. Parents of elementary- and middle-school-aged children were not yet facing the so-called model minority in college admissions, so they were more open to appreciating this cultural influence rather than sensing it as a threat.

Charles said of his family's involvement at a private learning center that many Asian Americans attended,

> We're a very small minority. I find that kind of great. It's an environment where parents are looking out to make sure that their children are doing exactly the same kinds of things that I want, that they're pushing them in ways that [youths] wouldn't push themselves, or, in some ways, the school wouldn't. I guess I identify a little bit with an immigrant mentality. I just take comfort that there are other parents who have similar kinds of values. I identify with that strongly.

Enrolling one's children in private math lessons signified much more than another after-school activity, whether basketball or dance; it meant that they were a better kind of parent. Even though born and raised in the United States, he speaks of his difference from his peers in the same manner that immigrants refer to their separation from US-born natives, of being a "small minority" with "an immigrant mentality" and a "comfort" found in being with parents with "similar kinds of values." More than just respecting immigrants, these parents often identified with them and not their fellow white Americans. He "strongly" believes in this difference from his white peers.

## Class Upbringing and Extracurricular Priorities

What led these white US-born parents to identify as or with immigrants rather than with their neighbors and to judge hyper education in moral terms? There are circumstances particular to each family, such as having seen one's much older children not progress through school as one had hoped, but a common thread was a parent's sense of difference from peers based on an assumed class upbringing. These individuals had grown up without high incomes or were keenly aware that their parents had grown up middle or working class. They differentiated between earned income and wealth. In line with the standard narrative around American mobility, they believed that they or their parents had moved up in class status through hard work and a commitment to education. It's how they ended up in their affluent neighborhoods. They thought their white neighbors took their wealth for granted and grew up privileged. Extra schooling served, then, as a way to remember their upbringing and pass on its lessons to their children. Cindy believed she was distinctive from others in her neighborhood and shared similarities with immigrants:

> I value education very highly. It's top of the list—family, education—because I come out of a working-class background. And so I know that that was our way, one of the reasons. Education and the idea of a meritocracy. And so that's where I come from, and that's why that influences my choices. And maybe that's more like other folks who might come here and have that same concern.

Vicky grew increasingly agitated in our interview as she reflected on the white families in her neighborhood relative to immigrants she reads about:

> When you look at the valedictorians in the Boston public schools, you know how they publish that in the [*Boston*] *Globe* every year? It's like every single one is an immigrant.[19] You know, they're working really hard, and they're doing really well, and there's, like, something to that work ethic that I do think nonimmigrant families have lost a little bit. . . . I mean, I live in kind of an affluent area. [Children in the area will] go through school. Their parents will pay for private college, and they'll end up on Wall Street, and they'll end up doing fine. But that's

not how the rest of the world works, and I don't want my kid to ever depend on that. . . . [Having my children in math classes with immigrants] makes me feel like I'm doing something right, because I do think the nonimmigrant kids might be spoiled a little bit.

Parents saw kindred spirits in immigrants who had "made it" through traditional lifestyles.

Helen, who equated math classes with Greek school, hoped that hyper education would provide her child with an "immigrant mentality" that might otherwise be missing given their now elevated class status:

You can say immigrants are more hardworking. They had to work harder. My husband came here with—it's like [a] traditional immigrant story. He left Lebanon during wartime, had like $5 in his pocket, went to college in the US. He didn't speak English, so, I mean, there's that, like, hardship component and that competitive component. And that's one of the things we're very aware about, that, you know, our kids don't have that need. If they want a new pair of jeans, they can get it tomorrow, you know? All their friends have Wiis and Porsches. It's like, how do you make sure that they still have that immigrant mentality? So I don't know. I think it's obviously the hardship component. Like, my husband wasn't given everything. You've got to work hard for it. So how do you teach a little spoiled brat that they have to work hard?

In this way of thinking, an emphasis on academics will prevent kids from becoming "spoiled," instill a competitive spirit, and offset the fact that parents cannot or will not provide full financial support (even as they can afford comforts). Extra academics served as a surrogate for an immigrant ethos to create appreciative, hardworking children. Immigrants had attained the American dream through similar commitments, and their children should follow suit, in contrast to their brattish friends with "Wiis and Porsches" who will "end up on Wall Street" thanks to their financial privilege.

Because supplemental education was not merely or even primarily fun for most children compared to their other activities, investing in it offset class privilege rather than reinforced it in parents' minds. Both Karen and her husband, parents of a ten-year-old daughter and twin boys age seven, had PhDs and lived in the Boston suburbs as engineers. She said,

> Our school has some very, very rich people. Their kids, in my opinion, will always have the tools to get help if they need to, monetarily. I am not like that. I have to work hard for the money, and so I will push my kids as much as I can, because I will not have the monetary means to help them later on. It may be judgmental to some of the people, but that's very true. . . . I think my family is not wealthy. My grandparents worked really hard. They're Holocaust survivors. My parents worked really hard, and, you know, they never paid for my college, so you have to do it yourself. . . . I think that we can [provide] help more to our kids now than what my parents were able to help us, but we did that through hard work. I want to maintain that for my kids. I want them to appreciate that too.

She draws a line from her grandparents' survival of the Holocaust to her parents' work ethic to her children's math class: all instill a core belief in hard work that marks a properly raised adult. This emphasis on self-sufficiency and hardship contrasted with parents' impression of their peers, whom they criticized as prioritizing children's enjoyment and as taking wealth for granted (whether verifiable or not). So even if they had houses, cars, clothes, occupations, and incomes comparable to their white neighbors, they did not identify as a single group. Ed, who called whites lazy, elaborated:

What I mean is, after having been here for two or three generations, and they have trust funds and inheritances, they don't think they have to work anymore. They think that they'd rather go skiing. They've got the money. They want their kids to spend the winters up in New Hampshire when they're not in school, a weekend's vacation, and they don't see the urgency for learning the way that maybe their grandparents did when they first came here.

He frames his established peers as having trust funds and, with that, having lost any sense of "urgency" that drove their grandparents' generation. In contrast, these parents were still building their finances, like immigrants.

Families did not have to grow up poor, working class, or even lower-middle class to sense status differences. Charlotte aligned her move from the Midwest to the East Coast with immigrants moving to a new land, echoing rhetoric about immigrants lacking access to opportunity and studying "twice as hard" as native-born people:

I think if you're an immigrant and your children are first generation, I'd assume or expect that there might be a sense that your child doesn't have the same advantages culturally and access. If you grew up in the Boston area as a white family who may have had family members going to top schools, you have built-in advantages. So I don't think [these local whites] feel as pushed to provide something extra like [extracurricular math class]. I mean, my husband and I are both from the Midwest. I'm from Indiana, and he's from North Dakota. We don't have this connection to [an] East Coast prestigious school.

In effect, she does not identify as much with white American privilege as she thinks her peers can. She believes that Boston-bred professionals have real privileges in terms of wealth or connections, unlike her and immigrants.

## Humanistic Rather Than Robotic

Just as parents can be too relaxed in their commitment to their children's education, they can also be too intense. White parents judged others based on not only *whether* they promoted academics but also *in what manner* they did so. As explained earlier, educators bemoaned hyper education in part for the stress it placed on youths. These parents, however, did not feel that after-school academics caused stress. They believed that only when parents pursued such education with indifference toward their children did it have negative psychological outcomes. Tanya said,

> I'm not, you know, what you'd call a tiger mom or something. You know, I don't push, push, push to the point if they're unhappy. But I think as long as she's happy doing all these things . . .

White parents wanted to raise children in a humanistic, sensitive fashion. The other side of this binary was supposedly authoritarian Asian "tiger moms." Asian Americans may be envied for being hardworking rather than lazy, but they were often read as extreme in their parenting style.

Virginia, whose middle-school son was gifted in math and made it to the highly competitive MATHCOUNTS, said,

> [Asian parents are] pushing their child, versus us just letting the child do his own thing. . . . I'm going to say specifically Indian and Asian. [They] are really, really pushing their kids through the summer programs, through online classes. And I don't know why. I know that getting into MIT, getting into Harvard, those are their top goals. And so I think that's why they push, and that's why they get them into these competitions, and they want to see them be top in these things, because they can put it on their applications for college. It's not my strategy. . . . So for [our son], everything he does is self-motivated, self-

driven. So anything he does online—Khan Academy studies, when he was in third, fourth, fifth grade—he'd ask for all those. It's always him. So for him, it is healthy.

Virginia distinguishes herself from others because the motivation is internal for her son. In contrast to many Asian Americans who may spend fewer hours in extra education than she does, her family is "healthy."

Amanda, a mother in a Boston suburb, noted that while her participation in her local math center literally put her in the same room as Asian Americans, she felt a significant distance between them:

> I'll tell you that I don't know that many [Asian American parents] because they do not reach out to interact with me. So it's a funny thing to be kind of the minority in the room. And they'll look after each other, and they will engage [each other]. It's not as if they're not friendly, but they're not seeking it out [with me] And there's this sort of intensity that they bring to it that I don't think is necessary. And maybe the big dividing line is that no matter what background you come from, if you're more achievement-oriented and less enrichment-oriented, then I guess I would be less like that person. So we're not as achievement-oriented, but a lot of people at [the learning center] are. They are into the competitions, the tests, the SATs for seventh graders. So we are a family who doesn't look like everyone else there, and then our purpose for being there is, it's not [like] some other folks. . . . I'm not going to make [my kids] do certain things so that it's just good for them. It depends on what it is.

While Asian Americans want their children to outcompete others, as is common among parents,[20] they become caricatured as caring only about excelling on a test rather than what their child has an interest in. Amanda has not spoken to them and does not know their stories but assumes "a lot of people" enroll their seventh graders in the SATs. As fitting the racialized "forever foreigner" image, Asian Americans are criticized for not reaching out to her, even as they have in no way been unfriendly. Nor has she made an effort to converse with them given that they are engaged with "each other."

Parents consistently referred to "balance" in how they raised children. Tanya, who wanted to keep her child competitive with Asian Americans aimed at entrance into MIT and Harvard, went on to say,

> I think that's amazing, you know, how many people will really do anything to try to get here and have the opportunity to study [at MIT, Harvard, etc.]. . . . I do think that we also need to be careful in that it's a balance, right, and kids are kids. I mean, they can't study and work all the time, so I hope that we're pretty balanced.

She feels that unlike Asian Americans, her children are not robots; they cannot "study and work all the time." Paula said about her daughter's Chinese American friends,

> I think with a lot of [Chinese American] families, "You study and you bring home the good grades." It's kind of the culture of some of her friends' families. [There is a] competitive pride to accomplish, and also math is a strong foundation for a lot of more STEM-related careers. . . . I know that she has some friends that all they do in their free time—one friend, all she does in her free time is even take more advanced math classes and more advanced science classes. . . . I do a very fine balance. . . . I [say to my daughter], "Hey, I'm trying to give you your freedom, but I don't want you to be disappointed in why you didn't have a good outcome in school."

Presumably due to Asian ancient culture, taking higher-level classes is all that some Asian Americans "do in their free time." Whites, on the other hand, embrace a liberal ideology and offer children freedom, a sense of individuality, and personhood unconstrained by a domineering culture, while also being attentive to practical considerations. In reality, Asian American youths enjoy much of their childhoods, as discussed later.

Immigrants were, in the end, respected as signifiers of what was possible, not as real individuals. White American parents believed their concern with their children's happiness separated them from their stereotyped image of Asian American parents. They felt they struck—or at least cared to strike—a balance between the immigrant and American sensibilities. Ed continued to say, "Whites are lazy. I like to say whites are lazy; Asians are crazy."

## Harkening Back to the "Olden Days"

In white parents' language of respect for immigrants yet critique of Asian Americans, they reveal their deeper symbolic interpretation of advanced education. The real group these parents identify with through hyper education is Americans of a bygone era, who more easily could balance hard work with the freedoms of childhood. As seen above, parents referenced the work ethic of their parents and grandparents, the "greatest generation" of sorts. Immigrants are more a foil than a literal group they identify with; white parents do not talk about transnational ties, generational conflict with parents, learning a new language, or other immigration narratives. They may not know or even interact meaningfully with many immigrants. Instead, they refer to a romanticized recollection of a simpler time. The image in their heads is of warmhearted families working together at home or on the fields, with unspoiled kids studying by candlelight because they appreciate hard work. Immigrants serve as a proxy for that bygone era, presumably all having arrived to the United States with $5 in their pockets and unable to speak English but making it with grit and a sense of urgency that enabled them to overcome hardships. Ignored in this narrative is the high level of education and employment or the university placement most of these particular immigrants arrive with.

For instance, Vicky, who appreciated the number of Asian American valedictorians, confessed that she did not have firsthand familiarity with many immigrants but was most interested in having her eight-year-old child grow up to be self-sufficient, which extra schooling facilitated. She thought that was easier in earlier days:

> I don't really know that many immigrants. The immigrants I do know, I know my nanny from El Salvador; she and her husband work so hard. They're newly minted US citizens. . . . I think my own kid is capable of more—like, I still tie his shoes. You know what I mean? I think, like, in the olden days, you know, kids were farming at age eight, seven, you know? I get mad at myself as a parent for not having more independent kids, but I kind of strive for that.

Farmers exist in the popular imagination as indicative of a hardworking, well-grounded persona, akin to the immigrant persona of today. This mother has no farming background but romanticizes an old-fashioned, "bootstrap" America. Such children learned to be responsible and hardworking while also enjoying their youth. The nanny and her husband—the only immigrants Vicky knows—are working toward their own American dream.

More than just being independent, the image of the "olden days" farmer contrasts with the plugged-in generation in affluent suburbs that allows for fun but without teaching responsibility. A common concern today regards too much "screen time" for children. These parents contrasted the popular use of leisure electronics with the supposed immigrant mentality that leads to academics and better lifestyles. Julie, the mother of three children aged six to twelve, took pride in how "behind the times" she was:

My father was not an immigrant, but he didn't grow up wealthy. For everybody in our family, you have to work really hard, and you have to study really hard, and that's important. Maybe it's the immigrant mentality that when you come to a new place, you have to work really hard to achieve. . . . We do not have any iPads in the house. We have one computer, and we have one TV, and we don't have an Xbox, and we don't have—I don't even know what all these little gaming things are. . . . You know, if you take away the computer and the TV, there's a lot of hours left in a child's day to do things that they enjoy.

Parents want a bygone era without "gaming things," and they invoke immigrants as symbolic of that. Like so many parents I spoke to, this mother conflates immigration with lacking money yet still achieving upward mobility. It is not immigrants per se with whom parents identify but a narrative of hard work and overcoming long odds (including even the Holocaust, as Karen said) in contrast to the temptations children are surrounded by today. Math classes helped instill that mind-set and lifestyle. Importantly, children will have "hours left in [the] day to do things that they enjoy."

## The Many Motives

It is easy to frame hyper education as a foreign practice limited to Asian Americans as educators often did, for they are overrepresented in the practice, and such a notion fits the tiger parenting stereotype. Yet that is incorrect. US-born whites engage in the same spaces and often for similar reasons as Indian Americans. While some white parents begrudgingly pursue additional schooling partly in response to Asian Americans increasing the educational bar in their neighborhoods (as do some Asian Americans), that is just one of several rationales, and it is rarely done without an appreciation for the activity. Parents consider after-school education as offering their children confidence in math, especially for girls, and practical skills to help them with test scores and intellectual growth. Schools appear insufficient and have misplaced priorities. Families also consider hyper education as a form of concerted cultivation—that is, like Indian Americans, they seek out such options even when there are no external pressures to do so. There is a sense of fulfillment that comes from being well rounded. Math classes sit next to guitar lessons and skiing for some children in the minds of parents. The earlier scene of kids enjoying math games at the math center celebration is one example.

Adults' strategic choices—in this case, to pay for activities that children rarely choose for themselves—cannot be reduced to an accumulation of capital and credentials à la sociologist Pierre Bourdieu's popular contention.[21] Here we see that even activities that have clear practical incentives have deeper cultural motives, again consistent with Indian American parents.[22] Their families' upward mobility into their current economic status is central to their identities, as is often the case for those who distinguish themselves from peers based on their values.[23]

Parents, ironically, turn to an activity that costs money and further privatizes education as a means to instill humility and perspective. At first blush, affluent parents agonize over raising children with a sense of entitlement, interpreted as consumption without regard to costs or need and as not believing one must work hard to be successful.[24] Children easily can grow up spoiled rather than valuing hard work and helping others.[25] Here, however, giving children privileged experiences of private math centers and educational advantages works to raise hardworking kids who will have a competitive mind-set rather than become overly entitled. The growth of extracurricular education will continue as long as it seems to provide more than just good grades, possibly regardless of the actual academic advantages it ostensibly aims to serve.

While there is a surprising amount of overlap between Indian American and white families, their choices and outlooks have significant divergences. Indian Americans' position as ethnic minorities drives their felt need for their children to excel in school above others, as explained earlier. It also informs their moral judgments around hard work. White Americans have similar critiques of the school system but do not experience them the same way or worry about them from the same point of view. Similarly, their critique of their professional peers follows a comparable rhetoric but stems from a different relationship to other whites, which allows for a harsher critique. Both groups worry about children doing drugs, not respecting elders, and not valuing hard work. But whites articulate more of a concern for having spoiled, overindulged children, while Indian Americans worry more about teen sex and guns.

RACE AND MORALITY: Race is central to how parents decide whether other families and even themselves are morally proper. Fitting the classic "model minority" stereotype, Asian Americans are praised for their work ethic and respectful demeanor. For parents here, the fact that their white children sit alongside Asian American youths means they are raising their children well. Immigrants—even immigrants of color—serve as a positive reference group for the majority.[26] Whites prefer school districts with majority white students and with few African Americans, and they prefer neighborhoods with similar class levels to themselves.[27] This does not mean, however, that they conflate all people of color as being the same. They identify with Asian Americans despite not being immigrants themselves.

Not only do parents praise Asian Americans, but they actively criticize fellow white upper-middle-class professionals as immoral. Taking from Asian American Studies, the opposite of the model minority are not whites but African Americans, for the model minority stereotype serves to penalize African Americans as unworthy. As seen for Indian Americans, antiblack assumptions inform white parents' critiques of affluent whites as overindulgent and delinquent. Their critiques of their white peers mirror antiblack stereotypes:

they are dissolute parents who do not respect education, they do not adequately supervise their children, they do not work hard enough, they are spoiled (whether through inherited wealth for white professionals or government welfare for supposed poor blacks), they are not monitored properly by their parents; they overcommit to lowbrow distractions like sports, and they run the risk of using drugs and alcohol. The ways in which black families nurture and support children are completely overlooked.[28] White peers become a version of stereotyped blacks in a discursive sense (not in a material or political or social sense). Again, given that antiblackness is prominent in the United States, it is not surprising that critiques of students take on antiblack references. These are even sharper critiques than those made by Indian Americans, who questioned and often looked down upon American culture as polluting but did not directly criticize whites as much. In other words, they were willing to give whites some benefit of the doubt in how they parented, but fellow whites were not.

It is fitting, then, that just as immigrants and working-class whites draw boundaries from blacks in their neighborhoods or workspaces, these white professionals act in similar ways toward their white neighbors.[29] Private learning centers serve as an ethnic space of sorts, and the students there are fictive kin. Thus the conflation of enhanced math and the synagogue and Greek school, for instance, for all spaces prevent a downward cultural assimilation to one's surrounding, corruptive environment.[30]

This is not to suggest that the parents held racist views toward blacks. They went out of their way to compliment poor minorities, even if in stereotypical ways. For instance, Ed criticized whites as lazy but said that poor African Americans have

tremendous potential, because they've got a burning desire to succeed. I believe a burning desire to succeed is an edge that the white kid doesn't have anymore. I'm generalizing. . . . What I've seen is that they're beaten down by the system.

Antiblack notions travel and need not be limited to the presence of black people.

While white parents identify with immigrants, it is only to an extent. Conceiving of Asian Americans as authoritarian follows standard stereotypes of them as the model minority: so dedicated to educational progress that they lose any balance and real personhood.[31] Not all parents who raise hardworking children are moral parents. "Tiger-parenting" Asian Americans go about this in a supposedly tortuous fashion, treating children like robots. Moral parenting entails not only which activities one pursues but how one pursues them, at which Asian Americans fail. These white parents consider themselves the most enlightened, for they care about their children's well-being but still recognize—and try to remedy—the deficiencies of the school system and surrounding culture.

What parents truly seek through supplemental education is not an alignment with immigrants but a connection to the "good-ole'-days" when self-sufficiency happened naturally on the "family farm." The nostalgic, all-American past also had easier rules to follow: hard work and clean living would lead to class mobility.[32] There is a popular imagination of the nuclear family that is no longer typical.[33] With an unsettled global economy and immigration pressures, even affluent white parents see instability in their children's futures.[34] Education centers serve as a substitute for that nostalgic past, for they help secure socioeconomic reproduction with a moral grounding of valuing hard work that might otherwise be in doubt.

# PART III

# Good Behavior

# 6

## "Everyone in the Family Was Involved"

"Veldschoen," Namita said to her daughter Geeta as they sat at the kitchen table on a warm summer morning in August 2013.

"What's a veldschoen?" Geeta asked.

Namita looked at her computer. "A heavy, rawhide shoe made without nails and usually without an insole. Veldschoen."

"Very comfy shoes?" Geeta probed.

"Mmm-hmm."

"Veldschoen. V-E-L-D-S-C-H-O-E-N. Veldschoen," Geeta rattled off.

"Spruit," Namita asked.

"S-P-R-U-I-T," Geeta quickly responded.

"Now we are doing the 'uu' sounds, like uu, oe, or ew. Like zuurefelt."

"Z-U-U-R-E-F-E-L-T," Geeta again sped through.

Geeta, fourteen years old, was preparing for the 2014 South Asian Spelling Bee finals. She had appeared in the Scripps National Spelling Bee the year prior, placing in the top fifty. Her dog scampered into the kitchen of their modest yet comfortable sunlit house. Namita was a stay-at-home mother, and her husband worked as a computer engineering professor at the local state university. Their younger daughter, who had also participated in the ethnic bee circuit at the regional level but had not made it to the finals, was upstairs in her room. Geeta and her mother were going through a list of words of Dutch origin, and any time Geeta missed a word, she would write it down in her spiral notebook. As she spelled, Geeta picked up the dog, scratched his back, and nuzzled noses with him. Namita kept reading out words. She had a warm tone and demeanor, not critical but focused. There was little side conversation, no joking around, no criticisms nor profuse praise. This reading of words had become a daily ritual at this point. They studied for three hours each morning, taking a break around lunchtime and then resumed for two to three more hours.

Geeta smiled often during our hours together. She spelled, asked for definitions, asked for parts of speech, and the like without a sense of stress or fear of failure. When she missed a word, she didn't get mad at herself or vent in frustration. She would just jot it down, spell it out loud correctly, and keep going. Contrary to stereotypes that these children are forced into studying while they would rather be doing almost anything else, this was Geeta's interest. Namita was more than along for the ride; she was an active participant, making her child's interest her own. She worked as her daughter's unpaid coach (and cook). About a quarter of competitive spellers I met had a stay-at-home mother, often with a college degree or higher. Namita invested in spelling aids, put in time, organized her day around the coaching, and provided nutrition during the spelling workout. She set a firm but generous tone, with many smiles even as her voice remained steady and serious.

Hyper education was more than a hobby or weekly class for many of the youths. Especially for those who participated in academic competitions, it was part of their personal identity. Rather than a solo effort, their participation stemmed from familial and community support that helped create a sense of normality around studying. For about a third of the children, initial participation in academic competitions was their idea. For another third, parents enrolled their children in them without giving them a choice. For the final third, it was a combination. In regards to learning centers, parents mostly initiated enrollment. With the binary of safety versus risk in parents' minds, these efforts helped put their children on the safe side and ensure the good behavior they wanted.

## Family Involvement

Milan, a father of two daughters in middle and elementary school an hour outside of Boston, shared,

> During the school year, after completing homework and other schoolwork, my older daughter devotes most of the time to spelling bee study. She mostly studies on her own: reading the dictionary, studying roots and rules of various languages, and going through lists. My wife finds words she thinks are interesting and hard. Then we quiz her on the words she finds. My younger daughter helps with pronouncing the words. During weekends and vacations, my older daughter spends most of the day studying, filtering through lists and working on the hard words.

As seen here and in the documentary *Breaking the Bee*[1] on Indian American spelling bee families, youths studied with their parents and siblings, with parents quizzing, using whiteboards, and laughing together.[2] Parents also took copious notes during competitions so as to figure out what to expect next year. For instance, at the 2016 South Asian Spelling Bee finals, I saw one family make a color-coded Microsoft Excel sheet with each word used in the bee, in order, and which ones were missed. These became the tools for future word lists.

The family helped make the intense process of hyper education feel habitual and normal. Parents with children in learning centers or other organized outlets played different roles for their children than for those engaged in independent studies, such as spelling bees. Parents of children in organized outlets, such as MATHCOUNTS, rarely served as coaches for their children's math enrichment; the official math teacher or math coach served in that role. Parents still supported the activity by dropping off and picking up their children, asking questions of the teacher and their children about progress, monitoring homework, and paying for the classes.[3] Parents most committed to extra math often had STEM-related occupations and educations, so discussing math at home or in the car felt natural. Some took an active approach. One mother checked her daughter's math-center homework right after she completed it rather than waiting for the instructor to do so at the next session so that her daughter could learn quickly from any mistakes. Most parents did not check the answers, instead just checking to make sure it was done, just like regular schoolwork.

Practically every child committed to extra scholastics referred to their family's efforts toward studying. Mothers typically spent more time with the kids, whether because they stayed at home or had shorter work schedules or prioritized more kid time. Sanjay, a former Scripps champion and now an adult, referred to his mom as "the organizer":

> It was my sister and my mom. My mom, she was kind of the organizer. "You have this many letters in the dictionary left to study. You have this much time. You're going to divide that evenly; that means you have this much time per letter." My mom made time tables for me. That first being this is how much time you have for the letter A. Letter A was pretty big; it took me a large amount of the summer. So she's like, "Oh, OK, let's do smaller letters." And that's how slowly we built up the speed. . . . Every single day for dinner, our dinner conversation would be like. "Oh, what letters did you do today? How many words did you cover? How many pages did you write down?" Questions like that, and

it's really like everyone in the family was involved. It really was a whole family effort.

Sanjay's and his family's efforts paid off.

Kavita, a mother of three children, talked about how she taught her children math:

> Most of my teaching is when I'm cooking and cleaning. I don't sit with them. I put three glasses of ice; now I want to put double the water; how much water do I need to put in? I do this while driving, cooking, when brushing their teeth. I'm driving most of the time with three kids. "Did you notice the name of that road? What was the shape of that sign," which I would ask when they were younger and learning shapes.

Her active verbal engagement with her children suits the concerted cultivation style of much verbal communication with children.[4] Mothers must balance housework and childrearing, rarely having time to do just one. Here, she manages to turn everyday activities—both hers and the kids'—into learning moments, with an emphasis on math and logic. A gendered form of parenting, not just a division of labor, emerges. The amount of mental energy it takes is significant.

Even when youths had solitary study routines, family members proved invaluable. Mayank, a former Scripps champion, explained,

> This is how I studied lists. I would go through each word of the list; if it were unfamiliar to me, I would look it up in the dictionary and read its definition, all of its available pronunciations, and its etymology— trying to soak up as much as possible about the word. Oftentimes, I would Google a particular word (for example, "colichemarde," a type of sword) and read up on articles about that word or sentences that

used that word—anything to develop a solid comprehension of the word. . . . But what I've described above is a seemingly independent, solitary process of studying, which is far from the truth. In my early years of preparation, my mother was absolutely invaluable; she often quizzed me on the Paideia. On spellingbee.com, there used to be a site that featured audio files of professors and National Spelling Bee pronouncers Alex Cameron and Jacques Bailly going through each word of the Paideia; I would often give myself written tests with those audio files, and my mom would grade them and let me know if I made any mistakes.

Parents routinely said that their children knew spelling and math better than they did. Still, parents found a way to assist.

Mothers also utilized their backgrounds in engineering to progress their children's achievement. Former Scripps finalist Chetan Reddy benefited from his mother, Geetha Manku, beyond her support, organizing, and quizzing. She used her electrical engineering and business training to develop a software program that conveyed words with their language of origin and definitions, thereby giving Chetan an easy way to learn.[5] She coauthored word lists with her son and husband with words commonly used in competitions. These included words of French origin, Greek origin, German origin, and more. Similarly, Jyoti Patel, the mother of former Scripps finalist Samir Patel (also from the Dallas / Fort Worth area, like Chetan), worked with her husband to publish their own word lists, in part with an algorithm developed by her husband.[6]

Even when children's interests and talents seemed unique to them, without parental assistance, parents became involved to nurture their children. Sarah, a white stay-at-home mother whose son demonstrated extreme proficiency in math at a young age, had more awareness of her son's talents and time to advocate for him than did her husband:

FIGURE 6.1. Ashrita Bhumireddy and her mother, Sirisha, study in her room in Andover, Massachusetts, September 2014. Photo by Pawan Dhingra.

It made us laugh because I'm not strong at all in math. My husband's an English teacher. So it's not like math has been a part of our world, and it's not something that we focus on. It really is just a gift that we saw in [our son]. I'm a stay-at-home mom; I was able to see that gift and work with him and get the materials that he needed and advocate for him once he was in school. I said [to his second-grade teacher], "If he already showed the ability to be learning at advanced levels, beyond these other kids who he just lives in class with, how does [staying in the same class] benefit him?" I'd say about two months into the school year, they realized, "OK, you're right and we'll work with this. We'll get him into a higher class; we'll do more for him."

Mothers were actively involved, and often so were fathers. Fathers created problem sheets or word lists, quizzed their children, attended competitions, and the like. They would help create systems for their children to break down words or equations and piece them back together.[7] Fathers also engaged with kids during more play and leisure times, which is typical of fathers' engagement with their children.[8] A middle-school boy, Janak, recalled a classic father-son tradition as a spelling opportunity with his father when he was seven years old:

> I guess in the early stages, we'd just be playing catch or something, and he'd be quizzing me some words while we'd be playing.

Family outings became opportunities for studying. A former Scripps champion, Neeru, showed me a menu from an Italian restaurant that she had held onto for years. At the restaurant with her family as a young girl while preparing for a spelling competition, her father took the opportunity to quiz her on Italian-origin words: rigatoni, chardonnay, spaghetti, merlot, and more. She had written the words on the menu and took it home as part study guide and part souvenir. Many years later, it was brittle in my hands, and she was nostalgic for the ways in which her family had made bee preparation part of her daily life.

Vijay Reddy, Chetan's father, quit his job and opened up GeoSpell, a tutoring business in the Dallas/ Fort Worth area to prepare students for spelling and geography competitions. While open to all students, he and his wife cater to fellow Indian Americans. Their clients are also from the Houston area, and even those outside of Texas take his online courses and purchase his training books. Weekly tutoring is $120 per month. He stood proudly next to contestants at the 2018 Scripps National Spelling Bee finals that he and his wife had helped along the way, including the champion, Karthik Nemmani. In 2019, he helped three of the co-champions. GeoSpell hosts its own competitions as well.

It is not surprising, then, that parents became almost as enamored by the competitions as did the children. At South Asian spelling competitions, I saw parents even without their children line up to meet Scripps champions. They pulled out their phones and took selfies as if the winners were celebrities.[9] When talking with Chandu, a Scripps champion and now a high school student, at an SASB event, a father of a speller couldn't help but interrupt us:

I have to shake your hand. Oh, it's such a pleasure, such an honor! I have to take a picture of you some time. My wife couldn't be here; she would be so happy.

Parents were willing to go to great lengths to facilitate their children's success. Some flew across the country, such as from California to North Carolina or from Texas to Massachusetts, so children could participate in a preferred South Asian regional competition to try to qualify for the finals (e.g., if the date scheduled in their area would not work for them, or if they wanted more time to prepare and so chose a later-scheduled competition, or even if they thought the other location would have fewer contestants than their own location).

Because these academic pursuits matter so much to parents, they can become bitter if kids fail. Geeta made it several rounds at the SASB finals that August on a stage of highly competent spellers. But she did not win. Disappointed, she still maintained her light air afterward. She gave hugs to her competitors (the other girls at least). She mocked herself for missing the word but didn't beat herself up. Her maturity showed when she quickly turned away from her loss and supported those still on stage. Namita, on the other hand, wore her disappointment more expressively. While she did not cry at her daughter's loss, she found nothing to smile about, instead staying mostly quiet for the rest of the competition, even during breaks. She sat in her chair with her daughter standing next to her. Toward the end of the competition, her daughter expressed interest in repeating all this next year. Namita, however, replied, "No. I'm not going through that again."

This parental commitment to educational support is consistent with other scholarship on Asian Americans. In part, educational achievement is an immigrant phenomenon; children of immigrants tend to do better in school than their peers with equal resources.[10] Asian Americans' high average educational achievements have been attributed to their emphasis on education in the home (e.g., parents spending time with children on their homework), use of supplemental education (e.g., tutoring, test prep classes), high expectations of academic success, and parents' own above-average level of educational attainment.[11] Still, all sorts of middle-class families are actively engaged in children's academic and extracurricular lives, not just Asian Americans.[12] This is not to say that differences between Asian Americans and others do not exist, such as in parenting styles.[13] But the differences occlude their overarching similarities in active parental involvement, especially for high-income families.[14] Regardless of nationality, parents had high expectations and engaged in a variety of common educational techniques, such as requiring children to read twenty minutes per day during the summer and school year, going to museums, cooking together, and more.[15] Informally, white parents also engaged their children's intellect through daily habits. Elizabeth, a white mother with children in a math center, relayed an observation her friend had made:

A mother asked me, "Are you a teacher?" I said no. She said, "Well, you talk in a way that is like a teacher." I had said to my son, "We are going to get three things off the shelf." That was how I was saying we were going to get three things. It wasn't, "We are going to get some stuff from the shelf." We are precise.

Time and mental energy were not the only kinds of investments. While the story so far has been one of family commitment, this only works within a context of financial stability. The "tiger mom" is not an answer to middle-class anxieties about sustained or upward socioeconomic attainment.[16] Parents' education level and employment status have a positive effect on children's educational development, including for language and literacy.[17] Even for Asian Americans, parents' income has a deciding role in affecting children's commitment to education.[18] The socioeconomic status of a family and their networks has a durable effect on school performance over other relevant factors, such as class size, school size, or percentage of student attendance.[19] Registering for and attending academic competitions can start to add up financially, even for regional competitions. Kavita said about the Indian American competitions her children participate in,

> It costs $600 to $700 for regionals registration and travel. For the finals [last year], it was $3,000.

As mentioned earlier, parents also purchased math and spelling software programs, problem and word lists, and other study guides for their children. Tutoring ranges from $20 to over $100 an hour. Paying for coaching was another popular option, especially for those most committed to the competitions, with rates exceeding $200 an hour.[20]

More broadly, socioeconomic class influences one's residential location, quality of local schools, peer exposure, and more. Families need the income and time to invest in opportunities for children, even including the gasoline to drive children to and from classes.[21] They need enough income to afford a family member to be home to supervise their child or to hire a caretaker. Without resources of money and time, families cannot readily support their children.

## All Work and Some Fun

For all the time and effort parents put into creating a commitment to academics, the kids put in more, especially for competitions. Mahipal said of his son who competes in MATHCOUNTS,

> [He studies math] ten hours a week. He does it on his own. We get him problem sheets from the MATHCOUNTS handbooks and whatever papers he can find online. We start preparing for competitions like AMC 8, AMC 10.

The time pressure can be intense. As one parent expressed in a group conversation at an SASB finals in 2013,

> School is a very heavy workload. He does math. He goes to a gifted academy, so there is a very heavy workload school. He does MATH-COUNTS; he does spelling.

It was not uncommon for youths serious about the competitions to study practically every day after school, anywhere from 30 minutes to a few hours, with four to eight hour days on weekends, especially as the competition approached. Spellers would focus on spelling rules of different languages and memorize the many exceptions to the rules. Those in ethnic bee finals did not stop preparing until the late summer. Youths would study for math competitions alone or in teams, often during the school year and commonly in after-school math clubs.

Elite spellers mastered the most recent Paideia (or Spell It!) lists of about 3,800 challenging words; the Consolidated Word List of almost 25,000 words; various other word lists constructed by spellers and/or purchased from third parties (e.g., from Hexco); and possibly even the *Merriam-Webster's Unabridged Dictionary* itself, with about 470,000 words. Some used flashcards. One speller typed a challenging word into her computer again and again until she memorized it. Most devised their own lists. At the SASB finals, Sonia shared,

> My best way of remembering the words is just, like, [to] force it into my head. I just close my eyes and think [of] the words a lot of times until I'm sure I know it.

One speller learned one hundred words a day from the Consolidated Word List when starting out in fourth grade and completed the list in about a year's time. Another explained his studies this way:

> The words from the most obscure languages initially gave me trouble, because, like, patterns from languages like Latin or Greek are somewhat more reasonable and they're not as unpredictable. And after some studying, I think I knew a lot more words in these obscure languages. . . . Then they weren't so hard.

This study process could be brutal, even for those most motivated. Pari, a middle-school girl, said when we chatted at an NSF finals competition,

> I just liked the way words, like, let me express myself. Sometimes it feels like a really fun time. I mean, like, using a lot of words. But at the same time, it feels a little boring, like, going through the dictionary and nit-picking every word—that seems hard. But I think that, overall, I take the positive side of it, so it doesn't feel as much of a chore as some people would find it.

Even those who won national spelling bees referred to studying as having many painful, boring stretches. Mayank said,

> When I had yet to be hooked to the bee in the fourth grade, studying the Paideia was utter toil. I often gave it a cursory ten-minute scan once a day whenever my mother kindly asked me to.

It was common for kids just starting out in competitions to want to enroll but then not want to prepare. Parents had to remind and convince their children to study.[22] Two fathers joked in the hallway of the NSF Boston regional in 2014 that they had to constantly nag their children to practice even though the children had been excited about participating at first. Even when hyper education clicks for youths and they want to pursue it, they can protest and get bored. Parents are the ones who help them keep up with it. One sixth grader, Malika, provided an example:

> There were lots of days that I felt like "Oh I don't really want to do this." But well, with the persistence of my parents, yeah, I did that every day for almost a year for thirty minutes or an hour. I remember there was this twenty-three-thousand words in a list and we were trying to get it done by a year. So they would always be pushing, "Oh we need to finish this by the end of this year. We need to finish this. You can't take days off."

While many students only prepared during the season of the competition, not year-round, they still sacrificed personal and social time. A common point was that youths formed their social lives around their study schedules, such as befriending children who were free when their study sessions allowed for breaks, at times missing out on what felt like meaningful experiences. Reshma, a former Scripps champion, recounted,

Yeah, I didn't, like, run with the cool kids or anything [in middle school]. And at that time, it seemed like such a big deal, like, "Oh my God, I'm missing out on this vital part of childhood." But now that I look back at it, I'm just, like, I wouldn't want to be hanging out at the mall, because, what's at the mall? Like, I don't have money, so I can't just, like, buy a lot of stuff. And then there's only, like, so much you can do at the mall. Kind of everything got just built up in one year—like, [at] thirteen years old, everything matters so much.

So much of adolescence—in particular for girls—is spent with friendships that can involve sports, sleepovers, and academics, and shopping in the suburban mall remains a quintessential site.[23] But these were sacrifices the youths put up with.

Those involved in math competitions such as MATHCOUNTS came together at set times during the week and studied in groups, which provided some camaraderie. Still, school friends stayed at school and home friends at home. Youths even sacrificed the ability to make friends. Sanjay said,

When we started middle school, the workload increased and everything. So we'd have more homework per day. So we started, like, not going out to play with friends and just worked at home. I didn't get to play with my friends.

While this is certainly sad in some respects, those committed to these activities had a hard time quitting them because the practice became so ingrained into their lifestyles, just like any other extreme extracurricular activity. Both guilt and enthusiasm led them to continue. As Sameera said at the 2015 SASB finals,

Maybe like when I first started, [quitting spelling] crossed my mind once or twice, but it wasn't really an option. I mean, I spent so much time on it that to go back now, it's like, well it's almost like a waste of my time. I mean, it's not really wasted because I've learned stuff from it. Yeah, so quitting now isn't really an option for me.

To quit would mean that one could have been doing something else all that time. The fear of admitting that to oneself, plus their continued enjoyment of the activity, kept them going.

Parents insisted time and again that their children enjoyed their academic activities and that they would not make them stay in them if they did not. Still, parents also urged their children to stick with the activities if they did not terribly mind them. One middle-school girl, Shanta, said about her parents' commitment to her spelling,

> If I really wanted to quit and I had a good reason, they probably would let me. But if it's just like I want to do something else, it's like, just stick with it. I just wanted time to do other things, like, say, pursue music or, like, just do something else. [My parents said], just keep working at it. You'll have time to do [other things].

A fifth-grade girl, Uma, who made it to the SASB finals and the Scripps bee, echoed,

> I think once you're in this deep, the only reason you really have to quit spelling bee is if there is something else you really want to do.

Parents forcing children into academic competitions against their children's will does happen, even if not frequently; children can resent their participation in hyper education. In a chat with a father and son at an NSF regional competition, the son had missed a friend's birthday party to compete in the math exam, much to his discontent:

Math is very boring. I'm like the number-one student in math in the whole entire first grade at my school right now.

Q: Really? Are you glad you came?

Not that much.

Such force is more the exception to the rule and mostly is found at the regional level of competitions; children who put in the time to make it past the regional level genuinely enjoy the academics. The tiger parent mentality can be real but is not generalizable to a culture. Nor is it isolated to one ethnicity. Max, the director of a math center, said,

It's a real thing, but it's not just with Chinese parents. I look at what my [white American] friends are doing with their kids, and they're investing in different things. Music, plays, or whatever it is that helps the kid get into Harvard. I think it's not just—it's obviously the stereotype of the perfect Chinese child who plays violin, who plays piano, plays tennis, and does math. That's kind of a stereotype, but these exist in other areas too. If you're looking at the upper-middle-class [whites], the kid is on a traveling soccer team. They don't do math.

I spoke with a group of three girls at the 2016 SASB finals, and they said about their parents,

They would support me in anything I wanted to do and tell me to do the best I can. And it doesn't matter if it's spelling, or math, or badminton, but [they would tell me] just to do the best I can.

They might tell me that I should study, but they wouldn't be that mad [if I stopped].

They would support me in whatever I want.

For the most part, children participated with some intrinsic interest and some parental pressure. The ratio of one to the other varied by family and even over time within the same family. The pressure from parents was higher for children in the private math classes than in the competitions. Parents often said that if their children protested attending math programs, they would stop the programs and instead supplement in other ways. Across my many initial conversations with Indian Americans and whites, parents said that their kids enjoyed attending math classes, so the idea of stopping was not actively discussed in their homes. As our conversations progressed, however, and I came back to the question of their kids' enjoyment, many confessed that their children enjoyed the classes more when they started, and some were not sure if they would stick with them given the lack of enthusiasm.

Diane, a fourteen-year-old white girl in suburban Boston, attended a math center and had a mixed attitude common among the children. When I asked her if she participated because she needed the math assistance or because she was excited by it or because her parents made her go, she gave a multifaceted answer with a clear leaning:

> I think it varies. Most of the times my parents want me to do it because they think that it works best for me. But sometimes I find it useful and applicable to what I'm learning in school, and sometimes I don't. . . . What I think I enjoy is the teachers are willing to help you. What I don't enjoy is how long it is. Some days I don't mind going. Maybe if it were only for like an hour or a half hour, but the fact that it's four is too much [including both the two-hour class and the two-hour homework assistance session she voluntarily attends].

Teresa still enjoyed attending an after-school math class, but her enthusiasm was higher when she started in second grade than now, three years later. She said, "I just wish I had more, like, [free] time." Her younger brother, in elementary school, would have liked to consider other extracurricular options, but his parents kept him in math. I asked him if he would still go to the math center or choose to play a sport if his parents gave him the option:

> I'd probably do soccer, but, like, if soccer, like, wasn't as good as a sport, then I'd do [the math center].
>
> Q: If you told your parents you didn't want to go next year, do you think they would still make you go, or do you think they'd say, "OK, don't worry about it"?
>
> Uh, they'd still want me to go.

Some parents used threatening techniques to keep their children engaged. A white mother at a math center mentioned that she forbids soccer for her son until he completes his weekly math assignments. Clearly her son was not enthusiastic about participating in the classes.

## Conflicted Cultivation

I mean, honestly, I think I do regret that I focused on spelling to such a degree. I mean, if I had at least given science [serious consideration], or even things like accounting, or at least understanding how to set up my own business when I was a little kid. These are all things that excite me right now, but I just didn't even think about it, because, you know, I was focusing on nothing else. I do regret that I only focused on that one goal to the exclusion of anything else. You know, I was homeschooled. I knew I had aptitude and logic in subjects, and so I would kind of cram through. I would get all my other subjects done in a pretty short amount of time, and then I would focus most of my day on spelling. I keep wondering, Wouldn't life have been so different, you know, if I had actually done something that was, you know, more relevant to today? I don't know.

Now an adult, Parag, a former Scripps Spelling Bee champion, regrets having spent so much time on spelling, something so removed from his current interests as to be a significant waste of time. He is left wondering what could have been. The sacrifices children make for competitive academics leave some of them wondering if it was all worthwhile.

Kumar, an Indian immigrant father whose company helped financially support academic competitions but did not have his own teenager involved in them, also criticized the practice of academic pursuits:

> I don't want somebody to be a genius. In the Indian families, it's all about kids, very restrictive in what activities they're supposed to be doing. It's all about studies. Kumon, [and] if not Kumon, then other instruction, other tutors, math, geometry, algebra, science, biology, whatever. It's all about academics! I want somebody to be street smart, quick, you know, because that's what this world is all about.

While I concentrated my conversations on those families who pursued extracurricular academics, I also included those who did not in order to demonstrate that there is not a singular point of view among Indian American professionals. Asian Americans are not monolithic in their parenting. Some do not push their kids into academics, because they regret how they had been forced to do so when young.[24]

Yet even those parents who promoted hyper education questioned their decisions and worried about the same outcomes that

Parag mentioned. While most parents felt relatively confident in their parenting strategy, a large minority openly discussed potential pitfalls. A mother at a group interview opened up to say,

> I don't think [academic competitions are] for all Indian children. For some, yes, but when we drag kids to these things, I believe we are losing the creativity part. We are losing artists, composers, musicians, authors. We are not training them; we're drilling them. I am worried more about how they do at my home; I'm more worried about when they go off to college. So am I giving them the right motivation and drive by doing this thing, or am I just making up a competitive kid? Are they looking around to be helpful, to serve, to innovate, to create for the whole international community rather than just Indian?

There could be a cost to ensuring children's good grades and good behavior. The concern was that the sense of alienation from one's work waiting for children when they became adults in a white-collar office could be happening to them now. The work world drains the "creativity part," and these parents wanted their children to be helpful and serve a community. Academic competitions have the same negative effects. Like some other parents, this mother had her children in academic competitions and simultaneously questioned the value of them. Is the goal to make youths more competitive or to nurture children's empathy and creativity?[25] Parenting oriented toward the former made it harder to accomplish the latter.

The mother's concerns are echoed by critics of "tiger parenting," such as educators and parents who want to limit academic competitiveness in schools. Her self-doubt shows that parents engaged in hyper education are not mere racial caricatures; they are sensitive to the same qualities that they are accused of disregarding.

Nityanand shared an anecdote with me and another parent at a 2014 spelling bee:

I met with a girl; she graduated from New York University. She said she was studying sociology, and her friend studied English. So I asked the English guy, who is now taking a course in computer science, "You graduated from a good high school, then you went to New York University. So you were doing [an] English major as an undergraduate, what was going into your mind? You want to be a teacher, a professor, you want to do a master's?" "Well, no, I never thought about that. I was good at English, and I liked studying English literature." So this is good and bad. Good in the sense that if you do what you like to do, then you innovate. So we [Indian Americans] do what is the hardest thing, which is what is the job that gives me the most money, I should be doing that. So we go after that. Here, they say no. They do what they like to do.

Just like studying sociology or English literature without a plan to become a teacher is "good and bad" in this father's mind, so is having children accrue more and more human capital to prepare for a job that provides the most income. The innovators and creative thinkers have followed their passions, and parents here wondered if they were handicapping their children from that possibility.

As I talked with Krishna at the 2014 SASB finals, he said he was proud of his daughter's math and spelling but noted,

I was the last person to be interested relative to my wife. My wife initiated it, and I wasn't a fan because you have to buy fifteen thousand words. What's the point? You won't use those words. My wife felt you should keep the kid motivated all the time on something, something different than the rest of the folks. [White Americans] don't put the focus on education, but they are good at presenting themselves. Being a bookworm is useless.

Another father commented, "We are losing social skills." Most academic pursuits do not prioritize interpersonal engagement and communication, especially in daily practicing. This works against the exact goal of extra education, even for STEM careers, to further youths' socioeconomic mobility.

Instead of inspiring innovation, these parents worried that they were going to stunt their children's growth. A mother said during a group interview,

> I see that a lot, especially in Asian kids. They perform extremely well in elementary school, middle school, and high school. They get into one of the best colleges. The first year is very good. The second and third year, actually when they are supposed to perform, they just cannot do it anymore. They are just way too tired, way too exhausted, just want to opt out; they just scrape through or something like that. I've seen a lot of kids do that.

She echoes the earlier concerns of elementary-school teachers, who mentioned exhaustion, stress, and burnout. Knowing when to push and when to ease up was "a very difficult decision" that parents grappled with, as one father said.

Some confessed that they felt more confused than their adolescent children, for they worried so much about their academic progress. Nidhi, a mother whose children participated in NSF, said,

> I don't think it's the kids. It's us who really are lost. We don't know where our kids are, and we always want to know whether my kid is best in the class. I don't think it's the kids who are missing out; I think it's the parents who are missing out.

Another father opened up within a group setting:

> I'm a B-I-C-A: "Born in India but Confused in America." I feel like it's a common pressure on both sides. We see our children, and they are slightly in a different direction [than we were]. They want to read more books; they want to play more sports. But we say that isn't the

right way. Maybe we are confused so much, and we are making our children more confused.

Playing off of the popular reference to second-generation Indian Americans as "ABCD—American-Born Confused Desi"—this father turned the tables on his generation. In contrast to scholarly and popular imagery of Asian immigrants, they can be racked with doubt, like all parents. While his confusion has cultural dimensions, it would be a mistake to interpret it only through that lens. All kinds of middle-class parents overschedule their children while they purchase books on "slow parenting," try to declutter their homes, and work to have family dinners.

Even as some parents wondered out loud about their strategies, many of them quickly stated that despite any reservations, enrichment education was in their children's best interests and worth doing. A father had spoken earlier in a group conversation about his concern that after-school academics were taking away from free time and creating too much pressure. Despite offering a window of self-doubt, he was quick to justify his practices:

> It's not time consuming. It's not an obnoxious and tedious chore for [my son]. He said that it is helping him, and we would rather be in support of him. We would support no matter what he thinks and wants to do. And it's a good thing, right, to be able to know how to compete and to deal with all of this pressure?

It was easy for some parents to discount any guilt. Ahmad, who had two daughters involved in math and spelling, said,

> Of course, sometimes we feel bad about that. The other kids are playing outside, and our kids are studying at home. Of course, it pays off for whatever sacrifice they had done as a child, and they feel good

about that too, and they don't think [it's a] bad thing. . . . They will de-velop their personal, professional skills and [learn] how to grow.

Hyper education is easy to defend according to many parents—that their children enjoyed it enough, that they had enough time for other activities, and that it was ultimately a worthwhile struggle to develop "personal [and] professional skills." One father commented, "The reason why I'm here [at an NSF event] is more to challenge [my son] on the creative thinking part." He believes academics instilled creativity. Not everyone agrees, including some former spellers who have achieved at the highest level.

## The Simple Pleasures of Life

Yasmin, a middle-school girl who started spelling when she was eight-years-old, explained her motivation to study when we were at an NSF finals:

> [It's] not just to win and memorize words so that way they can get the money. But it's more to use them practically. Like, I mean, some of the words in spelling bees are like camp words—you won't see them again. But even then, there are some words that you can use in everyday conversations.

Kids liked using the vocabulary they learned, whether in conver-sation or in school essays. In other words, spelling was personally fulfilling. They enjoyed the way sounds and letters came together, the origins of words, the connections between seemingly disparate words, and more. Because they wanted to use the words, one youth explained that the 2013 change to Scripps rules, in which contes-tants would be tested on the meanings and not just the spellings of the words, was a welcome one:[26]

Yeah, I think it's the knowledge of the words and, like, vocabulary. I'm glad actually that the Scripps added the vocabulary portion this year because I think that's one of the key reasons why people do spelling bees.

In talking with an editor of a press, whose job it is to deal with words, she bluntly asked me, "What's the point of a spelling bee when I have spell-check on my computer?" Likewise, one could ask, What's the point of learning advanced math in sixth grade if I have a calculator that will solve multidigit multiplication for me? The youths involved in these pursuits have passionate answers to these and other skeptical questions of why they sacrifice time, outings, and even friendships for these pursuits. Despite parents' concerns over what children are losing as they promote hyper education and children's own laments, there was much to appreciate in what they had gained.

Sameera appreciated the broader aspects of language: "It's really interesting how all these words are linked at one point, their etymology." Each speller had a favorite word and loved to share it. Reshma said,

> The activity [of spelling] itself was fun. Because you found there's actually a word for something, like "Tohuw." That's one of my favorite words; it means "chaos," and it comes from Hebrew.

News profiles of spellers invariably asked what their favorite words were and how to spell them. Each time, the newscaster reacted with amazement. Children enjoyed that look of surprise and, in fact, tried to create it. As a fifth-grade speller, Usha, said to me,

> I like throwing new words at people—new words that I've learned—and just looking at their confused faces, you know?

Kids even compared their pathway to the spelling bee finals to the character Harry Potter. As a middle-school boy explained to a few others at the SASB finals,

In *Harry Potter*, Harry doesn't just [win] from the start. He starts running away, finding better ways to approach the situation. He figures out a way for Voldemort to beat himself. And that's how it is in the spelling bee. You don't go to beat other people. You just have to keep spelling your own words. You have to keep living and outlast other people.

For those engaged in spelling bees and math competitions, the competitive dimension also made it all the more enjoyable. Robert, a white boy, competed in MATHCOUNTS. His mother explained,

So Robert has just been involved in so many competitions. It just fuels his interest in math and his wanting to learn more about math and his desire. . . . He loves it all.

Another youth, Vineeta, echoed when at an NSF finals competition,

[The competitive element is] really important.
Q: You're not just spelling for the sake of spelling? You're spelling to win?
Yeah! That's like a good 30 percent of it.

As professional athletes often say, the sacrifice involved is worth it for the sake of pursuing a championship. One boy stated in passing,

Um, I didn't get to play with my friends, but I thought, you know, spelling is one thing that I can actually be good at. So I thought, yeah, I should continue for the whole. I think that the real motivation is competing and trying to win.

Just as in sports, winning is worth the sacrifice.[27]

Geeta offered a gendered take on the relevance of competition:

So I personally think being a girl in these competitions is fun. I mean, I know a lot of times society tells girls that you just have to be pretty and, like, I know that's hard for any one young girl who wants to know [and] do academic things, but I don't really feel, like, bad, bad. You know, I've never felt that way.

Such an attitude is incomprehensible in the popular imagination, where the kids are simply word geeks or victims of tiger parents.

Spellers enjoy the learning and sharing of words, at times more than other pursuits. As Uma explained,

The things that other kids enjoy, we don't enjoy just like them, and . . . we have other interests—like, we would rather be spelling than, like, shopping or something.

Little compared to the thrill of being on stage for these children. They engaged in a ritual back-and-forth with the pronouncer to understand the word and break it down into its parts.[28] They enjoyed the spotlight, for the most part, for it affirmed that their countless hours of hard work had paid off. I asked Chandu what went through his mind as the confetti was falling after he won the Scripps National Championship, and he said,

Before, I had watched previous spellers who had won on *Jimmy Kimmel*, so I thought it would be nice if I could go on *Jimmy Kimmel*. So I was just thinking about stuff like that.

Making it to the Scripps finals and appearing on ESPN prime time was often part of spellers' hopes, for only a few believed they had a real shot at winning. When I asked Chandu why he became interested in spelling bees when in elementary school, he said,

> Oh, I saw it on ESPN and I thought it was cool. At that age, I just wanted to be on TV. [*Laughs*] . . . Then I discovered that I was actually pretty good at it, so I just stuck with it.

The worst part was waiting for one's word to be announced as a speller's turn got closer and closer. Geeta, who made it to the Scripps finals in 2014, recounted,

> As I get closer to the microphone, I definitely get more nervous because it's your turn and, like, it's so random. Like, you never know what the next word is going to be. It can be the one kid who gets like probably a hard word for that round, or you can get a very nice easy word and just sail onto the next round. So it just gets more nerve-racking. I don't know if anyone ever saw me shaking, but you would be shaking on the inside. My heart would be pounding. The silence before you get any word is always a little nerve wrecking because you know that's the last couple of seconds where you don't know whether you were given the time. Because that's when, like, your mind really opens to wild guessing, like "What might the word end up being?!"

Being on stage also can be exhausting. She went on to say,

> When you get really tired, after, like, maybe ten rounds, and you're just going back and forth, anyone could get out.

Spellers enjoyed talking with one another about their strategies, what kinds of words they liked or hated, and more. They had different tactics for how they dissected words on stage. Many asked for the meanings first, others the parts of speech, and the like. Their habits took on a pattern the audience then came to expect. Some captured the imagination of the audience with silly remarks or a gesturing style of standing and spelling. In the process, they honed skills needed for twenty-first-century adulthood, such as being media savvy and learning the art of self-presentation.[29] The camaraderie on stage was easy to see. Spellers high-fived one another as they walked back to their seats after spelling a word correctly. They talked during breaks.

Even if youths never raised a trophy, they believed their math and spelling furthered their academics, another motivation for their sacrifice. Academic subjects, from science to English, were easier because of their expansive vocabularies. Often cited was the help competitive spelling and math provided on future SATs and other standardized tests. A parent said, "At a later stage, my niece told [me], it really helps in SATs. It's a platform. Every year. Keep training." Students also reported other practical benefits from their years of studying, such as time-management skills, the importance of setting goals, self-confidence in one's abilities, and other attributes associated with serious engagement in extracurricular activities.[30]

With all of this studying and accumulated knowledge came some well-deserved boasting. When I spoke with a group of girls at an SASB finals in 2016, they took turns taking pride in their abilities:

My mind is better than spell check.

I was once typing an essay for English and I got so annoyed with the spell check that I went up on the internet, I figured out how to disable it, and I disable[d] it, and I haven't enabled it again. Like, I just got rid of it.

I love to correct my teacher.

Math competitions provided useful skills as well, both in terms of practical mathematics and as a way of thinking. Chandu, who also participated in math competitions, had this to say:

> If you're in math competitions, I'm thinking you have to break down the problems and try to understand and figure out what you need to use to solve the problem. So it's kind of similar in that way.

## Getting a Life

Mayank, now in his twenties, shared,

> The bee's greatest value is probably the vast network of strong friendships it helps build. Ask the contestants of the bee as they're leaving the contest what the greatest part of the experience was, and the majority will respond, "Meeting an amazing bunch of people." As a budding teenager, to go to a congregation of 250-plus kids whose love of spelling and whose precocity for academics matches mine was an absolute dream come true. It's for this reason I often feel bad for kids who decide to lock themselves in their room for the entirety of the bee to study for the contest; they're missing the true joy the bee can offer. To this day, I keep in contact with many of the spellers from my year as well as many from past years.

Youths engaged in the competitions lost opportunities to socialize with peers in their neighborhoods. This made the friendships they formed through after-school education all the more valuable, which is especially noteworthy considering that the competitions are often seen as solo ventures. Parents quickly recognized this too. Robert's mother shared,

> Being in these competitions and seeing these same kids over and over, we often see the same kids from MATHCOUNTS and spelling bee;

there's a big connection between those. So that is another fun aspect to being part of this math competition community.

Another parent at a MATHCOUNTS finals opened up to say in a slow, sincere tone that he was happy his son could be at the competition all the way from Alaska, for it gave him a community of people with similar interests and experiences, unlike at his high school.

Commonly, youths not only dedicated hours alone or with their family to studying but created a community of peers across the country who, via contemporary technology, formed groups or pairs who studied together.[31] Because spellers competed against the dictionary rather than against each other, they had little to lose by studying together. Sanjay described the Google-based group he and other spellers created:

> In the Google group, we all, like, sometimes share lists and, like, quiz each other on words. So that would really help us for the competitions. And I guess that it's a good connection between all the spellers, and our views to share from everyone's side. So . . . it's really an informative group.

Parents also appreciated how peers and teachers could motivate their children to study and not complain about participating.[32] Malika said, "Ever since, like, fourth grade, my class and my teacher [have] been really supportive of me doing spelling." Saroj said at an NSF group conversation in 2013 of his seventh-grade son involved in math,

> If half of his friends would not be doing it, that would then lead to the question of, Why the heck am I doing it? Most of his friends do this as well, so when he asks around, everybody is saying, yeah, I'm going to do this or something.

A mother at the Boston regional of an ethnic bee in spring 2015 said that her son wanted to repeat the finals mostly to hang out more with the friends he made at the previous year's finals. In fact, part of the reason why youths study so much is so that they can come back to the finals and meet friends who study as much as they do. The social camaraderie was not limited to Asian Americans. The Scripps National Spelling Bee takes pride in the good-natured socializing it creates in formal and informal ways, as do other competitions.[33] Kids who participated together keep in touch for years after Scripps. Geeta reflected on the fun at the bee a few years later:

> We would run around the hotels together—you know, kind of explore, just hang out together. We went on this tour on the bus. We talked; we had fun. I know that us girls would be, like, braiding each other's hair and stuff. We visit each other's hotel room to play cards, watch TV, that kind of thing. . . . The people I met from Scripps, I talked to them weekly, emails and Facebook. Talk about school, about our lives. When Scripps was airing this year, my inbox was filled up with, "Oh this person got this word wrong, and it's such an easy word."

Youths found enhanced learning a mix of joy and pain. For most, the experiences were not dissimilar from how youths talk about sports training. They have sacrificed quite a bit and have invested much of their identity and family resources, especially into the competitions. They find the academics intrinsically interesting, they make social connections, and the competitive element provides additional motivation, especially if they see no other option for personal excellence. Youths who are heavily involved even have difficulty not studying. Seema explained how she and her brother, both competitive spellers, struggled with downtime:

So my brother and I once experimented with this. After the South Asian Spelling Bee last year, we decided just to take the whole two weeks off before school started. Like, my brother had tennis, and I had my arts and crafts stuff that I had on my to-do list. I guess after, like, five days, the sixth day we just sat at home and we were bored; we had nothing to do whatsoever. And we basically had to spend our time, like, you know, bothering each other with cheesy jokes or anything, and it's just—yeah, it doesn't work.

For Indian Americans, especially high-achieving youths and professional parents, the community of fellow academic high achievers helped make youths feel more part of their ethnic group. Nityanand compared friendships made in kids' neighborhoods to those made at the Indian American competitions:

These are very well-adjusted kids. They have a set of friends [at home]. But I think this is more valuable to them because they're absolutely like-minded. They come from the same culture and background, and they can connect at a different level. That does not take away from the people or friends that they have in their other life as well.

Vineeta said,

Where I live, most of the people are very supportive, and they're all mostly Indians also, so they are working on something. I have lots of friends who spend four hours a day on math. They go to math camp nationals and stuff like that. They do four hours a day on science and go to science fair or whatever. So most of my friends did put some of that time into something else. We are relating there.

Children did not need their local peers to be engaged in the same intellectual activity to feel connected as fellow "geeks."

Ironically, despite spelling and math competitions being competitive spaces, they were safe spaces for the participants socially. Multiple parents and children at these competitions said that much of their value was the opportunity to be among like-minded peers. I will never forget how quickly friendships formed among the boys and among the girls at these competitions. Because the SASB is a two-night affair in a motel, with much time for socializing, it was easier for children to form bonds. It was common on the first night to see the twenty-six or so children move tables and chairs around so as to sit together, often with boys grouped on one side and girls on the other. Parents sat together in the ballroom at circular tables. Breakfast and lunch on the second day were also served in the ballroom, giving families more opportunities to talk and laugh together.

## Hyper Education as Normal

Long hours and significant dedication are the essential ingredients to success in academic pursuits. Parents themselves wondered out loud if they were truly ensuring children's good behavior or were creating unintentional risks due to insufficient attention to the humanist dimensions of personhood—creativity, street sense, passion. Those in weekly math classes often participated with less enthusiasm than did those in math or spelling competitions. Even competitors considered stopping at various points. Some parents, both Indian Americans and whites, forced their children into these activities despite children's regrets, but this was more the exception rather than the rule.

However, the real story is not about achievement but about how children come to see intense hyper education as normal despite its esoteric nature and long hours. They found such academic achievement personally meaningful, but it was support from their family and community in particular that sustained them through daily life.

Even if parents questioned the worth of hyper education, they often encouraged it and tried to make it enjoyable. Ritual practices and group trips to competitions made it a family affair. Parental support often was gendered, with mothers providing more support, but both parents engaged.

Facilitating this pull toward academics were families' financial resources, parents' elite educations, time to provide tutoring, and the like. In other words, there is no lesson to be learned here that family alone makes educational achievement possible regardless of personal circumstances. On top of that, the community dimension provides networks that give families guidance, opportunities, and inspiration. This sense of group pride and the normality of these pursuits make the contrasting reception from the media and school peers all the more difficult to manage.

# 7

## "I Have No Time for Haters"

The following are some of the tweets in response to the victories of Indian Americans in the Scripps National Spelling Bee:

> *I root for a white kid to win the #spellingbee. I root against every Chinese, Japanese, Korean, and Indian. I'm not ashamed to say this.*

> *Is this the national spelling bee or slumdog millionaire? #spellingbee #confused*

> *When was the last time a true American won the spelling bee? 1815? Not meant to be racist, but come on . . . ?*

> *every year them mfs from India come over to America and take our Spelling Bee away smh we need to regroup Merica.*

> *Nothing more American than a good spelling bee. Oh wait all the Caucasians are eliminated.*

> *Only one white kid left in the spelling bee, let's go buddy make America proud.*

> *Hey America step your game up looks like we getting beat out at the #spellingbee by India.*

> *Why is there only people from India in this fucking spelling bee?*

> *America: Still incapable of producing kids who can win its own spelling bee. Bravo, Uncle Sam.*[1]

Despite the bee representing a supposedly multicultural, meritocratic America, the full picture contains continued racial divisions and resentment toward immigrant communities.[2] The racist tweets became so bad that the normally reserved director of the Scripps bee, Paige Kimball, released a statement after the 2015 finals wishing that all youths would be understood without reference to ethnicity:

> I look forward to the day, as do I think many of our South Asian partici-
> pants, when they are called what they want to be called—Americans. . . .
> The bee is one of the truest forms of meritocracy, and we support
> every kid no matter where they come from. . . . It's unfortunate that
> people have some not very nice things to say on social media.

Nor is this the first time that the national spelling bee has encountered pushback based on the race of the champions. The first national spelling bee actually was in 1908 in Cleveland, more than a decade before the first official bee took place in 1925.[3] It was sponsored by the National Educational Association and was held at its convention. Marie C. Bolden, a thirteen-year-old African American girl from Cleveland, won the contest. A national spelling bee did not take place again for almost twenty years, partly out of racist protest to this outcome.[4] Nor was this the only relevance of race. During and after Jim Crow segregation, many African American students were denied equal access to the Scripps finals due to the discriminatory practices of local newspapers.[5] Math competitions face similar racist critiques for supposedly lacking "American" winners, given the number of Asian American finalists and champions. Carter, a leader within a national math competition, referred to accusations not only from the general public but even from leadership within his organization:

> Some people, especially in the leadership, I've had people come up to
> me and say, "You know this is terrible. We don't have any Americans
> on the stage." And I'm like, "No, we actually have 100 percent Ameri-
> cans on the stage. They're all American."

The long-standing image of Asian Americans has been as foreigners, and the frequent assumption has been an inability to speak English. Spelling bee victories prove the stereotype wrong, for Indian Americans are dominating competitions using the English language. And yet rather than being accepted as Americans, the victories are interpreted as evidence of their continued foreignness, for only non-Americans would care so much and be so good at this kind of competition. Race continues to define Asian Americans as foreigners no matter what they do—whether they struggle with English or have an unparalleled command of it. Despite, or because of, their good behavior, they encountered pushback.

Notwithstanding competition directors' calls for Asian Americans to be seen as being like everyone else, the youths remain framed on the wrong side of two axes: American versus foreign and well rounded versus one dimensional. Parents hoped to make their children safe through hyper education, yet unforeseen risks include a possible stigma along these binaries. On the one hand is the respect and appreciation of their parents and community members and on the other hand is unfavorable public treatment. Youths are left to bear the brunt of the disconnection, with an emphasis here on those in academic competitions, often spelling bees.

## Mainstream Media Depictions

The model minority image of Asian Americans is as academically one dimensional. Whether praised or reviled for their academic progress, Asian American youths are reduced to geeky students who lack other interests, made all the more apparent by their immigrant backgrounds.[6] Social media provides the most visible and overt example of their mistreatment. Respected media outlets reinforced the notion of these youths as spectacles to marvel at for their bizarre abilities. For example, math competition winners appeared on daytime talk shows and "competed" with the hosts on math questions. The setup was obvious: the winning math student (normally a cis-identified Asian American or white boy) would demonstrate his freakish abilities, and the well-groomed, full-of-personality hosts (normally cis-identified whites) would get a laugh—and the audience's empathy—for not knowing the answers.[7]

Interviews with and articles on winners comprise predictable questions: How do those Asian math [or spelling] kids do it? How much do they suffer? Do they really enjoy this? Here, the youths' race and academic interests intersect to make them deviant as foreigners and geeks. For instance, an article on CNN.com on why Indian Americans per se perform so well in the spelling bee began, "While you were out taking your kid to baseball practice or music class, Puthenveedu Jayakrishnan was helping his twelve-year-old daughter spell words that don't readily surface in daily life."[8] The "you" refers to the "average" reader, assumed to be an able-bodied, white (or at least non–Indian American) family without a commitment to spelling but instead interested in "standard" American activities. Similarly, on May 29, 2015, CNN anchor Brooke Baldwin asked Professor Shalini Shankar if spelling bee competitors would prefer to win the Scripps bee or the Little League World Series.[9] Again, the assumption was that one could be either typical, cool, and adept in the "all-American" pastime of baseball or geeky, foreign, and uncool; Asian Americans are the latter.

When youths at the 2016 Scripps bee did the "dab," a popular gesture of one's arms and head that mimicked NFL superstar Cam Newton, it was replayed on social media. The 2015 Scripps co-champion Gokul Venkatachalam made a name for himself through the Air Jordans he wore on stage, the LeBron James jersey he wore underneath his buttoned-up shirt, and even his hip handshake.[10] In 2016, co-champion Nihar Janga threw up his arms in the form of an X upon completing his winning word in reference to then NFL star Dez Bryant.[11] Each of these became a brief media sensation, for we do not expect geeky, unmasculine boys to be able to mimic stereotyped black male performance, given the association of black masculinity and hypermasculinity. The spellers are not unaware of how claims to athletic stardom can give them attention. Gokul Venkatachalam later told me that his sporting of the athletic gear was intentional. He was well aware of the juxtaposition he was making between the nerd and the jock. "I knew that [the sports attire] would be something people would pay attention to," he said. The model minority knows what the score is. Media attention to these kids' symbolic presentations is meant to compliment them as prototypical American adolescents, defined by heteronormativity, athleticism, fashionable tastes, and heightened social skills.[12] Such attention, however, underscores the assumed robotic, asexual nature of the typical spellers, for why else would such overt recognition of "coolness" be noteworthy except because it is entirely unexpected? Asian Americans' cultural fit in society is in doubt *not* because they do not achieve—but because they do.[13]

## The Culture of Coolness

While these are the media trends, we cannot assume that these binaries of American versus foreign and well-rounded versus one dimensional define children's personal experiences, for there is no such thing as an inherent stigma.[14] In fact, there are increasingly popular depictions of youths who are praised for their academic achievements (e.g., the film *Akeelah and the Bee*). In high school and college, being a "nerd" and being either masculine or feminine are not necessarily contradictory. For instance, "computer geeks" and "comic nerds" have a certain level of coolness as intelligent men or creative women.[15] This is not to say that geek culture is not still marginalized even within circles of higher education.[16] But there are not singular types of experiences.

Given the possible variety of reactions to youths' extracurricular academics, how did they experience their social environments?

As journalist and author James Maguire[17] wrote about spelling bee participants,

> Competitive spellers generally get one of two responses at school. Either kids are totally ignored about their spelling interests, or they will actually get ribbed about it. That happens quite a bit, surprisingly. The students will actually get teased somewhat mercilessly.[18]

Fortunately, none of the youths I interviewed reported physical bullying or being actively mocked. They could disregard negative social media and did not feel attacked personally. For instance, Chandu won a Scripps National Championship but did not dwell on possible negative reactions in social media, saying, "I guess we're all American, that's one thing. I didn't really think about these tweets too much."

Even as youths tried to downplay public racism, they were well aware of the stigma or possibility of stigma against them as one-dimensional geeks and foreigners in their schools. There are constrained definitions of coolness at this age group, including being athletic, fashionable, socially dexterous, and affluent.[19] I sat with a group of six girls at the 2016 South Asian Spelling Bee finals. They recognized the limited social definitions of coolness in school. Shanta said,

> I'm not really like [other girls in my school]. I think differently; I'm a different person. It's really amazing how much people judge you based on appearance, and, well, in my opinion, I don't really care about how people judge me based on how I look. I care about how they judge me based on, like, how I really am.

In addition, geeks did not prioritize standard types of beauty.[20] These girls tried to reject socially defined femininity. Another girl, Alka, offered,

Yeah, and in our school, half the girls in my class care more about how their hair is than what they are learning in math. And then they complain about, "We don't get this [academic topic]"?

Their interests in academics created a singular social image as victims of authoritarian parents. Usha said,

I enjoyed book reading, and when I read books, many people think it is because I'm forced to read books. But no. I like reading books, and it's one of my passions to do. So whenever I'm reading, they say, "Don't you ever like to have fun?" Well, I'm having my fun my own way, because I love reading books, and that's what I do to have fun.

The pride youths had in their accomplishments was mixed with embarrassment about their lack of cultural "coolness" as defined by their peers, even as they enjoyed playing video games, socializing with friends, reading across genres, and other activities.[21] Tom, a middle-school math teacher who led a competitive math team, echoed the point made by these girls:

These kids are not worried about their appearance or their status. They are very proud and comfortable with being smart. There are some kids who don't want others to know they're smart, and other kids wear it as a badge of honor. For some of the kids, in their culture, math is very important. Or it's the friends they're with and they want to be like their friends. At this age, they want to fit in; they don't want to be different. It's hard to make math cool.

Adults and kids resented the seeming double standard that their academic interests received relative to popular pastimes. A father noted with cynicism that if his son was practicing baseball batting for hours, he would be applauded for his dedication. Carter defended the practice of quickly solving complicated math equations relative to playing sports:

> So take baseball, right? I mean kids play baseball, [and] no one balks at that, but when are you really going to hit a ball traveling sixty miles an hour in the air? . . . For a math competition, what are you exercising? What skills are you honing in practicing to do that activity? And the answer is, you're becoming a better problem solver. . . . I mean, that's the most important thing you do in life.

The problem was not just that youths had geeky interests in the eyes of some but that they became defined by those interests. Seema, a sixth-grade girl, explained,

> Most people know me as the speller, and then every once in a while, I'll bring up something that came up in dance class at school, and everybody asks me, "You do dance?" And it [shouldn't be] that surprising, actually. I spend, in normal school days, I spend maybe six hours a week doing dance. And because my reputation is so primarily based on spelling, nobody even believes that I do dance.

Oftentimes, the youths became locked into a single role that carried undue expectations and emotional burdens. Vineeta said,

> I think for me it's . . . I think the part that I find most prominent is that I have a reputation to live up to. If I'm typing something, like, we have this partner essay in social studies, and I was typing it up because I'm good at spelling. I made a typo on a word, I think it was *dedendum* or something, I made a typo on that word and I put D-I instead of D-U-M. It's just a typo and then my partner gets supermad at me because I apparently spelled the word wrong. She got supermad at me because I spelled the word wrong. So it's like a reputation you have to live up to. It's kind of frustrating.

Not surprisingly, high-performing students seldom receive praise for their abilities and accomplishments from their peers.[22] While very rare for the kids I spoke to, bullying and teasing of Asian Americans have become problems in schools.[23] Yet even when youths received respect from peers, it came with strings attached. Usha shared,

> I feel like the smart people are actually the cool kids in my type of area. So everybody basically comes to us. If they need any help on any assignment, we're the first, you know, they basically think of. It's sort of annoying at times because they're constantly coming to us. At the same time, it's not like you're making a bunch of friends, be-cause they only try to be friendly toward you when they need you, and then they're like "OK [bye]."

She begins by referring to her group as the "cool kids" but then points out that no one wanted to actually befriend them.

Sameera noted the further burden of race, beyond mastering for-mulas or the dictionary over the baseball bat:

> Like, everyone thinks that you know everything just because you're Indian. They expect you to excel in all academic fields.

The model minority simulates a human but is not a real human.[24] Instead, the Asian is a robot, which is what gives "it" the ability to excel and yet be denied the respect given to a human.

Ajit, whose daughter made it to the Scripps finals, explained why racism followed them:

> The tree that bears the most fruit gets hit by the most thorns. We didn't even know so many people were watching us. ESPN makes it so everyone knows about it: the local newspapers, TV stations. It's too much. [It] breeds jealousy.

Sanjay lamented,

> In my opinion, I feel like there are a lot of stereotypes of Indian peo-
> ple in today's society. What I really want people to know about the
> Indian American community is that we're not the grade-grubbing,
> stingy type of people that we get portrayed as in the media. . . . We're
> not asocial kids that hole themselves up in their rooms and just study
> all day.

Even the spelling bee itself could be losing some of its storied
status, as it has browned and become associated with overly intense
Indian Americans. Reshma noted,

> Then I went to Scripps [for the first time], and it was this mainstream,
> amazing competition. And it promised, like, legitimacy for the spell-
> ing bee. And then you win it, and it's this great thing. But, um, like,
> talking to some of the older bee winners [lately]—there were actually
> nine former bee winners at a recent bee, and we all talked. They said
> the spelling bee was really, really cool in their day, and it's not nearly
> as cool today. That was talked about.

When I mentioned this comment to another former competitive
speller, she replied, "I can totally see that point. I kind of agree with
them." While still popular television, it is viewed as less and less
"mainstream."

## When Educators Single You Out

Mayank showed me a picture of a line of students waiting to greet
him at his school, as he wore a coat and tie, upon his return as
the Scripps national champion. In it, he is smiling widely. He
added,

Another invaluable source of preparation was the organizer of my middle school's spelling bee, our seventh-grade teacher of the humanities. Ever since I won the regional, I would spend an hour after school every Monday in his room; we would pull out Webster's Third, and he'd quiz me straight from the dictionary.

Assistance and respect from teachers meant a lot to youths. Another former Scripps champion, Chitra, explained that a teacher got her interested in spelling bees in the fourth grade:

I read a lot. I love books, and my teachers noticed that I would get like 100 percent on like all my spelling tests. My fourth-grade teacher showed me this competition, and I went and somehow got second.

Math teachers led MATHCOUNTS teams out of a sincere belief in their importance for youth academics. A fifth-grade girl, Jasmin, had been attending an after-school math center since second grade. Now in fifth grade, she had advanced math skills relative to her peers. When I asked her what her schoolteachers thought of her participation in this learning, she replied,

My teachers enjoy it. Like, I can help out some other kids. Like, if they're helping someone out, they'll ask me if I can help someone.

Her abilities made it easier for the teachers, for she could act as a teaching assistant. These anecdotes are not surprising. How youths of color experience stigma at school varies by race. African Americans and Latinxs are criticized by teachers but earn respect from peers; Asian American students are criticized by peers but often earn respect from teachers.[25]

And yet this is not the whole story. Educators can look down on or question youths for their commitments when youths go beyond what is expected in school. As seen earlier, educators regret the pursuit of hyper education when children seemed stressed, along with the work it can create for them. They seemed resentful at times. Reshma relayed,

> Teachers will say things like, "Oh, I, uh, I hope she's not in my class because then she'll correct everything that I spell wrong."

Sanjay recalled,

> I would get twenty books from the library, and I remember the librarians would always raise their eyebrow, "Can this kid really read all these books in three weeks?" And I would be able to, because that's what I wanted to do.

A mother noted mixed impressions from teachers. Some appreciated that her son could push the envelope of grade-level mathematics, while others resented the exact same thing. The previous years' teachers

> really appreciate [having my son] in their classes. He would start a conversation that the teacher never would have. I mean, this math teacher this year did not [appreciate him]. And on the one hand, I understand because they are teaching to a test.

In effect, youths committed to extracurricular education exceed school norms. Recall the school principal who declared with certainty, "I can't believe you're going to find kids who are passionate about long division. I just don't believe it." In other words, children who are passionate about mathematics or spelling are not normal. When I shared this principal's statement with Kristina, the founder of a math center, she could hardly hold her temper. She sat up in her chair and said,

That is what's wrong with this culture. Her assumption that no child wants to do it is what's wrong with this culture. It makes my blood boil! The assumption is that math is something that is not fun. That assumption is what's wrong with this culture. What the principal said really bothers me.

The idea that youths would not want to actively pursue academics made her "blood boil," and it went to the heart of her distaste for American mainstream culture.

Two dominant cultures often exist within schools.[26] One is of the teachers, security guards, and parents—that is, the "adult" approach to school as a place that students should treat in a deferential fashion. The second is the "peer" culture of the youths that defines what is cool, including music, fashion, and physical strength, along with caring about school performance. The students committed to hyper education reveal a third culture that is more attentive to educational accomplishment than even that expected by adults. It can be met with approval or criticism, depending on the educator and the school. But what is consistent is that the performance marks the group as distinctive.

Feeling mocked and unwanted because of one's accomplishments was rare. It was the other side of the coin that youths experienced more frequently, of being singled out and complimented for their unique abilities. Educators praised students for their achievements, but even that praise signaled that they deviated from the norm. For instance, Jiya was asked over the school loudspeaker to come to the principal's office. She was in third grade, still young and not yet in the peer-driven time of middle school when stigma becomes more pronounced.[27] When we talked in her home (where she told me this anecdote), she had an expressive, joyful personality, proud and vocal with a sense for the dramatic, with her frequent hand gestures and up-and-down vocal tones. She said that when she arrived at the principal's office, the principal took delight in asking her to spell a word. It was a nice honor to be recognized by the principal for one's skill and achievement. Jiya took pride in that moment. It is easy, however, to imagine that peers could mock her for such attention at some point, for her spelling drew her down the hallway to the principal's office. It signals that her skill could be paraded through the school as if part of a circus act. Lalima recounted how her daughter, a former competitive speller, felt under similar circumstances:

> Teachers ask her to spell words for them. She doesn't feel good about it. She should be proud of it, but they [are not]. The friends don't care. People think it's rote memorization. They say, "Oh an Indian won." [It] wouldn't be this way if they were not Indian.

Teachers have stereotypes of Asian American students as extremely studious and deferential and are even taught these stereotypes as a form of cultural awareness training.[28] These seeming compliments by teachers unintentionally fuel that racialization. A consequence of youths standing out relative to peers, as parents wanted them to, is a social division from other students and even teachers that often falls along racial lines.

## Working to Be Cool Enough

Geeta said in regards to the social media attacks on Twitter and the like,

> I think that's ridiculous that people get angry about the minorities winning or Indians winning the spelling bee in general. Because I think that kind of . . . that's totally racist. [The Indian American winners are] American kids first of all. I think a lot of times when people say these kinds of things, it is racist, but it's also them, like, you know, maybe they haven't done much in their lives, so they are lashing out on twelve- or thirteen-year-olds.

Indian American youths and their parents ridiculed those who made racist attacks, but unlike other minorities, they were less likely to use confrontation in their responses.[29] Because racism against them appeared inevitable, their parents had a resigned approach to it: the best strategy was to ignore the outbursts, for they were the result of jealousy, and the kids agreed.

HIDING THE STIGMA: Even as they ignored social media outbursts, youths still had to find ways of handling the social effects of their academic commitments around peers. Reshma did not disclose her amazing accomplishment of winning the Scripps bee, but not because she was humble:

> If I won, like, a golf tournament, like if I won the Master's? [*Laughs*]
> Yeah, I'd talk about it.

Her reaction fits a gendered pattern of girls hiding their stigmatized academic achievements and boys using humor to distract from them.[30] Chitra said,

> When I was a speller, that was one thing you totally hid. I remember, like, not even wanting to tell people what I was doing over the weekend when I was competing in the regional spelling bee. It was that big of a liability.

After-school learning carried little value among youths in what sociologist Allison Pugh[31] calls the "economy of dignity." That is, it did not help youths feel a belonging or status among peers in the same way as having the latest video game console or making the varsity softball team does. The opposite could be true. It was common for one's friends to know that one studied words and/or math outside of school. But youths downplayed the number of hours and how much one knew. One middle-school-age boy had made it to the Scripps finals and to the SASB finals. He spent eight to nine hours per day studying, especially closer to the contest dates. As was common among youths I spoke with, he did not tell his friends how much he studied. Nor did he use words he knew in public conversations, in order to avoid looking weird.[32]

Even when in small, interconnected schools, youths felt the need to downplay their investment in extra studying. Seema reported,

> It's a really small school. It's like a tight-woven community. I think that everyone knows what everyone is doing. Like, I could probably tell you what my friends are doing right now.
>
> Q: So everyone knew how many hours a day you spent spelling?
> I wouldn't say [they knew the] hours. I think that they know that I was interested in it and probably spent thirty minutes or an hour a day.

Even those just enrolled in learning centers and not competitions cautiously spoke of their participation, especially if they enjoyed it. A white sixth-grade boy, Jason, selectively shared his experiences with peers:

> It really depends on the person [as to whether I tell them about my participation]. There are people who just absolutely despise [the math center], and they think that anybody who's doing this is wrong to do so. They think it's fine to play soccer or whatever, what other teenagers do. . . . Like I said, it's not the most popular subject. I mean, if people who do it a lot are talking, I think it's fine discussing it. But other people, I guess, more the athletic crowd, they really don't like to talk about it.

As is common among so-called geeks and other groups who could hide their stigma, youths engaged in impression management and downplayed their defamed behavior in certain contexts.[33]

The stigma carried beyond just academic pursuits. Some Indian American youths wanted to hide their ethnicity in part as well. Vineeta recalled,

> Once someone told me that I had a little bit [of an] Indian accent when I talk, so I quickly kind of tried to change my speech patterns. I mean, I know a lot of Indian girls who straighten their hair and that kind of thing. I never have to straighten my hair, but I try to see what the girls wear or maybe stuff like that.

The association of Indians as both foreigners and geeks left some embarrassed. Some mimicked whiteness to fit in.

Youths' goal was not to emulate the popular kids, and they were mindful of their parents' aversion to assimilating. Still, they wanted to avoid sticking out as deviant. Children affirmed a well-rounded persona by participating in athletics and the arts, which also helped downplay their academic singularity.[34] Sarah described her son:

> So he was a baseball player up through seventh grade, [and a] basketball player through seventh grade. He's one of the popular kids in his school. So his intelligence is appreciated and respected by his whole school community. . . . He's the most humble person that you'd ever meet. He does not brag. He does not ever make anyone feel dumber than him. He's very thoughtful, he's very careful in how he speaks and what he says to people, so he doesn't ever make them feel that he knows more than them.

Youths who could outperform others in sports earned respect, thus making their book smarts an added benefit rather than a detriment. Even as Sarah's son's athletic skills are recognized, which is presumably made easier for him as a white boy, he must be careful of how he speaks so as not to appear *too* smart and incur resentment. While boys more often than girls use sports in order to fit in with peers, girls referenced it as well. Generally, youths argued that even if they were not heavily involved in sports, they could pass some arbitrary threshold of what was "enough" to feel well rounded. It is important to not set up a binary between hyper education and sports. Many youths cared about both[35] Parents also made sure to involve their children in a sport. A parent said during a group conversation,

> A lot of the kids here, they don't just do spelling. They do sports; they do drama. They have a lot of other interests.

THE BRAIN SPORT: In a group conversation at an SASB event, one young boy presciently referred to the spelling bee as "the brain sport" and said that as such, it is well suited for Indian Americans, who are competitive but cannot excel in traditional sports.[36] The room of parents and other youths nodded in agreement.[37] Being competitive spellers was "like [being] Olympic athletes," said a youth in another group setting, only harder:

> In the Olympics, you get all those events and competitions [in your sport] outside of the Olympics. Basketball players play for sixteen years. But we only get five years of competing [due to grade restrictions].

Another volunteered,

> Michael Jordan could miss every shot in the first quarter and still come back and win the game. For spelling, there is class, school, district, national levels—you miss one letter at any of those levels and you are out for the year. And spelling bee is an international competition, not even national.

Youths knew they should not be ashamed of their educational interest and therefore looked for ways to connect it to popular definitions of cool (rather than hide it). A common tactic was to articulate their participation in competitive academics as a type of sport, which created a more competitive image.[38] Comparisons to the Olympics and other sporting events were common. One father, as I passed him in the hallway and expressed sympathy for his son, who fell out of the 2014 SASB finals early, volunteered that spelling is the most "brutal of sports." If you make a mistake in golf, football, or most any other sport, you can make up for it. But in spelling, one mistake dooms you. When I mentioned to middle-school student Chirag at the NSF finals in 2013 the common stigma associated with academic "geeks," he rebuffed that people would not mock someone who swam hours a day if trying to become a professional swimmer. Our conversation came to an appropriate end when he said, "I have no time for haters."

A highlight for Scripps spellers was making it to the finals in part because it was broadcast on ESPN primetime; such programming affirmed the sports connection.[39] The celebrated sports channel also broadcasts the MATHCOUNTS finals live on its website. As an ESPN producer told me, these fit with their programming priorities, albeit surprisingly, since they are technically not sports. The channel turns the spelling bee and math competitions into a sports spectacle, with hushed whispers by correspondents, profiles of competitors, and confetti raining down on the champion(s).[40] ESPN has made it suspenseful enough to draw in viewers. In 2011, the Scripps finals brought in 952,000 viewers ages 18–49, its highest number yet, topped by the following year at 1.06 million viewers.[41] In 2014, 1.096 million adults watched the finals (while that seems huge, about the same number who watched the niche sport of Impact Wrestling, at 1.079 million viewers).[42] For MATHCOUNTS, kids are referred to as "mathletes," and they come charging into the ballroom for the finals competition in their state teams, waiving state banners, and declared as the "starting lineup."[43] At the end, the top teams are announced, with the top three receiving medals.

Even the lessons learned from competitive academics mimic those from sports. As Girish, a father of an elementary-school-age daughter said to me at an SASB finals in 2014,

> Playing a sport is not about getting the ball. It's about how you interact with others, it's about learning winning and losing, it's about learning about team playing. You don't want to take that away.

The Indian American comedian Hari Kondabolu has a routine on the Scripps National Spelling Bee, or "as I like to call it," he joked, "the Indian Super Bowl." As he told a reporter, "There aren't any South Asian athletes. I mean Jeremy Lin was Taiwanese-American. I took ownership of that. It's as close as we've gotten." Joking about the 2013 Scripps champion Arvind Mahankali's plan to compete in physics competitions after having won the spelling bee, he said, "He's a two-sport athlete!"[44]

OTHER WAYS OF FITTING IN: Beyond sports, kids connected hyper education to other popular pursuits. Sonia, a middle-school-age girl, noted while at the SASB finals in 2015,

> I like to act, and the confidence that spelling has given me from public speaking on the stage actually helps me a lot when I'm auditioning or on the stage and doing a role. If I hadn't done spelling, I don't think I would have been confident enough to develop other interests.

Another Scripps and ethnic bee participant ran for and won his student-body presidency. He also credited the bees for giving him the confidence to speak in front of others and the sense that he can accomplish what he sets his mind to. The activity they are stigmatized for becomes an asset, at least in their minds. Again, the youths did not seek to adopt the behaviors of the popular students but instead saw hyper education as accentuating their other, more accepted interests.

Parag, a past Scripps bee champion, said,

> I liked the fact that it was Americanizing. I mean, you know, it made me feel like I would be just as American, just as accepted by the kids around me, because I could spell and knew the intricacies of this language that was theirs, you know? You know, this language is more ours than yours. So I thought that that was a pretty big—to me that was a really big thing.

In his opinion, demonstrating a fluency in English helps rebut the notion of Indian Americans as foreigners (at least until the stereotype of Indian Americans changed to mark them as deviant for knowing English so well). He yearned for acceptance as an American. Rather than adopt a postcolonial attitude, of rejecting the need to conform to nationalist symbols and rhetoric, youths argued that their enrichment education—and spelling bees in particular—affirmed their adoption of American norms. Past Scripps champion Neeru, now an adult, argued,

> Spelling bees are a uniquely American tradition, and that Indians have so overwhelmingly filled the ranks of champions in recent years is remarkable. To some extent, it is a validation of our efforts to assimilate into American life, a stamp saying that "we've arrived."

Youths draw from the standard immigrant bargain narrative: they deserve respect and belonging as a trade-off for fitting into dominant institutions.[45]

Sanjay believed that by excelling in the spelling bee, they were emulating rather than threatening other American youths:

As Indian Americans, we come here, [and] we're trying to assimilate into this other culture. I think, you know, a lot of times we see the spelling bee as what American children are trying to excel at. Because we're trying to assimilate, we're trying to become closer to the culture, that's where we naturally gravitate toward. . . . A lot of the families, their parents are immigrants. Now they're here in America. So I think that their children are winning or doing well in the spelling bee shows that we can be—we can succeed in the country.

I stood next to Mahesh, the father of a champion, minutes after the victory. After the confetti fell and the trophy was handed to his daughter, she was asked by the media what she would do with the award money that she received, to which she confessed she wasn't sure. Her father scoffed at the question. She wasn't in this for the award money, he told me. She became engrossed in spelling in order to improve her English skills, for she felt committed to excel in the language. They believe they should be welcomed as full Americans, having mastered the American language. So much anti-immigrant rhetoric stems from an (often uninformed) critique of immigrants' knowledge of English.[46] Spelling bees are a cultural performance that demonstrates national allegiance, similar to adopting food, traditions, and other symbols. While these arguments were not necessarily persuasive to their racist critics, families held them as meaningful.

## Our Own Definition of Cool

Children's first major strategy to rebuff a sense of deviance involved asserting that contrary to their images as geeks or foreigners, they could connect with their classmates, were well rounded, enjoyed some popular pastimes, and were American. This meant hiding their academic pursuits as well. For their second major strategy, youths did not try to defend themselves against outside critiques. Instead, they went on the offensive. One way was to befriend those who agreed with their particular definition of normal—that is, those on the same general side of the well-rounded versus one-dimensional binary as they were.[47] When I asked Gopi at an NSF finals in 2013 how he handled that stigma around his math studies, he replied,

> Well, I guess, in that sense, then, yes, I was comfortable knowing that other people are going through the same thing that I am. But even then, I just viewed it more as fun than work.

When asked if he ever worried about his social image given his investment in spelling bees, Janak said,

> Uh, that's never really been an issue for our community, or like for me, because where I live, most of the people are very supportive, and they're all mostly Indians also. . . . Well, most of my friends spend four hours a day on math. They go to math camp nationals and stuff like that. They do four hours a day on science and go to science fairs.

He immediately refers to an Indian American community of high achievers as his social world, making stigma not an issue.

Shanta in effect code-switched between different sets of peers, a common practice among minority youths:

> I have lots of friends who have different interests. Most of my friends at school, they're interested in sports and drama and all the other things. So when I go to them and say I do spelling, they think there's nothing fun about it. But I also have other friends—people would call them nerdy or geeky. But they are interested in, like, math and science and other subjects. So when I say spelling, they think, oh it's just like other subjects. So they probably have their own interests. So they don't complain about the fact that, you know, I like spelling and spend a lot of hours on it.

Uma added,

> You'll see some people [in my friendship circle] who are smart. I mean, of course you'll see some people who are smart, and then you'll see some people who are music geeks, who are art geeks. Like, I have this whole variety of friends, and I still find a way to talk with them because I have all these different interests.

If they did not have a peer group that embraced them, they tried to create it.[48] Yasmin said,

> OK, well, my way is that I don't be friends with the people who everybody likes. I will maybe reach out to the new kid in the class sitting in the back, and I'll try and strike up a conversation with them. It doesn't matter, like, if everybody hates them. If they're a good friend, then they're my friend.

Reminiscent of their parents, youths articulated the cultural binary of being moral rather than immoral. This gave youths another way to take pride in their behaviors without having to convince peers that they were "cool enough." Mahindra, a former competitive speller who sat with me in his parents' home in Dallas, said, "I think the culture in which Indian Americans are raised has a lot to do with the success we have achieved." Sameera articulated the parenting differences she believed divided her from white professionals:

> I mean, [Indian parents will] say, "We'll give you an iPad if you use it the right way," not "We'll give you an iPad because you got an A, and then you can play it all you want." If you play too much, you won't have time to play when you're older. If you don't study good while you're a kid, you might not get the best of jobs, and you might get an average job. Instead, a doctor [as a profession] will give you a lot of money. So

FIGURE 7.1. Relaxed South Asian Spelling Bee dinner before the national finals, Somerset, New Jersey, August 2016. Photo by Pawan Dhingra.

if you study hard when you're [a] kid, you can live the rest of your life, and adult[hood] is way longer than childhood.

To be moral meant to have the right values and be forward-looking with regards to one's education, future employment prospects, and personal behavior. This perspective allowed youths and their parents to not simply feel equal to mainstream peers but to be superior to them. Mayank explained,

I don't think Indian Americans excel in the bee because they have some unique intellectual capacity. But I definitely believe they possess a few advantageous cultural traits. First and foremost, Indian immigrants make a child's studies one of the—if not the—largest priorities in the child's life, and this allows the kid to cultivate a work ethic conducive to success in the National Bee. . . . The Indian immigrant community is doing a great job instilling many of the right values in their children—hard work, dedication, and perseverance. The success also reflects well on the nation of India; that is, it shows that the people of India are equipped with the qualities conducive to thriving and flourishing outside of the homeland.

Minorities generally look for ways to assert superiority over the majority.[49] They often invoke a normative inversion—that is, they express their superiority over the majority by prioritizing norms and practices that they value and believe that the majority should value but does not, thereby making the dominant group the morally inferior one.[50] For example, Native Americans argue that rather than deny their indigenous past, tribal descendants should proudly claim their heritage and argue for land-based and community-oriented ways of life distinct from dominant American culture.[51] "Black is beautiful" is another powerful example. Minorities also chastise the majority for its discriminatory and immoral practices and so strip away their pride in their economic and political successes.[52]

And yet the families here do not embrace a normative inversion; they do not argue that the dominant values and practices are misguided and should be abandoned. Instead, their argument is, in effect, the opposite—that youths epitomize desired ways of life and deserve respect as such. Youths internalize the same binary articulated by parents. Excelling in math or spelling indicated having the "right values." Such attributes were an essential Indian trait, stretching back to an ancient homeland, according to Sanjay:

My parents, they grew up in India and they come here as immigrants, and you know definitely the job situation is harder for them. As immigrants, their degrees are foreign. My parents don't hold degrees from

English universities. That portion of their life was a bit harder for them. . . . To be Indian American, it means a lot to me. I carry it with a lot of sense of pride. The heritages really formed my identity. I think that Indian Americans in the United States are seen as [a] hardworking group of people. You know, we really work hard to achieve success.

The model minority narrative involved not just an essentialist culture, of being a "model" group, but also an ability to overcome challenges as a "minority."[53] That their parents could come to this new land and succeed meant that they were exceptional people in a meritocratic land.

Youths are not simply arguing that they are better than their peers, as common when rebutting stigma; they are better at what their peers and other Americans value—a commitment to hard work, an ability to overcome challenges, and a drive to achieve in school and the labor market. As a youth commented, "You don't see any of these kids, you know, dropping out of high school. Like, everyone's pretty self-sufficient." Their peers purportedly are failing in what they should want to excel at. What we see is an endorsement of a generic stereotype and immigration narrative. The blank nature of the narrative allows it to feel obvious and truthful. This "model minority" repertoire is made possible by their class privilege, and socioeconomic class influences which stigma responses resonate with them.[54]

## Pride and Prejudice

Scholars applaud immigrants' use of their ethnic attributes to improve their chances for success.[55] Yet youths' good behavior has emotional consequences that should be analyzed in addition to anxieties over earning enough "A's." The fact that parents treat academics as so consequential in keeping their children safe, even at times as a moral pursuit, affects children's self-identity and relationships. On the one hand, youths appreciate their families' involvement and take pride in how much they know. On the other hand, parents inadvertently create social and emotional risks, for youths have a harder time connecting with their school cultures as a result. They make major sacrifices in their free time, friendships, and status in order to be competitive in activities not understood or fully appreciated by others. They can approach education more intensely than even their teachers. High achieving students demonstrate a distinctive culture in school than has yet been sufficiently identified by researchers. Parents should be aware of the unintended consequences of pushing their kids to outcompete others in school.

Race further divides these youths from the general public—both social media and mainstream media—and their school cultures. Race works to maintain the supremacy of whites over others in part by defining minorities as deviant. In this case, Asian Americans exist as foreigners and one-dimensional geeks, each stigma informed by their racial status. Even compliments of them ultimately highlight their deviant pursuits and leave their other interests unnoticed, thereby pigeonholing them as not well rounded and as merely involved in the pursuit of memorization. Those who are recognized as "cool" by peers are exceptions to the rule, given their unique personalities, endeavors, or contexts.

In response, youths try to both fit into the prevailing definition of cool and argue for their unique superiority. They hide their endeavors and also contend that they are "cool" enough because hyper education fits into common pursuits of sports, theater, and the like, in effect upholding these extracurriculars as "normal" practices. Their goal is not to be like everyone else but to not stick out as deviant. At the same time by taking significant pride in their unique academics and building social worlds of their own, they highlight their good behaviors. They do not engage in a normative inversion but do the opposite—claiming pride in how exceptionally well they uphold agreed-upon ideals. In the process, they inadvertently put greater constraints on how to be a good Asian American, that is someone who must fit a model minority profile. Both of their types of responses reinforce the binary of proper versus improper behavior that makes an identity conflict possible in the first place. And yet in their day-to-day lives, they have no other options, and these navigation skills deserve commendation, for they help the youths feel at ease with their achievements.

# Conclusion

## *What Needs to Change*

In 2019, the Scripps National Spelling Bee broke. As pronouncer Dr. Jacques Bailly said during the late stages of the competition, "Champion spellers, we are now in uncharted territory." A few minutes later, eight co-champions were named. Immediately, pundits complained that the competition should figure out how to have just one winner. A frequent suggestion was to make the words harder.[1] As a society, we are uncomfortable with the idea of co-champions. We want a singular winner, even among elementary- and middle-school students, whether on the athletic field or in an academic contest. Winning and losing is taken for granted as part of childhood and education. Students compete against one another for college entry, the lead in the school play, internships, and more. States compete for federal grants to make their school systems "Race to the Top."

Within this logic of competition, hyper education makes complete sense, despite being treated as a foreign practice by many. In fact, as I hope I have shown in this book, hyper education fits with the United States' style of education and suits public rhetoric that the school system is failing children and needs both more quantitative assessments and assistance from the private market, including learning centers and corporate-sponsored academic contests. How well our schools teach is in doubt, according to pundits and politicians, so even good schools are not enough.

These parental choices contribute to educational inequality, which also fits within prevailing trends. Unequal access to quality education, the hoarding of resources, and unequal academic out-comes are, sadly, enduring markers of the American system.[2]

Hyper education also matches changing family dynamics. It is a form of concerted cultivation parenting, that is of providing kids multiple after-school activities and constantly nurturing their men-tal and cultural development. All types of parents embrace this style partly out of concern that their children otherwise will not succeed in school or the future workplace. Indian immigrants I spoke with (again, keeping in mind that not all Indian or Asian Americans have this educational or class background and mindset) similarly oper-ate on a binary of safety versus risk, albeit more pronounced than normally the case among whites and with an emphasis on academic extracurriculars. Yet rather than stereotypical authoritarian "tiger parents," they take into account children's interests and try to make additional education child centered. For them, a history bee has as much value as a spelling bee. Children often enjoy aspects of com-petitive academics, and parents typically quit advanced academics if children continue to protest. And like all parents with oversched-uled children, they worry if they are pushing their children too hard and into choices that, while providing certain advantages, come with more than financial costs (e.g., those that do not spark creativity, those that create stress). So hyper education generally suits stan-dard parenting practices, even if the outlet of academic-centered pursuits is seen as unusual.

Extracurricular education creates "good" kids, not just skilled kids. A commitment to scholastics was seen as practical and help-ing prevent unwanted outcomes like premarital sex, guns, drugs, and more. To not engage in hyper education or at least keep watch over children's academics made other parents suspect in their eyes. These Indian Americans worried about their children assimilat-ing into their upper-middle class cultures, which they critiqued in overlapping—not identical—ways as with stereotyped "black culture."[3]

A further sign that hyper education fits broader trends is that US-born whites, not just immigrants, increasingly practice it. The beliefs and practices of Indian American parents are not unique, contrary to popular and academic assumptions. Some white parents pursue enrichment education because they worry about their children's math scores relative to rising competition, especially for daughters. But it is also a type of concerted cultivation alongside guitar lessons and karate classes, as it is for Indian Americans. In addition, they too interpret their participation in moral terms. In fact, they make even harsher comments than do the Asian Americans about fellow white professionals who do not do the same. As found for Indian Americans, good grades is not enough to assure parents of their children's academic or moral safety.

We should not criticize supplemental education in a blanket way, for some children need and want outlets to be challenged academically. But if we do not want it to feel necessary to parents out of a fear of losing out and we want to push against the education arms race that benefits the select few, we should deal with the assumptions within contemporary education and parenting that enable and encourage hyper education.

## What Families Actually Resent

Despite hyper education's fit within contemporary educational, parenting, and cultural norms, it is still often seen as a problem by local parents and teachers for furthering academic competition and creating student stress. This disconnect between its alignment with current trends and the criticisms of it as a problematic practice suggests that detractors' real complaint is not with it but with something else.

The aversion to it by local schools, parents, and popular culture represents an objection to neoliberal ideology that defines not just advanced education but also the contemporary school system and family in ways that critics regret but rarely mobilize against. The problem is not that hyper education is foreign to education and parenting but the opposite—that it brings into relief reigning assumptions within them. In regards to education, schools have become increasingly competitive and rational, driven in part by government policies, the nonprofit-industrial complex, and public rhetoric. Critiques of after-school education as creating overtested youths obsessed with winning and as privileging private educational outlets are more aptly understood as critiques of educational reforms premised on these exact neoliberal ideals. Some districts pride themselves on advanced curriculums, AP course offerings, tracking, and the like, all of which add to student academic stress. Students constantly measure themselves relative to others. Families regret these consequences of contemporary education but take their complaints out mostly on extracurricular academics, for they stick out as elective and more clearly demonstrative of these problems. Concerns around student's mental health are valid and should be taken seriously. But the solution requires interrogating trends within the school system and corresponding non-profit organizations as a whole rather than only Asian American parenting styles, for those trends both encourage the constant measuring of one's progress in a hierarchical format and incentivize enrichment education.

Similarly, parents criticize tiger parenting as a distinctive problem rather than adequately confront how the trend of neoliberalism has transformed contemporary parenting in some regretful ways. Concerted cultivation by white parents and others often leads to overscheduled, stressed-out youths. Enrolling children in AAU basketball or multiple dance lessons instills in them cultural capital needed to succeed in school, makes it more difficult for other children who did not use the private marketplace of extracurricular activities to stand out as proficient in these activities, and exacerbate class inequalities.[4] Middle- and upper-class parents also invest in expensive educational toys, utilize summer camps, and move to neighborhoods segregated from poorer families in search of the highest-ranked schools.[5] Children are not simply too busy; their development is increasingly measured through their degree of skill accumulation. In these ways elementary-age kids are being prepared for future work. With rising income inequality in the United States and a lack of meaningful welfare support, the "winner-takes-all" system makes parents feel a need to invest in youths' long-term prospects or otherwise end up on the losing side.[6] Waiting until high school feels too late. Children eating dinner in the car while being driven from drama lessons to horseback riding is comparable to me eating lunch at my desk in that the meal ritual conforms to the larger project of serving a work mentality rather than the other way around.

Parents recognize problems with contemporary child-rearing, whether extreme or mild versions of helicopter parenting. This is evidenced by the numerous books and blogs on the stresses facing these families, including time crunches, expectations of perfection (on mothers in particular), concerns over children's college entry, and so on. Some parents, including celebrities, have infamously turned to bribing gatekeepers within the college admissions process.[7] But solutions remain limited to household-level decisions. When our children's soccer practices, piano rehearsals, and robotics classes become overly demanding, we manage them within the domestic sphere. We skip the occasional event, drop an activity from our children's repertoire, reference the amount of free time our children still enjoy, appreciate no-homework nights, insist our children love their activities, and savor our family vacations. All of that helps us maintain the belief that while our institutional cultures are changing, we are all right with that because their expectations are manageable and have not fundamentally altered our preferred ideals of childhood, at least not for those in primary school.

Most parents do not readily accept that they reproduce a neoliberal parenting model and, instead, are quick to criticize "tiger parenting" as a distinctive problem. Hyper education does not seem child centered (despite Indian American parents and children's references that it can be) but appears plainly geared toward human capital development and a future work self. What should be recognized is its overlap with mainstream contemporary parenting that is equally invested in preparing youths for work and adulthood, and critiques of it should be made correspondingly.

## Uncovering Racial Assumptions

The contemporary education system and parenting norms create undue stress and an overly competitive atmosphere for youths. Yet without also acknowledging the white normalcy within reigning education and parenting styles, including the stereotyping of Asian Americans as a foreign presence, schools and local parents will continue to give insufficient attention to their own culpability. The goal here has not been to simply reveal how middle and upper-class Asian Americans encounter race in local schools but moreover to draw attention to the white normativity embedded there that impacts all minorities as well as whites.

Asian Americans exist within a racial system as a group to be either respected or criticized, but in either case, they are used to maintain the status quo. They are applauded when their accomplishments support the notion of a meritocratic, color-blind society, such as when they appear as the "model minority." For instance, Heather Mac Donald, author of *The Diversity Delusion*, said the following to Fox News host Tucker Carlson on his show on June 6, 2019:

> If white privilege explained everything, please tell me how seven out
> of the eight of the recent national spelling bee example champions

were Indian Americans? If skin color were the scourge of people of color, they would not be able to succeed. In fact, why do they succeed, Tucker? Because they studied their butts off and that's what the inner-city kids have to start doing.[8]

In other words, because the "model minority" Asian Americans have achieved, so should other minorities. This criticism affirms the notion that the United States—in particular, its school system—is working fine the way it is.

Yet when Asian American achievement threatens white privilege, white educators and local parents respond by saying Asian Americans should calm down in their efforts and assimilate, and racial talk becomes more explicit rather than color blind. Asian American parents are stereotyped as authoritarian tiger parents obsessed with scholastics; they are even called "nuts." The school and local community, as a result, feel less of a need to be introspective about their own causes of student stress, as noted earlier. They also ignore the racial privileges they enjoy that push Asian Americans toward hyper education. For instance, Asian American families rarely benefit from privatized youth sports as do whites in these affluent suburbs, but this is not discussed in racial terms even as that impacts their chances for college admissions and drives them more toward academics. The possible racial barriers to college entry that Asian Americans face are not recognized either, even as that too encourages hyper education. The stereotype promise that Asian American students receive from educators can lead to false assessments of their abilities. White normalcy leads not only to these oversights but also to the assumption that nothing is wrong with whites whether they are on the top or the bottom of the racial hierarchy in their schools, while other students are told to change to mimic them. Unless the stereotyping of Asian Americans and the privileging of whiteness is understood and dealt with, local schools and

communities will continue to consider themselves as mostly supportive of students and not properly address the various causes of
student problems.

The investment of schools in whiteness is not surprising. Schools
have a long history of racial assimilation tactics on behalf of the
state, whether of Native Americans,[9] Latinxs,[10] African Americans,[11]
and other Asian Americans (e.g., of Japanese Americans during internment[12]). Minorities, like Asian American parents (in particular
tiger *mothers*) here, are often critiqued for not supposedly raising
their children to become healthy, heteronormative adults who suit
U.S. capitalism.[13] Also, as scholar Chandan Reddy has argued, the
state promulgates its own interests in the name of freedom and
liberal ideology.[14] With schools as a soft arm of the state, we must
ask how their claim of protecting liberal ideology—such as promoting liberal as opposed to authoritarian parenting models in town
hall meetings—accompanies other outcomes that serve the state,
namely, white normativity in educational processes and outcomes.[15]

Attention to the problems facing Asian Americans should not obscure the disadvantages facing other minorities, such as a hidden curriculum and disciplinary regimes that uniquely target black youths.[16]
Instead, this attention should demonstrate the reach of white supremacy, for it is at play even when whites are not the most academically successful. This book draws attention to how entrenched racial
hierarchies are. Schools and communities cannot engage in proper
self-reflection and address white privilege if they continue to frame
Asian Americans as model minorities or threatening foreigners.

## Alternative Approaches

There are alternatives to neoliberal parenting and education strategies that, if pursued in earnest, can help dismantle the felt need
for intense academic competition at this young age. At an individual
level, more families are resisting the call for organized activities,

with ideas like "free-range parenting."[17] Similarly, "slow parenting" emphasizes the benefits of families reducing their scheduled activities and letting kids enjoy free time and boredom.[18] A few parents can find ways to opt out of standardized tests.[19] Cities try to create more natural environments rather than sports fields to encourage exploration and "natural play."[20] The spirits of the ideas—of letting children grow up with more independence, camaraderie, and creativity—fit together.

While there is much to learn from this movement, it represents a lifestyle reserved for those with class and racial privilege.[21] Children of working-class and poor families often have more family chores or obligations and sometimes less safe neighborhoods to wander in. Affluent parents also presumably provide their children with a well-resourced school and can supplement at home with parental time, cognitive-development toys, and conversation, thereby ensuring they still outcompete many others. They also know how to advocate for themselves with administrators and are taken seriously. Still, at the individual level, such pushback is more useful than shaming Asian Americans as a way to speak against neoliberal parenting expectations.[22]

As for parenting, changes are happening at the school district level, but with mixed results. While some movements aim to reduce stress, such as by limiting course loads and homework, others are meant to help children handle stress, such as by offering breathing exercises and yoga classes.[23] Typically, these are districts where academic stress has reached a fever pitch and high achievements are expected, suggesting that these tactics will have only a limited, albeit still useful, impact.[24] Moreover, such practices do not alter schools' logic of building up children's capital in a competitive fashion, as measured by standardized tests and elite curriculums. Still, these changes recognize that the quest for more and more scholastic achievement can be questioned at the community level.

Resistance must go deeper than slow parenting and reducing homework. Alternative conceptions of education exist and can be drawn upon, ones that resist both neoliberal impulses and white supremacy. Indigenous communities have led the way in asserting the necessity of educational models premised on alternative genealogies.[25] An example is a "land literacy pedagogy" aimed to further self-determination for indigenous peoples.[26] More generally, education can focus not on students' development of capital and college entry but on social transformation.[27] Students can be empowered to help guide their own learning as inside experts on topics that concern them.[28] Educators sharing their struggles and motivations with one another models team-oriented approaches for students.[29] Project-based learning, for instance, can be utilized to promote ideals of equality alongside entrepreneurship.[30] The challenge is to reconcile this subaltern perspective with the increasing competitiveness, individualism, and whiteness of mainstream education systems of the state and the nonprofit sector and accepted by many parents.

Steps must be taken beyond trying to convince individual parents with racial, class, and cultural privileges to not advance their kids. Greater scrutiny should be applied to the zero-sum framing of contemporary academics, the increased privatization of education, the routine anxiety found in young children, the erosion of the public school as the authority on education in favor of charter schools, the oversized voice of the nonprofit industrial complex in education, the peer cultures that pigeonhole high academic achievers, and the devaluing of creativity and the arts (unless tied to STEM education). It is true that trends outside of the education institution impact families. Globalization will continue to increase competition for resources, whether college admissions or otherwise. Still, domestic institutions and policies independently further the cultural trends people regret and should be the target of parental critique.

The point here is that to challenge embedded racial hierarchies and to allow children afternoons full of skating, it might be necessary to rethink the function of the school system and corresponding parenting tactics. Because such a sea change is a daunting undertaking even at the district level, parents resisting this hyper education arms race are better served by making allies rather than enemies with those who partake of after-school academics and should recognize their racial assumptions.

## Immigrant Options

Addressing the competitiveness, increasing privatization, and white normalcy in the education system and contemporary parenting is a tall order. In the meantime, Indian American parents seek out hyper education to take care of themselves within the current system. In other words, they do not pursue it just because they are familiar with it from their upbringings. Hyper education *as a practice fits into* the neoliberal education system and concerted cultivation parenting in contrast to critiques by teachers and neighborhood parents. But *the motivation is as a tool of resistance* by immigrant parents to the white privilege surrounding them.

The adaptation patterns of middle- and upper-middle-class professional immigrants remain poorly understood. Immigration studies frame them within an assimilation paradigm and assume that they join mainstream institutions while keeping aspects of their ethnic culture in the private sphere. Critical race studies mostly ignores them as well and focuses on minorities more clearly marginalized by the state and racial capitalism. When attentive to minority professionals, the emphasis is on their continued racialization and limited real mobility and belonging, such as due to the glass ceiling, visa restrictions, one-dimensional media portrayals, residential discrimination, and so on. I have tried to demonstrate many Indian Americans' significant achievements in education, show how the achievement is buttressed by class privilege, and also explain the motivations and effects of hyper education.

Race matters in ways more complicated than typically considered. Parents do not express concerns about overt racism, do not worry much about a glass ceiling for their kids, do not prioritize math and science as objective fields less prone to discrimination, and even when asked do not refer to race as a motivation for their parenting strategies. Yet race clearly informs how they judge other extracurricular avenues to outcompete peers (e.g., sports), how they assess possibly uneven college entry expectations, and how they consider their children's need for human capital given their lack of social capital. They are aware that their kids get stereotyped as good at math. They worry about grades and the "Asian F" given how significant grades are in the rat race for college admissions, as they are made to compete with fellow Asian Americans for slots. Parents create their own Asian American style of concerted cultivation that stresses academics at least as much if not more than other extracurriculars. Standard pathways for children's success, with a concern for good grades yet a premise that kids' passions and route to excellence lie elsewhere, are presumed risky despite parents' economic privilege. Again, the point is not to dwell on the racial disadvantages facing Asian Americans per se but to demonstrate that those parents recognize and try to resist adopting all the parenting strategies of their white neighbors for children's mobility.[31] This is despite their neighbors' high class status.

Parents' resistance to standard ways of assimilating also surfaces in the moral judgments they make around extracurricular learning. They fear a "downward assimilation" in terms of their children's values and character. While such fears are normally assumed for working-class and poor minorities, they apply even when surrounded by fellow highly educated professionals. The fact that these critiques mirror racist stereotypes of African Americans further demonstrates how antiblack racism is embedded in what constitutes a "good student."[32] Their judgments of their white peers rely more on caricatured assumptions than on demonstrated reality, such as their white peers leaving their children's education up to them rather than being deeply engaged. Fellow whites share these assumptions and make comparable critiques of peers not invested in enrichment education. Hyper education, then, serves as a means to resist an assumed downward assimilation in terms of both mobility and morality.

If the goal is to limit immigrant parents' sense of supplemental education as a necessity regardless of children's initiation, educators and others must recognize the different levels of the playing field that some benefit from relative to others. Educators ask Asian American parents to relax, and they insist everything will work out for their children as it has for their own children (when doing woodworking and having a lot of time to play). But to what degree did their families' success depend on white privilege and being in the most developed, resource-concentrated country in the world at a time of clear global dominance? For many white professionals, social capital and cultural capital are taken-for-granted mechanisms for mobility. But is it realistic to expect ethnic minorities to find full mobility by applying themselves simply to the extent expected by schools, even those with strong academic reputations? They cannot rely on robust social and cultural capital, and they cannot effectively compete on the athletic field or community theater, in their minds. They worry about being held to a higher bar in college admissions. Similarly, calls for slow parenting must recognize the racial inequalities they are built on.

Indian Americans' identity as immigrants and minorities shapes their attraction to hyper education. But even US-born whites increasingly pursue it, often by their own volition rather than because they feel pressured by Asian Americans. The fact that supplemental academics takes on a moral valence for whites demonstrates how seriously families take it and how education signals what kind of family one is, even among families already in strong school districts. Hyper education will continue to grow given people's multiple motivations for it.

Critiques of enrichment education are justified, as for concerted cultivation parenting more generally, when it leads to overscheduled and overstressed kids. But no progress will be made unless parents' motivations are fully understood and dealt with.

## Think of the Children

Parents' use hyper education as a way to resist standard outcomes leaves youths in a predicament. Good behavior by children is not enough to earn acceptance. While excelling on the swim team earns you a varsity jacket and cheers from the audience, youths committed to more learning encounter double-edged praise. Many kids respond by presenting themselves as fitting into cultural norms or rejecting these standards and creating more daylight between them and others. Neither is an enviable option, even as they handle it well.

Asian American parents are well served by paying attention to this, and many already do. Popular and academic writing has missed the internal conflict these parents feel in how they raise their children; they worry about the implications for kids. Expecting children to conform to an educational pathway premised on surpassing school standards and then not anticipating social-emotional challenges is unreasonable in terms of both daunting academic levels and the social anomalies some experience relative to their peers. Ironically, parents' pursuit of financial and moral safety can put their children at emotional risk. Parents must better support their children as they ask them to stand out among others. Proactively or reactively talking with teachers and administrators about these concerns, not simply about the schools' academic standards, is useful, as is engaging with neighborhood parents.

Students' racial status as Asians privileges them relative to blacks and Latinxs but also facilitates caricatured readings of them. Spelling or math is not seen as something someone does; it is considered something someone is. As the "model minority," youths are framed as one dimensional and engaged in memorization tactics. Their other interests and talents are ignored. This is all the more reason why parents should consciously attend to their children's well-being and communicate about that with schools.

The pressure to better support such youths does not fall on the parents alone. The key reason why youths can feel stigmatized and must say they "have no time for haters" has to do with how they are framed in the media and in school environments. The mainstream media, not to mention social media, hangs onto notions of Asian Americans as a foreign presence to be explained, whether as model minority "whiz kids" or as victims of "tiger parenting." The media also subscribes to a dichotomy that celebrates well-versed and sporty youths but makes an academic commitment something to be justified. Obviously, popular culture's interest in sports exceeds that of its interest in math or spelling. But that is not a reason to frame the two as mutually exclusive options or to privilege one as deviant relative to the other, especially inside schools.

The reactions to Asian Americans reveal not just the prejudices they face but, more generally, white middle-class cultural assumptions in school cultures. Schools have an administrative culture that expects youths to conform to established academic pathways and procedures, and relatively conservative behavior, dress, and modes of expression.[33] These expectations disproportionately punish black and Latinx youths as "problem children."[34] Here we see that youths can be in tension with administrative cultures not because they do not live up to academic and behavioral expectations but because they exceed those expectations.

The youths should not suffer for their pursuits. Schools should recognize how they pigeonhole students into social types. Teachers and administrators must lead the way in celebrating youths' achievements without falling into the stereotype of Asian Americans as culturally prone to such successes; they must treat them as three-dimensional kids for whom academics is just one of their interests. Students should not be made to feel strange for going beyond school expectations (while also not being punitively disciplined if not living up to cultural expectations). Teachers should compliment but not dwell on these extrascholastic achievements. Schools should accentuate such youths' other interests and skills, such as by drawing attention to them when celebrating their academic accomplishments or by giving such children a platform to define themselves socially.

This focus on the needs of immigrant minority, middle- and upper-middle-class children who exceed school expectations should not obscure the larger challenges facing school systems. The goal should be not to make sure that some get ahead but to provide high-quality education to children of all backgrounds and to work through the racial and class inequalities between and within schools.[35] This investigation into hyper education reveals how race, immigration, and neoliberal ideology shape education choices for those who already have financial resources. It should be used as evidence of the entrenched nature of racial hierarchies and competitive incentives, not to feel sorry for one group over another. Other education models that resist these challenges have much to teach even if not adopted. Schools should aim to fulfill their ideal mission of leveling the playing field by serving as socially just institutions. Schools should enlist parents who are involved in hyper education as part of the broader community of parents, for they share many of the same motivations as others. All children ultimately could benefit.

Maybe then we can celebrate multiple co-champions rather than reserve the title of champion for just one person. Maybe we can come to see such an outcome as a positive sign, not a problem to fix.[36]

After each year's SASB finals, families return to the motel where everyone was staying, and it is time to let loose. There is a dance party with Bollywood music and open bar. Mothers dance together, couples dance, and the kids clearly have the most fun. Part of the ritual is for them to egg on Rahul Walia, the founder, to take part, which he does without too much convincing. He also is letting off some steam, having just finished a months' long tour of the country and the organization of the finals. Each time I have been there, he gets excited by the occasion, dancing and laughing with both the parents and the children. In 2015, I came up to him to congratulate him on the evening. He and I had talked earlier about the ridicule that Indian American children receive for their bee championships and how their academic excellence comes with a stigma. After a hug, I was turning to leave and he exclaimed in reference to our earlier conversation, "Pawan, there's no stigma with this!"

The dance party and dinner were just the beginning. Afterward, boys literally ran through the halls of the motel. Girls chatted together and ran as well, sometimes with the boys but mostly on their own. The morning after the finals competition, I learned that youths stayed up until 1 a.m., well past their normal bedtimes, asserting their independence.[37] Photos captured the cans of soda, the silly poses, and the numerous smiles. Some parents commented that they were asleep before their kids came into their room. The children had worked hard to deserve this, they said, and they like seeing their children have so much fun. For many parents, having a social space for children to relax with peers who held similar interests was worth the price of attendance. It was a space where youths in hyper education were embraced for being who they are.

# ACKNOWLEDGMENTS

A book is as much a way of giving thanks as it is a way to start a conversation. While the rest of the book explains what conversation I aim to have, here I focus on the immense thanks I have for those who helped bring this book to life. First and foremost, I want to thank the children, parents, educators, and others I spent time with in this research and writing process. Each one gave time that they did not need to, and without that generosity, this book would not be. People gave serious thought to our discussions. I hope that they find something useful in this piece for themselves, just as they have hopefully made it useful for others. I do not aim to represent any individual, much less an ethnic group or community or demographic. Instead, I used those conversations and observations to draw out themes that I think are central to contemporary middle-class parenting, education, and immigration.

I also want to thank those who took their time to engage me while researching and writing it. I cannot list them all here, as memory will fail me. Some of those are, in alphabetical order, Rick Baldoz, Freeden Blume Oeur, Ratnam Chatterjee, Margaret Chin, Cedric De Leon, Tomas Jimenez, Paul Joseph, Miliann Kang, Grace Kao, Philip Kasinitz, Jennifer Lee, Jennifer C. Lee, Min Jin Lee, Shelley Lee, Lisa Lowe, Samip Mallik, Helen Marrow, Pablo Mitchell, Konrad Ng and others at the Smithsonian Institution, Sameer Pandya, OiYan Poon, Elizabeth Raleigh, Sam Rega, Sharmila Rudrappa, Leah Schmalzbauer, Sharmila Sen, Shalini Shankar, Sarah Sobieraj, Stanley Thangaraj, Rahul Walia, Natasha Warikoo, Chris Weller, and Min Zhou. In addition to generous university visits, I have benefited from feedback at conferences of the American Sociological Association, American Studies Association, Association for Asian American Studies, the Eastern Sociological Society, Jeffrey Alexander and the Center for Cultural Sociology at Yale University, and Mary Waters and the Migration and Incorporation Workshop at Harvard University. Students have played a key role as well, including Sabrina Lin and Karina Thanawala.

I know it is customary to give thanks to one's editor, but I truly want to thank Ilene Kalish at New York University Press. This is my fourth book but my first with Ilene. I learned much about how to write from her as well as the ideas in the book. She gave a careful eye to the chapters and shared an affect that I can best describe as therapeutic. I hope our work together carries on. The three reviewers of the book deserve more than a free copy; they deserve an apology if it does not live up to their thoughtful comments.

No acknowledgments are complete without thanking individual family members. That is as true here as anywhere. I can be overly sensitive, quiet, passive-aggressive, or the like when talking about my work when in the middle of it, and the middle part lasts the longest. More than put up with me, they gave me needed feedback and generally kept my spirits up. Thanks so much to my mother, father, mother-in-law, Shalini, Jim, Arun, Koshi, Charu, Talvin, and Amitav.

# APPENDIX

## Research Design and Methods

I have interviewed and spent time with three distinct sets of individuals between the years 2011 and 2018: educators, parents, and children (including those now grown). I have talked with twenty-eight educators, including elementary- and middle-school teachers, school principals, school administrators, math center directors, bee and math competition organizers, bee and math coaches, and college admission officers. This is on top of informal yet informative conversations with other elementary- and middle-school educators when at academic competitions. Educators were primarily in the Boston area—in particular, suburbs with a much higher percentage of Asian Americans than the state average (of 6.3 percent in 2014) and a lower percentage of families and people living below the poverty level than the state average (of 8.3 percent in 2014).[1] The school districts in these areas are consistently rated as among the best in the state and in the country by *Boston Magazine* and *U.S. News & World Report*. Educators also were in Colorado, Florida, Illinois, New Jersey, and Texas. Families had typically moved to their particular towns based on the strong reputation of the school systems. Those involved in spelling bees were Indian Americans; those in math competitions were Indian, East Asian, and white; and those in math centers were whites, Asian Americans, European immigrants, and other minorities.

The rest of the interviews were with parents and children, primarily of Indian descent, who participated in math centers, spelling bees, and math competitions. I have talked and spent time with

Table A.1. Interviewees

| | |
|---|---|
| Indian American parents involved in spelling and/or math, individual conversations | 60 |
| Indian Americans at spelling and/or math competitions, group conversations | 85 |
| Whites involved in math centers and/or math competitions | 30 |
| Children, including former Scripps National Spelling Bee champions and finalists (not including informal conversations) | 29 |
| Educators, including public school teachers and administrators, center directors, and spelling bee administrators | 28 |
| African American, Chinese American, and Eastern European / Russian families | 2–4 each |

sixty Indian American parents engaged in hyper education, each such interview ranging between forty-five and ninety minutes. In addition, I have conducted eight different highly informative group conversations, lasting typically between forty-five minutes and one hour, at South Asian academic competitions (either just spelling competitions or competitions with spelling and math options), each with fifteen or more families present. These were Boston-area regional competitions and national finals competitions. On average, ten families per session participated. I also conducted a ninth group interview at a MATHCOUNTS finals competition for middle schoolers, with about two dozen South Asian, other Asian American, and non–Asian American (mostly white) families present, over half of whom contributed, with representation across all ethnic groups. So these group conversations led to about eighty-five more informants, making a total of 145 Indian American adults. Typically, Indian American families whose children did spelling bees also put time into math as well, whether in a learning center, math competition, or supplemental work at home. Those in math competitions may not be involved in spelling bees.

About a third of those Indian American parents lived in New England, and all lived in middle- or upper-middle-class suburbs.

The other two-thirds came from various parts of the United States, since the regional spelling and math competitions of the national final that I visited took place in a dozen metropolitan areas across the country. National spelling and math competitions brought in families I spoke with from around the country (California, Colorado, Florida, Kansas, Illinois, Minnesota, Mississippi, New York, Ohio, Pennsylvania, Texas, Washington, and elsewhere). Their geographic areas often—not always—map onto those with a highly educated workforce.[2]

The Indian parents were immigrants who arrived as married professionals in the middle and upper-middle class. They were disproportionately in science and technology fields. Most commonly they were in engineering, such as software engineers, mechanical engineers, computer systems analysts, electrical engineers, and the like, with a smaller proportion as physicians, professors, accountants, small business owners (e.g., motels), and stay-at-home mothers. They arrived through work or education visas, such as the H-1B, or as their spouses. All came with bachelor's degrees and most with or immigrating to complete master's degrees, practically all in STEM fields. Their visa statuses allowed them a pathway to citizenship. Practically all believed that they would stay in the United States. These parents came from a variety of states within India, both southern and northern India. All the fathers worked outside of the home, and around two-thirds of the mothers did as well. Most household incomes ranged from $100,000 to $400,000 depending on geography, occupation, and years of experience. This was a different immigration wave than the previous generations of Indians, who immigrated in large numbers since the Immigration and Naturalization Act of 1965. Most Indian immigrants since 1965 have come as highly educated. But previous generations seemed to have more physicians rather than computer programmers. This current wave of migrants also came from throughout India, not primarily the north. Immigrants from South India have been pronounced in recent decades and are frequently involved in IT, and many spelling bee champions have been of South Indian ancestry.

All families had at least one child in the elementary- or middle-school grades (below grade 9). Eighty percent had a child in the public-school system, and the other 20 percent were enrolled in private schools. Mothers and fathers made up an almost equal ratio of informants, and all were in heterosexual marriages to other Indian Americans. Practically all of the Indian American parents migrated to the United States as adults. I am not privileging the nuclear family or the heteronormative family as the model of immigration and belonging. While these were the people studied here, other kinds of family formations and sexualities exist within South Asian America and should not be neglected or downplayed as a result of studies such as this one.[3]

So as to move beyond a profile of just Indian Americans, I also have interviewed and spent time with thirty US-raised, white families who had children enrolled in private math centers (not spelling bees), a few of whom also did math competitions. They were of the same occupational status as the Indian immigrant informants. All of these individuals had college degrees, and most had postgraduate degrees, typically in STEM-related professions (e.g., structural engineers, biotech engineers, physicians, accountants, scientists), but also in law, finance, insurance sales, teaching, and other professional occupations. The few stay-at-home mothers had bachelor's degrees. Eighty percent had a child in the public-school system. Three-quarters of the white parents I spoke with were mothers, and one-quarter were fathers. Two individuals were divorced when we met, but the rest were in heterosexual marriages. As indicative of their class privilege, when asked how much they spent on children's activities, parents confessed they often did not keep track, and hardly any referred to finances as a reason to not pursue an extracurricular or pick one over another. In the course of the fieldwork, I also talked with a few African American parents, Eastern European / Russian immigrant parents, and a few Chinese immigrant parents. They fit the same occupational and demographic profile of the other adults. There is much to be learned from families of professional backgrounds in terms of not only social reproduction but also how they understand and maintain their privilege. Yet race and other social divisions are not attended to in the study of such persons, which this project addresses.[4]

The interviews with children were less structured. While I sat down with fifteen Indian American children, I also learned much from informal conversations with dozens more at academic competitions and after-school centers. These were conversations facilitated by or in the location of their parents. I also spoke with fourteen former spelling bee top-ten finalists and champions.

From 2010 to 2017, I also conducted ethnographic observations at eleven spelling bee competitions (both South Asian–centric and Scripps, and including three weekends with South Asian American families at finals competitions), a MATHCOUNTS competition for middle-school students, Boston-area locations of five nationally franchised math learning centers, three independent math programs, people's homes, receptions for spelling bee finalists in New York City, community meetings, learning center events, and other related settings. I also spent time in three families' homes, observing daily engagements and study practices. Beyond observing, I volunteered at bees, guided children to their competitions, assisted with setup and takedown, and more. I also enjoyed breakfasts, lunches, tea, dinners, and drinks with families.

# NOTES

## INTRODUCTION: THE GROWTH OF EXTRACURRICULAR EDUCATION

1 Nuckols 2016.
2 Chakravorty 2016.
3 These do not include the competitions geared toward certain Asian American populations. For example, see Korean-American Scientists and Engineers Association 2019.
4 Mori and Baker 2010.
5 Byun and Park 2011; McNeal 1998; Peng and Wright 1994; Ho, Park, and Kao 2018; Zhou and Kim 2006; Relatedly, Asia spends more on supplemental education than any region (Global Industry Analysts Inc. 2016).
6 Global Industry Analysts, Inc. 2016, 2018.
7 ASU GSV X n.d.; Global Silicon Valley 2016.
8 Kumon 2015a.
9 Kumon 2015b; see also BusinessWire 2014.
10 Cision PR Newswire 2016; Mathnasium 2016.
11 Goldberg 2017.
12 Moss 2014.
13 For-profit businesses in education fare better when not competing directly with schools but instead occupying related niches, as in the case of learning centers (Aurini and Davies 2004).
14 Practically all the names in this book are pseudonyms to protect people's confidentiality.
15 Zernike 2011.
16 Zhou and Li 2003.
17 Park et al. 2016.
18 Shell 2017.
19 Anderson, Funk, Elliott, and Smith 2003; Lareau 2003.
20 Kim et al. 2013. See also National Post 2016; and Su 2011.
21 Southgate 2013.
22 Davidson 2011; Zhou et al. 2004; Cooper 2015; Smith 2013.
23 Suratt 2017. Private school—presumably the site of intense academics—could become a refuge for those looking for a more relaxed educational environment.
24 Hwang 2005.
25 Jimenez 2017.

26 Spencer 2015.

27 Parmar, Harkness, and Super 2004.

28 Gonzales 2015; Putnam 2015; Boschma and Brownstein 2016; Ericson and Silverman 2001.

29 Zong and Batalova 2017; Radford 2019.

30 Desliver 2014.

31 Omi and Winant 1994.

32 Aurini, Davies, and Dierkes 2013; Ball et al. 2014; Ford, Baytops, and Harmon 1997.

33 Economist 2019; Pew Research Center 2015.

34 Nearly six out of every ten children are involved in some extracurricular activity (US Census Bureau 2014).

35 Hills 1987; Bainbridge 2018.

36 Spencer 2013.

37 Lareau 2003.

## CHAPTER 1. "OVERPROGRAMMED FAMILIES"

1 In Massachusetts, it is the Massachusetts Comprehensive Assessment System (MCAS), a standardized test for the state's public schools.

2 Galloway, Pope, and Osberg 2007; Lite 2014; Luthar and Becker 2002; Segool et al. 2013; Spencer et al. 2018.

3 Abeles 2016.

4 Newsweek Staff 2006.

5 Phelan, Yu, and Davidson 1994; Wagner, Cole, and Schwartzman 1995. See also Rosin 2015; Cullotta et al. 2017; and Flannery 2018.

6 Bethune 2014.

7 Flannery 2018.

8 NBC News 2014.

9 Spencer 2017.

10 Lambert 2018. For more on how schools, communities, and families may reduce stress, see www.stressfreekids.com; https://kidlutions.myshopify.com; and Price-Mitchell 2019.

11 Davidson 2011.

12 Qin, Way, and Rana 2008; Saran 2015.

13 Lung-Amam 2017.

14 Jimenez 2017.

15 Vincent and Ball 2007; Cha 2016.

16 Anderson, Funk, Elliott, and Smith 2003; Lareau 2003.

17 Hwang 2005.

18 Vincent and Ball 2007; Cha 2016.

19 Anderson, Funk, Elliott, and Smith 2003; Lareau 2003.

20 Lee and Zhou 2015.

21 Teranishi 2010; Yeh and Inose 2002. See also Counseling@NYU 2017 and Qiao 2017.

22 Hijioka and Wong 2012.

23 Lee et al. 2009; Lorenzo, Frost, and Reinherz 2000.

24 Bray and Lykins 2012.

25 Yi 2013.

26 Directors of learning centers said they tried to be sympathetic to teachers' complaints regarding the workload that results from after-school education, with limited results.

27 Jetten et al. 2017.

28 Ball et al. 2014; Lewis 2003.

29 The treatment of Asian Americans fits a racial project, as discussed by Omi and Winant (1994).

30 As the *New York Times* reported in 2006, Asian Americans in New York City suburban schools are a model group, raising academic standings and promoting cultural diversity.

School officials, teachers, and parents say that the expanding Asian population has strengthened their schools not only by raising test scores but also by promoting diversity and tolerance. See Doerner 1985; Plain Dealer 2003; Goleman 1990; and Quindlen 1987.

31 Brand 1987.

32 Blue Oeur 2018; Vargas 2018; Wun 2016.

33 Bonilla-Silva 2003.

34 Paul 2011.

35 Takaki 1989.

36 Franck 1997; Seigel 2005.

37 Faircloth, Hoffman, and Layne 2013; Jenks 2005; McHale, Crouter, and Tucker 2001; Tyler 1993. See also History and Educational Models in Early Childhood Education n.d.

38 Kim 1999.

39 Pong, Hao, and Gardner 2005.

40 Kim et al. 2013.

41 Dornbusch et al. 1987; Kao 2004; Li, Costanzo, and Putallaz 2010.

42 Chao 1994; Wu and Chao 2011; Yoshikawa, Mistry, and Wang 2016.

43 Choi et al. 2013.

44 Jambunathan and Counselman 2002.

45 Viramontez Anguiano 2004.

46 Kao 2004.

47 Martin 2009.

48 Feagin and Sikes 1994; Lareau and Horvat 1999.

49 Lewis-McCoy 2014; Ogbu 2003; Staiger 2004; Wun 2016.

50 Byrd 2011.

51 Tierney 2012.

52 Lewis and Diamond 2015; Sattin-Bajaj and Roda 2018.

53 Calarco 2018a; Lewis-McCoy 2014.

54 Gregory 2017.

55 Jaschik 2017.

56 Glenn 2009.

57 Noguchi 2016; Groves 2016; Spencer 2017.

58 Bernstein 2016; Spencer 2015.

59 Spencer 2015. This is part of a larger movement to "rescue" children from the stress of helicopter parenting. See Italie 2011; "Free-Range Friend." n.d.; New York Times Editorial Board 2015; Doyle 2016.

60 Modica 2015.
61 Parmar, Harkness, and Super 2004.
62 Smyth 2016.
63 Lewis and Diamond 2015.
64 Lee and Zhou 2015; Schneider and Lee 1990.
65 Steele and Aronson 1995.
66 Ochoa 2013.
67 Segool et al. 2013.
68 Bray and Lykins 2012.
69 Minero 2018; New York City Department of Education. 2002.
70 Apple 2004; Bondy 2011; Grande 2015; Wrigley and Carnoy 1986.
71 Adams 1995.
72 Del Moral 2013; Estrada 1981; Spring 2016.
73 Stevens 2009; Wiley 2000.
74 Bascara 2006; Lowe 1996.
75 Wilson III 2008.
76 Apple 2004; Solomona, Portelli, Daniel, and Campbell 2005.
77 Reddy 2011.
78 Gordon and Newfield 1996.

## CHAPTER 2. "IF THE SCHOOLS WERE DOING THEIR JOB, THEN WE WOULDN'T NEED TO EXIST"

1 Coleman 1961; National Research Council 2004.
2 National Center for Education Statistics 2009.
3 Berliner and Biddle 1995; Ritzer 1983.
4 U.S. Department of Education 2013; Ambrosio 2013. NCLB has been called a means to privatize the school system and implement free-market principles (Golann 2015; Mehta 2013). Private companies have long provided textbooks, teacher training, assessment procedures, and more to public schools and increasingly have taken over entire public schools (Molnar 2006; Harvey 2005).
5 Such reforms, ostensibly meant to identify the weakest schools and incentivize them to improve, punished them. Students depart schools considered failing and take public money with them, but such schools have a higher share of the poorest students, whose extra needs are not able to be adequately addressed. The bill was severely underfunded, making it almost impossible for already poorly resourced schools to meet high-achieving benchmarks (Duncombe, Lukemeyer, and Yinger 2008). Rather than guarantee that failing schools will get the support they need to turn around, those schools are closed within NCLB as inefficient uses of public money. As fitting neoliberalism, organizations (and individuals) are expected to better themselves with an entrepreneurial attitude, and if they do not, then they deserve to be shut down (Hursh 2007). Those schools fail within the marketplace of available options, which under NCLB included the expansion of charter and private schools.
6 Woodard 2013.
7 See Stewart 2007. NCLB was replaced by the Every Student Succeeds Act, which no longer has the tutoring requirement but still funnels money to learning centers. See also Weiss et al. 2009.

8 Wolk 2005; Molnar 2013. The effects of this supplemental education on low-income students in underperforming schools are questionable (Heinrich, Meyer, and Whitten 2010; Muñoz, Potter, and Ross 2008).

9 States could determine their own standardized tests and the standards that must be met by their schools, but the fact that student test scores would become the key measure of academic progress was—and remains—doxa.

10 Republicans and Democrats take direct aim at teachers' unions and collective bargaining more generally (Chait 2014). Governments similarly push legislation that allows noncertified people to teach, claiming that teachers who have passed licensing exams are not necessarily more qualified than those who have expertise in their content area (Stephenson 2017).

11 For example, in the "blue" state of New Jersey (New Jersey Department of Education 2012).

12 For instance, the principal, Rachel, explained that the Massachusetts Comprehensive Assessment System (MCAS), the state's standardized assessment of public school learning, deviated from the everyday assessments teachers used:

> It's very rare, if ever, that we give multiple-choice tests. The bulk of the MCAS is multiple choice. The other thing is that most learning, at least in our district, comes with asking students to ask questions of what they don't understand and providing them with feedback along the way. For the MCAS, the children sit down [and] take the test; the teacher is not allowed to provide any feedback along the way.

> Mimicking the critiques teachers have of hyper education, she sees standardized tests as being in conflict with more open-ended teaching and assessments. Even as schools may not value these assessments, they accept this state-sanctioned authority and assess themselves based on their performance (e.g., schools hang large banners on their buildings to parade that they are "blue ribbon" schools). See US Department of Education 2012.

13 Roach and Frank 2008.

14 Journell 2010; Overman n.d.

15 Lebesco 2011.

16 Wong 2015.

17 Caplan 2018; Hursh 2007.

18 Groark 2003.

19 Gates 2009.

20 As reported in the *Washington Post*, "The foundation has spent hundreds of millions of dollars developing teacher evaluation systems that use student test scores to help evaluate teachers, a controversial assessment method that many experts say is unfair and invalid" (Strauss 2014).

21 Strauss 2016.

22 Scores are used to evaluate not only students' knowledge but also their presumed motivation, intellect, and effort, as well as the quality of the schools. Ravitch 2017; Walker 2010.

23 Ravitch 2017; Strauss 2013b.

24 Skoll Foundation. n.d.

25 Khan 2012, 4.

26 Khan 2012, 7.

27 Khan 2012. His ideal model inverts the normal classroom, with "teaching" at home and "homework" taking place at school. Teachers and students who have incorporated Khan Academy into their classrooms and classwork report mixed results (Schwartz 2014).

28 Dintersmith 2018.

29 Trei 2005; Strauss 2013c.

30 Mathews 2000; Brown 2015; Finn 2014; Sanchez 2016; Gallagher 2002.

31 Students on average believe that they are not pushed hard enough, they put in fewer hours for school than international students, and their test scores are lower across various subjects, especially math. CompareYourCountry 2015; Ryan 2013; Boser and Rosenthal 2012; Loveless 2017.

32 Farkas and Duffett 2008; Journell 2010; Loveless, Farkas, and Duffett 2008; Newsweek Staff 2006.

33 Anderson 2016.

34 Darling-Hammond 2015; Oakes 1987.

35 Au 2011; Berliner and Biddle 1995.

36 Oakes 1985.

37 Hallinan 2014. See also Oakes 1987 (but see Gamoran 1992; Karlson 2015).

38 Ferguson 2008.

39 Alvarez and Mehan 2006.

40 Kalleberg 2009.

41 Jenks 2005.

42 Platt 1977.

43 Takanishi 1978.

44 Binkley and Capetillo 2009.

45 Binkley and Capetillo 2009; Harvey 2005.

46 Hurrelmann 1988.

47 Heynen 2007; Slater 2015.

48 Gregory 2017.

49 Vincent and Maxwell 2016.

50 Putnam 2015; Weeks 2011.

51 Gill-Peterson 2015.

52 Roediger 2017.

53 Lareau 2003; Stephens 1995. Selecting an academic competition or after-school program, driving a child to and from that space, helping the child prepare for the extra academics, and the like constitute the unpaid labor necessary to maintain the capitalist logic within and outside of the educational system.

54 Gunzenhauser 2006; Walker 2010. The state's testing mandate represents a rational approach to education that downplays and arguably undermines students' humanity by reducing their intellectual opportunities and output to a standardized test (Alcazar 2006).

55 Stevenson and Baker 1992.

56 Byun and Park 2012. The image of tutoring is as one-on-one support to a student struggling academically. While that is indeed the most common type, parents wanting more challenging academics or above-average test scores for their kids and who prefer structured activities also turn to these options (Byun and Park

2012; Davies 2004). Asian Americans utilize "shadow education" (e.g., SAT test preparation and tutoring), often for advancement rather than for remedial purposes, more often or as often as other racial groups (Byun and Park 2012).

57 Aurini and Davies 2004.

58 Baker 2009; Baker and LeTendre 2005.

59 Baker et al. 2001; Choi, Calero, and Escardibul 2012; Mori and Baker 2010.

60 Junior Kumon Program 2011.

61 Mori 2013.

62 Kumon 2014.

63 Vimeo 2016.

64 Davidson 2009.

65 Franchise Direct 2019; Kumon 2017.

66 Mathew 2008.

67 Aurini and Davies 2004.

68 Strauss 2013a; MasterClass 2016.

69 Massachusetts Society of Professional Engineers 2015.

70 Heitin 2016.

71 The first national spelling bee actually was in Cleveland in 1908, more than a decade before the first official bee took place in 1925, discussed later (see Maguire 2006).

72 The national spelling bee has historic roots in the United States. The contemporary national spelling bee started in 1925 and was founded by nine newspapers and hosted by the *Louisville Courier-Journal*. Frank Neuhauser, age eleven, won that year for spelling "gladiolus." Just as today, school children across the country competed for an opportunity to make it to the finals.

73 One afternoon a week was set aside for spelling competitions in some schools. Such practices were a carryover from Elizabethan education practices in England dating back to the sixteenth century (Read 1941).

74 Despite its British roots, the spelling bee is a truly American tradition (Read 1941). Not only has it been an active part of the school and extraschool experience for over two centuries, but the United States is the only country with a continued spelling bee practice. Moreover, how and why spelling bees take place arguably has an American rationale. In England, bee competitions focused, in part, on students' pronunciation of the words and so rewarded students based on where they were from (or at least, where they appeared to be from). In the United States, the more objective attention to spelling arguably signifies the nation's commitment to meritocracy, where one's origins purportedly do not matter because each person has an equal opportunity to achieve. To participate in a spelling bee, then, is to make oneself an American, contribute to the meritocratic legacy, and practice the Calvinist philosophy that through effort, one can take control over the life's uncertainty, just as one tames the uncertainty of the arbitrary American language.

75 Maguire 2006.

76 Stevens, Macaulay, and Miller 1873. Given that spelling competitions took on an entertainment quality, their popularity waned around the 1820s as other forms of nightly entertainment arose. Spelling bees had a more nostalgic than invigorating appeal. As New Englanders traveled west, they reinvented the

spelling bee tradition in frontier states like Indiana and Iowa. Spelling bees waxed and waned in popularity in the latter half of the nineteenth century. The popular book *The Hoosier Schoolmaster* helped revive the bee in 1875, with even Mark Twain introducing a bee competition in 1875 in Connecticut (although with dubious enthusiasm for the event) (McArthur 2011). The national bee adapted to new forms of technology. It had a revival in the 1920s and 1930s, in part because they carried well in radio format (Maguire 2006).

77 For instance, there is the Association of Christian Schools International bee, which has regional bees across the country.

78 Given that spelling competitions took on an entertainment quality, their popularity waned around the 1820s as other forms of nightly entertainment arose. Spelling bees had a more nostalgic than invigorating appeal. As New Englanders traveled west, they reinvented the spelling bee tradition in frontier states like Indiana and Iowa. Spelling bees waxed and waned in popularity in the latter half of the nineteenth century. A popular book, *The Hoosier Schoolmaster*, helped revive the bee in 1875, with even Mark Twain introducing a bee competition in 1875 in Connecticut (although with dubious enthusiasm for the event); McArthur 2011.

79 Scripps n.d., "Scripps National Spelling Bee Experience."

80 From 1974 to 1977, the taped finals showed on PBS in primetime; from 1994 to 2005, they aired live on ESPN during the daytime. For five years, from 2006 to 2010, ABC carried the finals.

81 Not only is Scripps bringing representatives of other nations to the United States bee, but it is helping organize bees for other countries, such as Jamaica, Japan, and Ghana. An English spelling bee has been held since 2009 in Shanghai, for instance, and Scripps is helping institutionalize it in China's international schools. China, Thailand, Indonesia, and Malaysia compete annually in the Asia Spelling Cup. India has had its own spelling competitions for years as well. Business Standard 2017.

82 Read 1941.

83 Maguire 2006.

84 For instance, a 2012 story by National Public Radio on Indian Americans' achievements in the bee quoted Srinivas Mahankali, the father of a finalist (and future champion) and his connection between children's success and Indian culture: "Memory is so much emphasized in Indian traditional learning systems." Schoolchildren often had to memorize poems so they could recite them—even in reverse. "It doesn't make any sense, but there were competitions to just chant it in reverse," Mahankali said (Smith 2012). Here, the act of not assimilating but instead embracing one's cultural background is applauded as helping children succeed.

85 García 2015. The documentary film *Spellbound* embraces this theme with its collection of ethnically, geographically, and economically diverse youths profiled in the film.

86 Today, to be eligible to attend the Scripps National Spelling Bee, the speller must not have won a previous Scripps championship, must not have passed beyond the eighth grade on or before February of the competition year, and must attend a school that is officially enrolled with the Scripps Bee. The speller must have been declared a champion of a bee-sanctioned final local spelling bee or be a

spelling champion whose application for participation in the Scripps National Spelling Bee's self-sponsorship program has received final approval by the Scripps National Spelling Bee. Contestants can be from abroad and from US territories, American Samoa, Guam, Puerto Rico, the US Virgin Islands, and Department of Defense Dependents Schools in Europe. (Scripps n.d. "International Spellers"). If spellers meet all of these requirements, they are eligible to continue down the path to the national bee. Once at the bee, spellers first take a twenty-five-word written spelling (and since 2013, also vocabulary) exam (known as round 1) and then spell live on stage (round 2). Rules have been known to change every few years. For instance, in 2013 and 2014, a written/computerized test was administered twice (in rounds 1 and 4). Based on the combined scores of the youths from those two rounds, some advance, while half to two-thirds do not. As of 2017, finalists again take a twelve-word written spelling and vocabulary test, which is used to break possible ties (Katz 2017).

87 Homeschool associations, groups, and co-ops follow the same procedures as other public, private, and charter schools.

88 In fact, school participation may be dropping in some areas. Jennifer, the longtime organizer of a Boston area spelling bee, recounted the difficulty of maintaining school commitment:

> So it was like seventy-five schools that were participating in ours. And then once Scripps started charging the schools, not just the sponsors, we dropped down to around fifty. And then by the last year I did it, I think we were down to thirty-four.

89 Brown 2019.

90 There was an increase in attendees from the 1970s to 1990, and participation again jumped up when it began being broadcast on ABC from 2006 to 2010 and then on ESPN primetime 2011 to the present. About two-thirds of contestants come from public schools, about a quarter from private or parochial schools, and about 5 percent are homeschooled. They vie for the championship cash prize of $40,000, plus more in savings bonds and books.

91 Additionally, if parents decide not to book their stay at the bee's official hotel, they must pay a $600 nonparticipation fee to the Scripps National Spelling Bee.

92 Scripps n.d., "Scripps National Spelling Bee Introduces Changes"; Scripps n.d., "RSVBee"; Scripps n.d., "Frequently Asked Questions."

93 The RSVBee route may grow in popularity for Scripps because corporate sponsorship, such as through newspapers, is harder to come by. Scripps is partnering with major media conglomerates such as Comcast. Comcast spelling bee sponsorships are rising across the country. According to Jennifer, newspapers—once the main sponsors of spellers—are doing so less and less. She recounted her conversation with Scripps about the challenge of finding a sponsor:

> I can't find a newspaper who's willing to sponsor this anymore; they said that they had just started to accept nonnewspaper partners. Comcast actually is the sponsor across the country, you know. There's still a lot of newspapers who sponsor them, or newspaper groups, but I noticed Comcast is, you know, scattered around the country representing, sponsoring.

Local newspapers in Portland, Oregon, Walpole, Massachusetts, and Canton, Massachusetts, for example, partner with Comcast to put on their bees.

A typical local spelling bee program costs about $5,000 a year for the sponsor, which includes recruiting pronouncers and judges, securing a location for the bee, flight and accommodations for the champion speller and one adult to go to the finals, and more. It is no wonder that struggling industries are teaming up with others to find ways to pay.

94 For example, Stuti Mishra, the 2012 Scripps runner-up, hosted a webpage with videos on how to deconstruct words from various language origins (Saturdays with Stuti 2016). See also Hyman 2013.

95 Shapira 2017.

96 Study books for academic competitions have become a business in and of itself. Individuals have quit their jobs and started businesses catering to youths preparing for competitions. They offer materials for purchase, such as books with Greek origin words commonly used in spelling bees: "GeoSpell Greek," n.d.; "GeoSpell Core: Spelling Bee Words," n.d.; Frost n.d.; Iyer n.d.

97 Hexco n.d., "How Do I Get Past?"

98 Hexco n.d., "Spelling Coach."

99 Hexco n.d., "Spelling Coach."

100 For example, The Art of Problem Solving specializes in study aids for math competitions.

101 For instance, Kelly Haven, a member of the Navajo nation living in Arizona, felt significant dissonance between herself and other youths at the Scripps bee even without accounting for private supplements. "Schools here are very different from schools out there," Kelly said. "Their schools, they have more money. So they can invest in art classes, music classes—stuff like that. We don't have that here. We just have regular classes" (Janetsky 2018).

102 Parents recognized and appreciated these results. Indian-only spaces suggested to parents that their children would compete against top-quality peers. Anjali, a mother of a speller, said,

Just given the legacy that is with we and the Asian kids and everything, you know, we know that we will be competing with the best that are out there, and that matters a lot.

103 Kulkarni 2017.

104 North South Foundation n.d.

105 India Herald 2017.

106 While one must have a parent of Indian heritage or a parent holding an Indian passport (or Person of Indian Origin card) to qualify for NSF, a parent or grandparent can be of any South Asian origin for SASB. While other South Asians have participated, it is practically only Indians who make it to the finals. Like Scripps (and unlike NSF), it has a for-profit wing attached.

107 He organizes interviews with the contestants during the day of the finals, which takes place in the evening and then air on the Sony Entertainment Television Asia network as teasers for the competition, which itself airs typically in October (three months after the competition is performed live) in more than 120 countries.

108 Davé 2016.
109 Field notes, New Jersey, August 16, 2013.
110 Dinces 2011.

CHAPTER 3. "YOU'VE GOT TO SURVIVE IN THIS WORLD"
1 Sharma 2012.
2 Najar 2011.
3 Friedman 2013; Lareau 2003; Rosenfeld and Wise 2010.
4 Anderson, Funk, Elliott, and Smith 2003; Bodovski and Farkas 2008; Bourdieu and Passeron 1990; Dunn, Kinney, and Hofferth 2003; Friedman 2013; Lareau 2003; Putnam 2015; White and Gager 2007.
5 Akos 2006.
6 Houlihan and Green 2010.
7 See Dhingra 2019 for an elaboration on this point. Also see Hirschman and Wong 1986; Lee and Zhou 2015; Lung-Amam 2017; Xie and Goyette 2003.
8 Laughlin 2014.
9 Fejgin 1994.
10 Kimball, Smith, and Quartz 2013.
11 Sinha 1995.
12 Kao 2000; Thangaraj 2015.
13 In recent years, the cap on H-1B visas, which is commonly used by Indian immigrants, has been reached within days of the start date (Jordan 2016).
14 Washington and Karen 2001, 191.
15 Messner and Musto 2016.
16 Holt et al. 2008; Levey 2009.
17 Field notes, Durham, NC, August 18, 2013.
18 This is an example of biopolitics, of the shaping of people's bodies to conform to expectations of the neoliberal state, where the accumulation of skills becomes required for lifelong productivity (Foucault 2008).
19 See also Lan 2018.
20 Sue and Okazaki 1990.
21 For instance, the organization The Indus Entrepreneurs (TIE), now with over 2,500 chapters worldwide, was started by and for Indian immigrants in information technology to find networks among themselves in part because of a lack of other forms of social capital.
22 Dhingra 2007.
23 Poros 2010.
24 Dhingra 2012; Subramanian 2000.
25 Raleigh and Kao 2010.
26 Goyette and Xie, 1999; Hirschman and Wong 1986; Schneider and Lee 1990; Sue and Okazaki 1990.
27 Espenshade and Radford 2009; Iyer 2017; Poon 2014.
28 Lan 2018. But see Park 2018; Jaschik 2017; and Nimetz 2017.
29 Lan 2018.
30 It is similar to other lawsuits filed against other Ivy League institutions. See Fuchs 2016; Belkin 2016. For more, see Woo 2012.

31 Biskupic 2018; Hartocollis 2018. The lawsuit is ultimately less about eradicating anti-Asian bias and instead more about barring affirmative action and any attention to race in college admissions.

32 Wu 2003.

33 Gersen 2019.

34 Okihiro 1994.

35 The critique of college admissions' possibly racist protocols is intended to have the school open up more to Asian Americans and does not necessarily lead to a critique of affirmative action, as alleged by conservative activists like Edward Blum.

36 Wu 2018. Parents can have concerns over a higher standard while still supporting affirmative action (Ramakrishnan and Wong 2018).

37 Golden 2017.

38 Feliciano 2005; Lee and Zhou 2015; but see Kasinitz 2016.

39 Verma and Gupta 1990.

40 Cram schools are taken for granted as an ethnic ploy to achieve academically. As Vivian Louie (2004) also finds, educational achievement has become synonymous with Asian America, so much so that Asian Americans who do not achieve as highly as they perceive other Asian Americans to be achieving can disidentify with their ethnic group (i.e., they believe they are not really Asian unless they do well in school). Cram and ethnic language schools provide a context within which people are around their coethnics and support their commitment to education. While noted as important, more scholarship should focus on these cram schools (Shrake 2010), as the understanding of these cram schools in the United States remains limited.

41 To date, Indian education has focused predominantly on engineering and other sciences. According to a British Council report, "Over the last decade, the diversity of courses offered by universities and colleges has narrowed, resulting in saturated markets for engineers, technology graduates and MBAs" (British Council 2014, 16), See also Dundes, Cho, and Kwak 2009.

42 Private liberal arts colleges have been established in India in recent years as a corrective to the STEM higher education opportunities to date. Dhawan et al. 2016; Saraswathy 2014.

43 Eckstein and Peri 2018; Asian Americans Advancing Justice Los Angeles 2014; Bahattacharjee 2018.

44 Connley 2018.

45 Ramakrishanan et al. 2017.

46 Evidence supports these parents' perspective that children can develop skills in math with effort and an open mindset rather than thinking that some children are good at math and others are not (Dweck 2008).

47 Kao 2000.

48 Smith 2012.

49 Vincent et al. 2013.

50 Portes and Rumbaut 2006.

51 Bonilla-Silva 2004.

52 They evince a minority culture of mobility—that is, a particular pathway to mobility designed to maneuver through relevant institutions based on their

types of capital and constraints as ethnic minorities (Neckerman, Carter, and Lee 1999). The white middle class is not the only middle-class group for minorities to integrate into or not. Depending on one's geographic location, immigrants can model themselves after (or distinguish themselves from) the black middle class (Clerge 2019).

53 Lacy 2007.
54 Waldinger and Feliciano 2010.

## CHAPTER 4. "HYPER EDUCATION DOES SOMETHING FOR YOU ON MORAL GROUNDS"

1 Elliot 2012.
2 Raj and Silverman 2007. While there is a low rate of teenage pregnancy among Chinese and Indian Americans (Kim 2001), that should not be read as indicating a more sober lifestyle or a lack of premarital sex. Abortion among Asian Americans is not uncommon.
3 Das Gupta 2006; Espiritu 2003; Purkayastha 2005.
4 Kasinitz et al. 2008; Portes and Zhou 1993. Some give back to their ethnic group (Vallejo 2012).
5 Friedman 2013.
6 Lan 2018.
7 Aurini and Davies 2004.
8 Read 2009.
9 Wallace 2015; Taylor and Rich 2015.
10 Apple 2004; Kozol 1991.
11 Koshy 2013.
12 A latent function of involvement in these spaces was the affirmation of social ties (Vincent and Maxwell 2016).
13 Alexander and Smith 2001.
14 Frye 2012.
15 Gibson 1988; Portes and Zhou 1993.
16 Waters 1999.
17 Anderson 1999; Newman 1999; Small 2002.
18 Kibria 2002.
19 Imoagene (2017) explains how well-educated Nigerian immigrants adapt when living next to African Americans rather than whites.
20 Portes, Fernandez-Kelly, and Haller 2005; Waters 1999.
21 Jimenez 2017; Ogbu 2003.
22 Bell and Hartmann 2007.
23 Levine and Stark 2015.

## CHAPTER 5. "WHITES ARE LAZY, ASIANS ARE CRAZY"

1 Swartz, Manning, and Gulya 2016.
2 Park et al. 2016.
3 Jimenez 2017.
4 Davies 2004.
5 Davidson 2011.
6 Sherman 2017.

7 Vincent and Ball 2007.

8 Lewis and Diamond 2015.

9 Bombardieri 2005.

10 Kalleberg 2009.

11 Byun and Park 2012; Heinrich, Meyer, and Whitten 2010; Chatterji, Kwon, and Sng 2006.

12 Friedman 2013.

13 Honoré 2010; Nelson 2010; Senior 2014.

14 While common among middle-class parents, both white and black working-class parents also engage in some elements of the same (Lareau 2003; Chin and Phillips 2004; Rosier and Corsaro 1993).

15 Jimenez 2017.

16 Brantlinger 2003.

17 Pugh 2009.

18 Considine 2011.

19 Actually, in 2018, about half of the Boston public school system's thirty-six valedictorians attended the region's schools from kindergarten onward, and under half (42 percent) were born outside the United States. SAMPAN 2018.

20 Friedman 2013.

21 Bourdieu and Passeron 1990.

22 Alexander and Smith 2001; Francis and Archer 2005; Frye 2012; Kaufman and Gabler 2004; Vaisey 2010.

23 Lamont 1992.

24 Sherman 2017; Swalwell 2013.

25 Khan 2011; Gaztambide-Fernández and Howard 2013.

26 Jimenez 2017.

27 Doane and Bonilla-Silva 2003.

28 Carter 2005.

29 Kefalas 2003; Lamont 2000.

30 The fact that parents criticize other whites in the vein of antiblackness demonstrates that cultural notions can travel and be applied to new groups when perceived as threats (Alexander 2006).

31 Okihiro 1994.

32 See also Williams 2006.

33 Hansen 2004.

34 Cooper 2014.

## CHAPTER 6. "EVERYONE IN THE FAMILY WAS INVOLVED"

1 Rega and Weller 2018.

2 Having American-raised relatives pronounce words was much more desirable, for spellers often did not trust the pronunciations of their immigrant parents.

3 Park et al. 2011.

4 Lareau 2003.

5 UT Dallas 2018.

6 Patel 2014.

7 Rajesh Kadakia, the Indian American father most profiled in the documentary *Spellbound*, is seen dedicating significant time and mental energy to help his

son advance in the spelling bee. He is portrayed as the driver of the competition, much more so than Darshana Kadakia, his wife, who assists in supportive and domestic ways.

8 Sayer, Bianchi, and Robinson 2004.

9 For example, parents lined up at the 2012 North South Foundation to meet and snap photos with Kavya Shivashankar. Parents also took photos with Sriram Hathwar at the South Asian Spelling Bee regional in Boston when he was there to support his younger brother. Gokul Venkatachalam and Sriram shook the hands of many youths and parents at the South Asian Spelling Bee 2015 finals.

10 Hao and Woo 2012; Kao and Tienda 1995; Raleigh and Kao 2010; Tran and Valdez 2017.

11 Lew 2006; Okazaki and Lim 2011; Peng and Wright 1994; Sy and Schulenberg 2005.

12 Lareau and Shumar 1996; Mau 1997.

13 Goyette and Xie 1999; Kasinitz et al. 2008.

14 Drummond and Stipek 2004.

15 Barnard 2004; Fan and Chen 2001; Feuerstein 2000.

16 Koshy 2013.

17 Hartas 2014; Schlee, Mullis, and Shriner 2009; Washbrook et al. 2012.

18 Goyette and Xie 1999; Louie 2004.

19 Caldas 1993; Caldas and Bankston 1997. Those with limited incomes who achieve well in school often have access to community resources, such as low-cost extracurricular education. See Lee and Zhou 2015.

20 Shapira 2017.

21 Bodovski and Farkas 2008.

22 As reported in CNN,

> In Fresno, California, Jayakrishnan, spends four to five hours a week with his daughter. They spell out words and he puts her through mock contests. Sometimes, his daughter protests.
>
> "How will spelling help me?" she asks. "I have a spell checker on my computer." "It's for your benefit," Jayakrishnan tells her. (Basu 2015)

23 Haytko and Baker 2004.

24 Lan 2018.

25 For more on the importance of empathy in children, see Borba 2016.

26 Critics argue that this major change was made to limit South Asian Americans' success in the written round based on the stereotype that South Asians just memorize spellings but do not care about the meaning of the words. Still, South Asian American dominance has continued.

27 Dhingra 2016.

28 Shankar 2016.

29 Shankar 2019.

30 Friedman 2013.

31 Guo 2006.

32 Fine 2001.

33 For instance, kids pound and battle with the MATHCOUNTS long balloons after the finals competition is over.

## CHAPTER 7. "I HAVE NO TIME FOR HATERS"

1 For more examples, see MacPherson 2015.

2 Heim 2015; Pandya 2017; Shankar 2019.

3 Eaton 2017.

4 There was much consternation that all-white teams would compete against racially integrated teams and even might lose to African Americans. After this transpired, the superintendent of the New Orleans school banned New Orleans students who had participated in the bee from competing in any more academic competitions in the North. In the words of a New Orleans clergyman, "The 'intense feeling' can be explained on one ground only: the Negro girl's victory was an affront to the tradition of Negro inferiority" (Greenlee 2017).

5 For instance, they participated in "separate but equal" bees with no pathway to the finals. In 2013, vocabulary questions were added to the preliminary rounds, a move considered by some as a way to limit the number of Indian American finalists, who presumably focus only on spelling. But the bee's executive director, Paige Kimble, says the change in procedure is one that helps reinforce the Bee's educational purpose (Wood 2018).

6 Lee 2009.

7 LIVE Kelly and Ryan 2018.

8 Basu 2015.

9 Gray 2015; MSN 2015.

10 Payne 2015. He later received from James a pair of his namesake sneakers, along with other items.

11 Curtis 2016. He later was invited to the Dallas Cowboys practice facility, where he met his sports hero and others (Mandell 2016).

12 Milner 2013; Pascoe 2007.

13 Immigrants' acceptance and even ability to immigrate depend on being perceived as fitting into standard family practices (Shah 2012).

14 Link and Phelan 2001.

15 While nerds have been normally associated with whiteness (Bucholtz 2001), current online and in-person settings, such as Comic-con, "Nerds of Color," and the like, have provided more diverse, self-described geek interest groups. See also Kendall 1999; and Tocci 2009.

16 Young 2014.

17 Maguire 2006.

18 Henkin et al. 2008.

19 Adler, Kless, and Adler 1992; Bishop 1999; Frost 2003; Link and Phelan 2001; Pandya 2017; Swiatek 2001.

20 Quail 2011.

21 At a South Asian Spelling Bee finals in 2016, the MC of the event interviewed a random selection of participants. He joked with the youths after a few of them listed reading as their favorite hobby to try to pick something else as a favorite pastime, which they all struggled to do.

22 Manor-Bullock, Look, and Dixon 1995.

23 King 2013; Sikh Coalition 2014.

24 Nakamura 2009.

25 These anecdotes are not surprising. How youths of color experience stigma at school varies by race. African Americans and Latinxs are criticized by teachers but earn respect from peers; Asian American students are criticized by peers but often earn respect from teachers. Ochoa 2013; Warikoo 2011.

26 Warikoo 2011.

27 Brown and Steinberg 1990.

28 For instance, a teacher in the documentary *Spellbound* says she has never had a problem with an Indian American student, again conflating ethnicity and academic performance and indicating that youths are read in racialized ways. See also Feng 1994.

29 Lamont et al. 2016.

30 Swiatek 2001.

31 Pugh 2009.

32 This is the same tactic used by gifted students hoping to avoid alienation. Coleman and Cross 1988.

33 Brown and Steinberg 1990; Goffman 1963; LeBel 2008.

34 Kinney 1993.

35 The documentary *Breaking the Bee* reveals other interests too.

36 The audience in the room applauded this remark. Field notes, New Jersey, August 15, 2013.

37 Individuals bring together contrasting identities in their daily activities and articulations, such as what they eat at work, how they decorate their houses, and more. I refer to this as a "lived hybridity." In the case of hyper education, youths created a lived hybridity by conceptualizing competitive academics as akin to sporting events, making themselves similar to athletes rather than to unmasculine geeks. See Dhingra 2007 for more.

38 Attempts to make "geeks" cool often resort to relying on how geeks can fit gender profiles, with men trying to appear very masculine and women trying to appear very feminine. See Kendall 2011.

39 The broadcast on ESPN has pushed the finals to later in the evening and possibly changed the spectacle in less obvious ways. At the 2012 finals, a father of a former Scripps champion whose second child was competing in the finals said that he thought the words in the semifinals round were much tougher than usual, and in the finals they would probably pick easier words because "they'll need to fill out two hours of primetime ESPN coverage."

40 Dhingra 2016.

41 TV by the Numbers 2012.

42 TV by the Numbers 2014.

43 Based on observations, 2015. See also MATHCOUNTS Foundation 2012.

44 Blair 2013.

45 Louie 2004.

46 Chavez 2013.

47 Manor-Bullock et al. 1995; Newman 1999; Young 2014.

48 It is common for maligned groups to seek out a sense of community in order to feel normal. See Delano Robertson 2014.

49 Espiritu 2003; Lamont et al. 2016.

50 Wimmer 2008.

51 Cornell 1988.

52 Kusow 2004.

53 Louie 2004.

54 Mizrachi and Zawdu 2012.

55 Neckerman et al. 1999; Portes and Zhou 1993; Zhou and Bankston 1998.

## CONCLUSION: WHAT NEEDS TO CHANGE

1 Fetters 2019; Nuckols 2019.

2 Apple 2004; Kozol 1991; Putnam 2015.

3 Jimenez 2017.

4 Friedman 2013.

5 Owens 2016.

6 Putnam 2015.

7 Smith 2019.

8 Media Matters 2019.

9 Adams 1995; Slivka 2011.

10 Moll and Ruiz 2008.

11 Ispa-Landa and Conwell 2015; Lewis 2003.

12 Ng 2002.

13 Ferguson 2004.

14 Reddy 2011.

15 Keisch and Scott. 2015.

16 Ferguson 2010; Wun 2016.

17 Druckerman 2014; Honoré 2010; Lythcott-Haims 2015; Skenazy 2009.

18 Conry 2016; Goddard 2015; Belkin 2009.

19 Pizmony-Levy 2019.

20 Goltsman et al. 2009.

21 Land 2016; Calarco 2018b. For instance, when their children are seen alone, affluent white families often receive the benefit of the doubt rather than being assumed to be negligent parents.

22 Atlantic 2018.

23 Kadvany 2015; Rosenberg 2004; Spencer 2015.

24 Forestieri 2017; Spencer 2017.

25 McCarty 2002.

26 Goodyear-Ka'opua 2013.

27 Darder, Baltodano, and Torres 2003; Grande 2015; Maynard and Weinstein 2019.

28 Ripp 2014.

29 Poth 2019.

30 Lenz 2016.

31 Lacy 2007; Neckerman, Carter, and Lee 1999.

32 Vargas 2018.

33 Warikoo 2011.

34 Rios 2011.

35 Hassrick et al. 2017.

36 Dhingra 2019.

37 Fine 2001.

## APPENDIX: RESEARCH DESIGN AND METHODS

1 US Census Bureau n.d., "State and County QuickFacts."
2 Moretti 2012.
3 Shah 2012.
4 Cousin, Shamus, and Mears 2018.

# BIBLIOGRAPHY

Abeles, Vicki. 2016, January 2. "Is the Drive for Success Making Our Children Sick?" *New York Times*. Retrieved from www.nytimes.com.

Abeles, Vicki, and Grace Rubinstein. 2015. *Beyond Measure: Rescuing an Overscheduled, Overtested, Underestimated Generation*. New York: Simon & Schuster.

Adams, David Wallace. 1995. *Education for Extinction: American Indians and the Boarding School Experience, 1875–1928*. Lawrence: University Press of Kansas.

Adler, Patricia, Steven J. Kless, and Peter Adler. 1992. "Socialization to Gender Roles: Popularity among Elementary School Boys and Girls." *Sociology of Education*, 65, 3: 169–87.

Akos, Patrick. 2006. "Extracurricular Participation and the Transition to Middle School." *RMLE Online*, 29, 9: 1–9.

Alba, Richard D., and Victor Nee. 2003. *Remaking the American Mainstream: Assimilation and Contemporary Immigration*. Cambridge, MA: Harvard University Press.

Alcazar, Alvaro. 2006. "The Challenge of Education in the Empire." *Humanity and Society*, 30, 2: 180–92.

Alexander, J., and P. Smith. 2001. "The Strong Program in Cultural Sociology: Elements of a Structural Hermeneutics." Pp. 11–26 in *The Meanings of Social Life: A Cultural Sociology* by Jeffrey C. Alexander. Oxford: Oxford University Press.

Alexander, Jeffrey. 2006. *The Civil Sphere*. Oxford: Oxford University Press.

Alvarez, Doris, and Hugh Mehan. 2006. "Whole School Detracking: A Strategy for Equity and Excellence." *Theory into Practice*, 45, 1: 82–89.

Ambrosio, John. 2013. "Changing the Subject: Neoliberalism and Accountability in Public Education." *Educational Studies*, 49, 4: 316–33.

Anderson, Elijah. 1999. *Code of the Street: Decency, Violence, and the Moral Life of the Inner City*. New York: W. W. Norton.

Anderson, Jennifer, Jeanne Funk, Robert Elliott, and Peg Hull Smith. 2003. "Parental Support and Pressure and Children's Extracurricular Activities: Relationships with Amount of Involvement and Affective Experience of Participation." *Journal of Applied Developmental Psychology*, 24, 2: 241–57.

Anderson, Jenny. 2016, November 4. "A New Study Shows That the Gender Gap in Math Abilities Starts Early—and Teacher Bias Makes It Worse as Time Goes On." *Quartz*. Retrieved from www.qz.com.

Viramontez Anguiano, Ruben P. 2004. "Families and Schools: The Effect of Parental Involvement on High School Completion." *Journal of Family Issues*, 25, 1: 61–85.

Apple, Michael W. 2004. *Ideology and Curriculum*. 3rd ed. New York: Routledge.

———. 2007. "Whose Markets, Whose Knowledge?" Pp. 177–93 in *Sociology of Education: A Critical Reader*, 3rd ed. Alan R. Sadovnik and Ryan W. Coughlan (eds.). New York: Routledge.

Archambault, Francis X., Karen L. Westberg, Scott W. Brown, Bryan W. Hallmark, Wanli Zhang, and Christine L. Emmons. 1993. "Classroom Practices Used with Gifted Third and Fourth Grade Students." *Journal for the Education of the Gifted*, 16, 2 (January): 103–19.

Asian Americans Advancing Justice Los Angeles. 2014. "Making America Work: Asian Americans, Native Hawaiians, and Pacific Islanders in the Workforce and Business 2014." *Asian Americans Advancing Justice Los Angeles*. Retrieved from www.advancingjustice-la.org.

ASU GSV X. n.d. "Bending the Arc of Human Potential." *ASU GSV X*. Retrieved from www.asugsvsummit.com.

Atlantic. 2018, April 12. "Letters: Legalizing 'Free-Range' Parenting Is a Step in the Right Direction." *Atlantic*. Retrieved from www.theatlantic.com/.

Au, Wayne. 2011. "Teaching under the New Taylorism: High-Stakes Testing and the Standardization of the 21st Century Curriculum." *Journal of Curriculum Studies*, 43, 1: 25–45.

———. 2018. *A Marxist Education: Learning to Change the World*. Chicago: Haymarket Books.

Aurini, Janice, and Scott Davies. 2004. "The Transformation of Private Tutoring: Education in a Franchise Form." *Canadian Journal of Sociology*, 29, 3: 419–38.

Aurini, Janice, Scott Davies, and Julian Dierkes, eds. 2013. *Out of the Shadows: The Global Intensification of Supplementary Education*. Bingley, UK: Emerald Group.

Bahattacharjee, Yudhijit. 2018. "How South Asian Americans Are Building a New American Dream." *National Geographic Magazine*, September 2018. Retrieved from www.nationalgeographic.com.

Bainbridge, Carol. 2018, September 26. "Should You Hothouse Your Child?" *Very Well Family*. Retrieved from www.verywellfamily.com.

Baker, David. 2009. "The Educational Transformation of Work: Towards a New Synthesis." *Journal of Education and Work*, 22, 3: 163–91.

Baker, David, and Gerald K. LeTendre. 2005. *National Differences, Global Similarities: World Culture and the Future of Schooling*. Stanford, CA: Stanford Social Sciences.

Baker, David P., Gerald K. Motoko Akiba, Alexander W. LeTendre, and Alexander W. Wiseman. 2001. "Worldwide Shadow Education: Outside-School Learning, Institutional Quality of Schooling, and Cross-National Mathematics Achievement." *Educational Evaluation and Policy Analysis*, 23, 1: 1–17.

Ball, Stephen J., Carol Vincent, David Gillborn, and Nicola Rollock. 2014. *The Colour of Class: The Educational Strategies of the Black Middle Classes*. London: Routledge.

Barnard, Wendy Miedel. 2004. "Parent Involvement in Elementary School and Educational Attainment." *Children and Youth Services Review*, 26, 1: 39–62.

Bascara, Victor. 2006. *Model-Minority Imperialism*. Minneapolis: University of Minnesota Press.

Basu, Moni. 2015. "Why Indian-Americans Win Spelling Bees: P-R-A-C-T-I-C-E." *CNN*, June 3, 2015. Retrieved from www.cnn.com.

Baumann, Gerd. 1996. *Contesting Culture: Discourses of Identity in Multi-ethnic London*. Cambridge: Cambridge University Press.

Bedor, Deborah. 2015. *Getting in by Standing OUT: The New Rules for Admission to America's Best Colleges*. Charleston, SC: Advantage Media Group.

Belkin, Douglas. 2016. "Asian-American Groups Seek Investigation into Ivy League Admissions." *Wall Street Journal*, May 23, 2016. Retrieved from www.wsj.com.

Belkin, Lisa. 2009, April 8. "What Is Slow-Parenting?" *New York Times*. Retrieved from https://parenting.blogs.nytimes.com.

Bell, Joyce, and Douglas Hartmann. 2007. "Diversity in Everyday Discourse: The Cultural Ambiguities and Consequences of 'Happy Talk.'" *American Sociological Review*, 72, 6: 895–914.

Berliner, David, and Bruce Biddle. 1995. *The Manufactured Crisis: Myths, Fraud, and the Attack on America's Public Schools*. New York: Perseus Books.

Bernstein, Melissa. 2016. "Children, Screens, and Why It's Time to Take Back Childhood." *TODAY Parenting Team*, October 22, 2016. Retrieved from https://community.today.com.

Bethune, Sophie. 2014, January 11. "American Psychological Association Survey Shows Teen Stress Rivals That of Adults." *American Psychological Association*. Retrieved from www.apa.org.

Binkley, Sam, and Jorge Capetillo, eds. 2009. *A Foucault for the 21st Century: Governmentality, Biopolitics and Discipline in the New Millennium*. Cambridge, UK: Cambridge Scholars.

Bishop, John H. 1999. "Nerd Harassment, Incentives, School Priorities and Learning." Pp. 231–79 in *Earning and Learning: How Schools Matter*, edited by Susan E. Mayer and Paul E. Peterson. Washington, DC: Brookings Institution Press.

Biskupic, Joan. 2018. "Lawsuit: Harvard Ranks Asian-Americans Lower on Personality Traits." *CNN News*, July 3, 2018. Retrieved from www.cnn.com.

Blair, Elizabeth. 2013, July 18. "Comedian Hari Kondabolu on Diversity, Race and Burger King." *National Public Radio*. Retrieved from www.npr.org.

Blue Oeur, Freeden. 2018. *Black Boys Apart: Racial Uplift and Respectability in All-Male Public Schools*. Minneapolis: University of Minnesota Press.

Bodovski, K., and G. Farkas. 2008. "'Concerted Cultivation' and Unequal Achievement in Elementary School." *Social Science Research*, 37, 3: 903–19.

Bombardieri, Marcella. 2005, January 17. "Summers' Remarks on Women Draw Fire." *Boston Globe*. Retrieved from http://archive.boston.com.

Bondy, Jennifer M. 2011. "Normalizing English Language Learner Students: A Foucauldian Analysis of Opposition to Bilingual Education." *Race, Ethnicity and Education*, 14, 3: 387–98.

Bonilla-Silva, Eduardo. 2003. *Racism without Racists: Color-Blind Racism and the Persistence of Racial Inequality in the United States*. Lanham, MD: Rowman & Littlefield.

——. 2004. "From Bi-racial to Tri-racial: Towards a New System of Racial Stratification in the USA." *Ethnic and Racial Studies* 27, 6: 931–50.

Borba, Michele. 2016. *UnSelfie: Why Empathetic Kids Succeed in Our All-about-Me World*. New York: Touchstone.

Boschma, Janie, and Ronald Brownstein. 2016, February 29. "The Concentration of Poverty in American Schools." *Atlantic*. Retrieved from www.theatlantic.com.

Boser, Ulrich, and Lindsay Rosenthal. 2012, July 10. "Do Schools Challenge Our Students?" *Center for American Progress*. Retrieved from www.americanprogress.org.

Bourdieu, Pierre, and J. C. Passeron. 1990. *Reproduction in Education, Society and Culture*. New York: Sage.

Bowles, Samuel, and Herbert Gintis. 2011. *Schooling in Capitalist America: Educational Reform and the Contradictions of Economic Life*. New York: Haymarket Books.

Brand, David. 1987, August 31. "Education: The New Whiz Kids." *Time*. Retrieved from www.time.com.

Brantlinger, Ellen. 2003. *Dividing Classes: How the Middle Class Negotiates and Rationalizes School Advantage*. New York: Routledge.

Bray, Mark. 1999. "The Shadow Education System: Private Tutoring and Its Implications for Planners." *Fundamentals of Educational Planning Series*, no. 61.

———. 2003. "Comparative Education in the Era of Globalisation: Evolution, Missions and Roles." *Policy Futures in Education*, 1, 2: 209–24.

Bray, Mark, and C. Lykins. 2012. *Shadow Education: Private Supplementary Tutoring and Its Implications for Policy Makers in Asia*, no. 9. Manila, Philippines: Asian Development Bank.

Brettell, Caroline, and Faith Nibbs. 2009. "Lived Hybridity: Second-Generation Identity Construction through College Festival." *Identities: Global Studies in Culture and Power*, 16, 6: 678–99.

British Council. 2014, February. "Understanding India: The Future of Higher Education and Kwak 2009. Opportunities for International Cooperation." *British Council*. Retrieved from www.britishcouncil.org.

Brown, Bradford, and Laurence Steinberg. 1990. "Academic Achievement and Social Acceptance." *Education Digest*, 55, 7: 57.

Brown, Emma. 2015, March 31. "Gifted Students—Especially Those Who Are Low-Income—Aren't Getting the Focus They Need." *Washington Post*. Retrieved from www.washingtonpost.com.

Brown, Oswald. 2019, April 29. "565 Spellers to Compete in the 2019 Scripps National Spelling Bee Competition." *Bahamas Chronicle*. Retrieved from https://bahamaschronicle.com.

Bucholtz, Mary. 2001. "The Whiteness of Nerds: Superstandard English and Racial Markedness." *Journal of Linguistic Anthropology*, 11, 1: 84–100.

Business Standard. 2017, January 9. "India's Largest Spelling Competition Is Back with Its 9th Season, Classmate Spell Bee Takes Indian Schools by Storm." *Business Standard*. Retrieved from www.business-standard.com.

BusinessWire. 2014, August 21. "Kumon Math & Reading Centers Expand into Reno Market." *BusinessWire*. Retrieved from www.businesswire.com.

Byrd, W. Carson. 2011. "Conflating Apples and Oranges: Understanding Modern Forms of Racism." *Sociology Compass*, 5, 11: 1005–17.

Byun, Soo-yong, and Hyunjoon Park. 2012. "The Academic Success of East Asian American Youth: The Role of Shadow Education." *Sociology of Education*, 85, 1: 40–60.

Calarco, Jessica McCrory. 2018a. *Negotiating Opportunities: How the Middle Class Secures Advantages in School*. New York: Oxford University Press.

———. 2018b, April 3. "'Free Range' Parenting's Unfair Double Standard." *Atlantic*. Retrieved from www.theatlantic.com.

Caldas, Stephen J. 1993. "Reexamination of Input and Process Factor Effects on Public School Achievement." *Journal of Educational Research*, 86, 4: 206–14.

Caldas, Stephen J., and Carl Bankston. 1997. "Effect of School Population Socioeconomic Status on Individual Academic Achievement." *Journal of Educational Research*, 90, 5: 269–77.

Campbell, James Reed. 1991. "The Roots of Gender Inequity in Technical Areas." *Journal of Research in Science Teaching*, 28, 3: 251–64.

Caplan, Bryan. 2018. *The Case against Education: Why the Education System Is a Waste of Time and Money*. Princeton: Princeton University Press.

Cardiel, Christopher Louis. 2012. "Are We Cool Yet? A Longitudinal Content Analysis of Nerd and Geek Representations in Popular Television." PDX Scholar *Dissertations and Theses*. Portland, OR: Portland State University.

Carnoy, Martin, Richard F. Elmore, and Leslie Santee Siskin. 2003. *The New Accountability: High School and High-Stakes Testing*. New York: RoutledgeFalmer.

Carter, Prudence L. 2005. *Keepin' It Real: School Success beyond Black and White*. New York: Oxford University Press.

Cha, Ariana Eunung. 2016, June 27. "Your Perfectionist Parenting Style May Be Detrimental to Your Child." *Washington Post*. Retrieved from https://washingtonpost.com.

Chait, Jonathan. 2014, July 8. "Teachers Unions Turn against Democrats." *New York Magazine*. Retrieved from www.nymag.com.

Chakrovarty, Sanjoy. 2016, May 30. "Why Do Indian-Americans Win Spelling Bee Contests?" *BBC News*. Retrieved from www.bbc.com.

Chao, Ruth K. 1994. "Beyond Parental Control and Authoritarian Parenting Style: Understanding Chinese Parenting through the Cultural Notion of Training." *Child Development*, 65, 4: 1111–19.

———. 1995. "Beyond Authoritarianism: A Cultural Perspective on Asian American Parenting Practices." Paper presented at the American Psychological Association Annual Meeting, New York.

Chatterji, Madhabi, Young Kwon, and Clarice Sng. 2006. "Gathering Evidence on an After-School Supplemental Instruction Program: Design Challenges and Early Findings in Light of NCLB." *Education Policy Analysis Archives* 14, 12: 1–47.

Chavez, Leo. 2013. *The Latino Threat: Constructing Immigrants, Citizens, and the Nation*. Stanford, CA: Stanford University Press.

Cheadle, Jacob E., and Paul R. Amato. 2011. "A Quantitative Assessment of Lareau's Qualitative Conclusions about Class, Race, and Parenting." *Journal of Family Issues*, 32, 5: 679–706.

Chin, Tiffani, and Meredith Phillips. 2004. "Social Reproduction and Child-Rearing Practices: Social Class, Children's Agency, and the Summer Activity Gap." *Sociology of Education*, 77, 3: 185–210.

Choi, Alvaro, Jorge Calero, and Josep-Oriol Escardibul. 2012. "Private Tutoring and Academic Achievement in Korea: An Approach through PISA-2006." *KEDI Journal of Educational Policy*, 9, 2: 299–322.

Choi, Yoonsun, You Seung Kim, Su Yeong Kim, and Irene J. K. Park. 2013. "Is Asian American Parenting Controlling and Harsh? Empirical Testing of Relationships between Korean American and Western Parenting Measures." *Asian American Journal of Psychology*, 4, 1: 19–29.

Chua, Amy. 2011. *Battle Hymn of the Tiger Mother*. London: Penguin Books.

Cision PR Newswire. 2016, June 17. "National PTA's New STEM Initiative." *Cision PR Newswire*. Retrieved from www.prnewswire.com.

Clerge, Orly. 2019. *The New Noir: Race, Identity, and Diaspora in Black Suburbia*. Berkeley: University of California Press.

Coleman, James S. 1961. *The Adolescent Society: The Social Life of the Teenager and Its Impact on Education*. New York: Free Press of Glencoe.

Coleman, Laurence, and Tracy Cross. 1988. "Is Being Gifted a Social Handicap?" *Journal for the Education of the Gifted*, 11, 4: 41–56.

CompareYourCountry. 2015. "United States." *PISA 2015*. Retrieved from www .compareyourcountry.org.

Connley, Courtney. 2018, October 11. "The 7 Fastest-Growing High-Paying Jobs Today." *CNBC*. Retrieved from www.cnbc.com.

Conry, Jaci. 2016, May 2. "The Benefits of Slow Parenting." *Boston Globe*. Retrieved from www.bostonglobe.com.

Considine, Austin. 2011, July 29. "For Asian-American Stars, Many Web Fans." *New York Times*. Retrieved from www.nytimes.com.

Cooper, Charlie. 2015, September 4. "Overly-Controlling Parents Cause Their Children Lifelong Psychological Damage, Says Study." *Independent*. Retrieved from www.independent.co.uk.

Cooper, Marianne. 2014. *Cut Adrift: Families in Insecure Times*. Berkeley: University of California Press.

Cornell, Stephen. 1988. *The Return of the Native: American Indian Political Resurgence*. Oxford: Oxford University Press.

Corsaro, William, and Donna Eder. 1990. "Children's Peer Cultures." *Annual Review of Sociology*, 16, 1: 197–220.

Cotter, David A., Joan M. Hermsen, Seth Ovadia, and Reeve Vanneman. 2001. "The Glass Ceiling Effect." *Social Forces*, 80, 2: 655–81.

Counseling@NYU. 2017. "Burdened with Worry: How the Pressure to Succeed Can Affect Asian American Students." September 25. Retrieved from https:// counseling.steinhardt.nyu.edu.

Cousin, Bruno, Shamus Khan, and Ashley Mears. 2018. "Theoretical and Methodological Pathways for Research on Elites." *Socio-Economic Review*, 16, 2: 225–49.

Cullotta, Karen Ann, Karen Berkowitz, Kimberly Fornek, and Suzanne Baker. 2017, November 13. "'No Worse Fate Than Failure': How Pressure to Keep Up Is Overwhelming Students in Elite Districts." *Chicago Tribune*. Retrieved from www .chicagotribune.com.

Curtis, Charles. 2016, May 27. "Dez Bryant Was Super Pumped When Spelling Bee Co-champ Did His 'X' Celebration." *USA Today*. Retrieved from https://ftw .usatoday.com.

Darder, Antonia, Marta Baltodano, and Rodolfo D. Torres. 2003. "Critical Pedagogy: An Introduction." Pp. 1–21 in *The Critical Pedagogy Reader*. New York: Psychology Press.

Darling-Hammond, Linda. 2015. *The Flat World and Education: How America's Commitment to Equity Will Determine Our Future*. New York: Teachers College Press.

Das Gupta, Monisha. 2006. *Unruly Immigrants: Rights, Activism, and Transnational South Asian Politics in the United States*. Durham, NC: Duke University Press.

Davé, Shilpa. 2016. "Winning the Bee: South Asians, Spelling Bee Competitions, and American Racial Branding." Pp. 228–43 in *Global Asian American Popular Cultures*, edited by Shilpa Davé, LeiLani Nishime, and Tasha Oren. New York: New York University Press.

Davidson, Alex. 2009, February 12. "Remedial Math." *Forbes*. Retrieved from www.forbes.com.

Davidson, Elsa. 2011. *The Burdens of Aspiration: Schools, Youth, and Success in the Divided Social Worlds of Silicon Valley*. New York: New York University Press.

Davies, Scott. 2004. "School Choice by Default? Understanding the Demand for Private Tutoring in Canada." *American Journal of Education*, 110, 3: 233–55.

Del Moral, Solsiree. 2013. *Negotiating Empire: The Cultural Politics of Schools in Puerto Rico, 1898–1952*. Madison: University of Wisconsin Press.

Delano Robertson, Venetia Laura. 2014. "Of Ponies and Men: *My Little Pony: Friendship Is Magic* and the Brony Fandom." *International Journal of Cultural Studies*, 17, 1: 21–37.

Desliver, Drew. 2014, September 30. "5 Facts about Indian Americans." *Pew Research Center*. Retrieved from www.pewresearch.org.

Dhawan, Ashish, Paramath Sinha, Vineet Gupta, and Sanjeev Bikhchandani. 2016, January 17. "Education: Renaissance of Liberal Arts Education in India." *Business Today*. Retrieved from www.businesstoday.in.

Dhingra, Pawan. 2007. *Managing Multicultural Lives: Asian American Professionals and the Challenge of Multiple Identities*. Palo Alto, CA: Stanford University Press.

———. 2012. *Life behind the Lobby: Indian American Motel Owners and the American Dream*. Palo Alto, CA: Stanford University Press.

———. 2016. "Indian Americans and the 'Brain Sport' of Spelling Bees." Pp. 127–51 in *Asian American Sporting Cultures*, edited by Thangaraj Stanley, Constancio Arnaldo, and Christina Chin. New York: New York University Press.

———. 2019, June 1. "The Scripps Spelling Bee Is Broken: Please Don't Fix It." *New York Times*. Retrieved from www.nytimes.com.

Lewis, Amanda and John Diamond. 2015. *Despite the Best Intentions: How Racial Inequality Thrives in Good Schools*. Oxford: Oxford University Press.

Dinces, Sean. 2011. "'Flexible Opposition': Skateboarding Subcultures under the Rubric of Late Capitalism." *International Journal of the History of Sport*, 28, 1: 1512–35.

Dintersmith, Ted. 2018. *What School Could Be: Insights and Inspiration from Teachers across America*. Princeton, NJ: Princeton University Press.

Doane, Ashley W., and Eduardo Bonilla-Silva, eds. 2003. *White Out: The Continuing Significance of Racism*. New York: Routledge.

Doerner, William R. 1985, July 8. "Asians to America with Skills." *Time*. Retrieved from www.time.com.

Dominguez, M. Melina, and John S. Carton. 1997. "The Relationship between Self-Actualization and Parenting Style." *Journal of Social Behavior and Personality*, 12, 4: 1093–100.

Dornbusch, Sanford M., Philip L. Ritter, P. Herbert Leiderman, Donald F. Roberts, and Michael J. Fraleigh. 1987. "The Relation of Parenting Style to Adolescent School Performance." *Child Development*, 58, 5: 1244–57.

Doyle, William. 2016, August 30. "Why Finland Is Rejecting U.S. School Reforms: Column." *USA Today*. Retrieved from www.usatoday.com.

Druckerman, Pamela. 2014. *Bringing Up Bébé: One American Mother Discovers the Wisdom of French Parenting*. New York: Penguin Press.

Drummond, Kathryn V., and Deborah Stipek. 2004. "Low-Income Parents' Beliefs about Their Role in Children's Academic Learning." *Elementary School Journal*, 104, 3: 197–213.

Duncombe, William, Anna Lukemeyer, and John Yinger. 2008. "The No Child Left Behind Act: Have Federal Funds Been Left Behind?" *Public Finance Review*, 36, 4: 381–407.

Dundes, Lauren, Eunice Cho, and Spencer Kwak. 2009. "The Duty to Succeed: Honor versus Happiness in College and Career Choices of East Asian Students in the United States." *Pastoral Care in Education*, 27, 2: 135–56.

Dunn, Janet, David Kinney, and Sandra Hofferth. 2003. "Parental Ideologies and Children's After-School Activities." *American Behavioral Scientist*, 46, 10: 1359–86.

Dwairy, Marwan, and Mustafa Achuoi. 2009. "Adolescents-Family Connectedness: A First Cross-Cultural Research on Parenting and Psychological Adjustment of Children." *Journal of Child and Family Studies*, 19, 1: 8–15.

Dweck, Carol S. 2008. "Mindsets and Math/Science Achievement." *Institute for Advanced Study Commission on Mathematics and Science Education*. Retrieved from www.growthmindsetmaths.com.

Eaton, Sabrina. 2017, May 30. "Cleveland Girl's Spelling Victory Created Racial Controversy, National Headlines in 1908." *Plain Dealer*. Retrieved from www.cleveland.com.

Eckstein, Susan, and Giovanni Peri. 2018. "Immigrant Niches and Immigrant Networks in the U.S. Labor Market." *RSF: The Russell Sage Foundation Journal of the Social Sciences*, 4, 1: 1–17.

Economist. 2019, January 3. "Why Children's Lives Have Changed Radically in Just a Few Decades." *Economist*. Retrieved from www.economist.com/special-report/2019/01/03/why-childrens-lives-have-changed-radically-in-just-a-few-decades.

Elliott, Sinikka. 2012. *Not My Kid: What Parents Believe about the Sex Lives of Their Teenagers*. New York: New York University Press.

Equity and Excellence Commission. 2013, February 2. "For Each and Every Child: A Strategy for Education, Equity, and Excellence." *Equity and Excellence Commission*. Retrieved from www2.ed.gov.

Ericson, John, and Debra Silverman. 2001, June. "Challenge and Opportunity: The Impact of Charter Schools on School Districts." *RPP International*. Retrieved from www2.ed.gov.

Espenshade, Thomas J., and Alexandria Walton Radford. 2009. *No Longer Separate, Not Yet Equal: Race and Class in Elite College Admission and Campus Life*. Princeton, NJ: Princeton University Press.

Espiritu, Yen Le. 2003. *Home Bound: Filipino American Lives across Cultures, Communities, and Countries*. Berkeley: University of California Press.

Estrada, Leobardo. 1981. "Chicanos in the United States: A History of Exploitation and Resistance." *Daedalus*, 110, 2: 103–31.

Faircloth, Charlotte, Diane M. Hoffman, and Linda L. Layne, eds. 2013. *Parenting in Global Perspective: Negotiating Ideologies of Kinship, Self and Politics*. New York: Routledge.

Fan, Xitao, and Michael Chen. 2001. "Parental Involvement and Students' Academic Achievement: A Meta-analysis." *Educational Psychology Review*, 13, 1: 1–22.

Farkas, Steve, and Ann Duffett. 2008, August 6. "Results from a National Teacher Survey." *Thomas B. Fordham Institute*. Retrieved from www.edexcellencemedia.net.

Feagin, Joe R., and Melvin P. Sikes. 1994. *Living with Racism: The Black Middle-Class Experience*. Boston: Beacon Press.

Fejgin, Naomi. 1994. "Participation in High School Competitive Sports: A Subversion of School Mission or Contribution to Academic Goals?" *Sociology of Sport Journal*, 11, 3: 211–30.

Feliciano, Cynthia. 2005. "Does Selective Migration Matter? Explaining Ethnic Disparities in Educational Attainment among Immigrants' Children." *International Migration Review*, 39, 4: 841–71.

Feng, Jianhua. 1994. "Asian-American Children: What Teachers Should Know." Urbana, IL: *ERIC Clearinghouse on Elementary and Early Childhood Education*.

Ferguson, Roderick. 2004. *Aberrations in Black: Toward a Queer of Color Critique*. Minneapolis: University of Minnesota Press.

Ferguson, Ronald. 2008. *Toward Excellence with Equity: An Emerging Vision for Closing the Achievement Gap*. Cambridge, MA: Harvard Education Press.

Fetters, Ashley. 2019, May 31. "The Youths Have Outsmarted the Scripps National Spelling Bee." *Atlantic*. Retrieved from www.theatlantic.com.

Feuerstein, Abe. 2000. "School Characteristics and Parent Involvement: Influences on Participation in Children's Schools." *Journal of Educational Research*, 94, 1: 29–40.

Fine, Gary. 2001. *Gifted Tongues: High School Debate and Adolescent Culture*. Princeton, NJ: Princeton University Press.

Finn, Chester E. 2014. "Gifted, Talented, and Underserved." *National Affairs*. Retrieved from www.nationalaffairs.com.

Flannery, Mary Ellen. 2018, March 28. "The Epidemic of Anxiety among Today's Students." *National Education Association Today*. Retrieved from www.neatoday.org.

Ford, Donna, Joy Baytops, and Deborah Harmon. 1997. "Helping Gifted Minority Students Reach Their Potential: Recommendations for Change." *Peabody Journal of Education*, 72, 3/4: 201–16.

Forestieri, Kevin. 2017, September 15. "Survey: Less Homework, Less Stress for MVLA Students." *Mountain New Voice*. Retrieved from https://mv-voice.com.

Foucault, Michel. 1978. *The History of Sexuality*. Vol. 1, *An Introduction*. New York: Vintage Books.

———. 2008. *The Birth of Biopolitics: Lectures at the Collège de France, 1978–1979*. Translated by Graham Burchell. New York: Palgrave Macmillan.

Franchise Direct. 2019. "Kumon Franchise Costs & Fees." *Franchise Direct*. Retrieved from www.franchisedirect.com.

Francis, B., and L. Archer. 2005. "British–Chinese Pupils' and Parents' Constructions of the Value of Education." *British Educational Research Journal*, 31, 1: 89–108.

Franck, Thomas M. 1997. "Is Personal Freedom a Western Value?" *American Journal of International Law*, 91, 4: 593–627.

Free-Range Friend. n.d. "Free-Range Friend." Retrieved from http://freerangefriend.com.

Friedman, Hillary. 2013. *Playing to Win: Raising Children in a Competitive Culture.* Berkeley: University of California Press.

Frost, Josh. n.d. "Practice Competitions for MATHCOUNTS." *Art of Problem Solving.* Retrieved from www.artofproblemsolving.com.

Frost, Liz. 2003. "Doing Bodies Differently? Gender, Youth, Appearance and Damage." *Journal of Youth Studies,* 6, 1: 53–70.

Frye, M. 2012. "Bright Futures in Malawi's New Dawn: Educational Aspirations as Assertions of Identity." *American Journal of Sociology,* 117, 6: 1565–624.

Fuchs, Chris. 2016, May 23. "Complaint Filed against Yale, Dartmouth, and Brown Alleging Discrimination." *NBC News.* Retrieved from www.nbcnews.com.

Gallagher, James J. 2002, June. "Society's Role in Educating Gifted Students: The Role of Public Policy." *National Research Center on the Gifted and Talented.* Retrieved from www.eric.ed.gov.

Galloway, Mollie, Denise Pope, and Jerusha Osberg. 2007. "Stressed-Out Students-SOS: Youth Perspectives on Changing School Climates." Pp. 611–34 in *International Handbook of Student Experience in Elementary and Secondary School,* edited by D. Thiessen and Alison Cook-Sather. Dordrecht, NL: Springer.

Gamoran, Adam. 1992. "The Variable Effects of High School Tracking." *American Sociological Review,* 57, 6: 812–28.

García, Jose. 2015. "Learning from Bad Teachers: The Neoliberal Agenda for Education in the Popular Media." *Critical Education,* 6, 13: 1–18.

Gardner, David. 1983. "A Nation at Risk: The Imperative for Educational Reform; A Report to the Nation and the Secretary of Education." United States Department of Education. Washington, DC: The Commission.

Gates, Bill. 2009, January. "Annual Letter 2009." *Bill & Melinda Gates Foundation.* Retrieved from www.gatesfoundation.org.

Gaztambide-Fernández, R. A., and A. Howard. 2013. "Social Justice, Deferred Complicity, and the Moral Plight of the Wealthy." *Democracy and Education,* 21, 1: 7.

GeoSpell. n.d. "GeoSpell Core: Spelling Bee Words." *GeoSpell Academy.* Retrieved from www.geospell.com.

———. n.d. "GeoSpell Greek." *GeoSpell Academy.* Retrieved from www.geospell.com.

Gersen, Jeannie Suk. 2019. "The Many Sins of College Admissions." *New Yorker,* October 7.

Gibson, M. 1988. *Accommodation without Assimilation: Sikh Immigrants in an American High School.* Ithaca, NY: Cornell University Press.

Gill-Peterson, Julian. 2015. "The Value of the Future: The Child as Human Capital and the Neoliberal Labor of Race." *WSQ: Women's Studies Quarterly,* 43, 1/2: 181–96.

Giroux, Henry A., 1983. *Theory and Resistance in Education: Towards a Pedagogy for the Opposition.* Westport, CT: Bergin & Garvey.

Glenn, Evelyn Nakano. 2009. *Unequal Freedom: How Race and Gender Shape American Citizenship and Labor.* Cambridge, MA: Harvard University Press.

Global Industry Analysts, Inc. 2016, October 5. "The Global Market for Private Tutoring Services Is Forecast to Reach US $227 Billion by 2022." *Global Industry Analysts, Inc.* Retrieved from www.strategyr.blogspot.com.

———. 2018, December. "Growing Role of Shadow Education in Helping Students Cope with Competition to Gain Admission into Elite Universities Drives Global

Growth of Private Tutoring Services." *Global Industry Analysts, Inc.* Retrieved from www.strategyr.com.

Global Silicon Valley. 2016, May 9. "ASU GSV Summit: K–12: The Math Revolution—Raising the Bar." *YouTube.* Retrieved from www.youtube.com.

Goddard, Joanna. 2015, May. "Trying Out Slow Parenting." *A Cup of Jo.* Retrieved from https://cupofjo.com.

Goffman, Erving. 1963. *Stigma: Notes on the Management of Spoiled Identity.* New York: Simon & Schuster.

Golann, Joanne W. 2015. "The Paradox of Success at a No-Excuses School." *Sociology of Education,* 88, 2: 103–19.

Goldberg, Carey. 2017, April 13. "Why Thousands of American Parents Are Sending Their Kids to 'Russian Math.'" *WBUR.* Retrieved from www.wbur.org.

Golden, Daniel. 2017. August 11. "Asian-Americans Are Indeed Treated Unfairly in Admissions, but the Culprit Is Not Affirmative Action." *Chicago Tribune.* Retrieved from www.chicagotribune.com.

Goleman, Daniel. 1990, September 11. "Probing School Success of Asian-Americans." *New York Times.* Retrieved from https://timesmachine.nytimes.com.

Goltsman, Susan, Laurel Kelly, Susan McKay, Patricia Algara, and Larry Wight. 2019. "Raising 'Free Range Kids': Creating Neighborhood Parks That Promote Environmental Stewardship." *Journal of Green Building,* 4, 2: 90–105.

Gonzales, Roberto. 2015. *Lives in Limbo: Undocumented and Coming of Age in America.* Berkeley: University of California Press.

Goodyear-Ka'opua, Noelani. 2013. *The Seeds We Planted: Portraits of a Native Hawaiian Charter School.* Minneapolis: University of Minnesota Press.

Gordon, Avery, and Christopher Newfield. 1996. *Mapping Multiculturalism.* Minneapolis: University of Minnesota Press.

Goyette, Kimberly, and Yu Xie. 1999. "Educational Expectations of Asian American Youths: Determinants and Ethnic Differences." *Sociology of Education,* 72, 1: 22–36.

Grande, Sandy. 2015. *Red Pedagogy: Native American Social and Political Thought.* Lanham, MD: Rowman & Littlefield.

Gray, Noah. 2015, May 29. "Theory behind Why South-Asian Americans Win Spelling Bee." *Twitter.* Retrieved from www.twitter.com.

Greenlee, Cynthia R. June 2017. "The Word Is 'Nemesis': The Fight to Integrate the National Spelling Bee." *Long Reads.* Retrieved from https://longreads.com.

Gregory, Sean. 2017, August 24. "How Kids' Sports Became a $15 Billion Industry." *Time.* Retrieved from www.time.com.

Groark, Marie. 2003, February. "New Grant to Expand Options for High School Students Being Left Behind." *Bill & Melinda Gates Foundation.* Retrieved from www.gatesfoundation.org.

Groves, Barry. 2016, April 12. "Asian-American Parents Bring Academic Pressure with Them." *Mercury News.* Retrieved from www.mercurynews.com.

Gunzenhauser, Michael G. 2006. "Normalizing the Educated Subject: A Foucaultian Analysis of High-Stakes Accountability." *Educational Studies: Journal of the American Educational Studies Association,* 39, 3: 241–59.

Guo, Aige. 2006. *Competition Preparation and Deliberate Practice: A Study of the 2005 National Spelling Bee Finalists.* Ann Arbor, MI: University of Toledo Press.

Hafner, Anne. 1990. "A Profile of the American Eighth Grader: NELS:88 Student Descriptive Summary." *National Educational Longitudinal Study of 1988*. Washington, DC: National Center for Education Statistics.

Hall, Stuart. 1990. "Cultural Identity and Diaspora." Pp. 222–37 in *Identity: Community, Culture, Difference*, edited by J. Rutherford. London: Lawrence and Wishart.

Hallinan, Maureen T. 2014. "The Detracking Movement." *Education Next*. Retrieved from www.cationnext.org.

Hamilton, Laura. 2016. *Parenting to a Degree: How Family Matters for College Women's Success*. Chicago: University of Chicago Press.

Hansen, Karen V. 2004. *Not-So-Nuclear Families: Class, Gender, and Networks of Care*. New Brunswick, NJ: Rutgers University Press.

Hao, Lingxin, and Han Woo. 2012. "Distinct Trajectories in the Transition to Adulthood: Are Children of Immigrants Advantaged?" *Child Development*, 83, 5: 1623–39.

Hartas, Dimitra. 2011. "Families' Social Backgrounds Matter: Socio-economic Factors, Home Learning and Young Children's Language, Literacy and Social Outcomes." *British Educational Research Journal*, 37, 6: 893–914.

———. 2014. "Parenting for Social Mobility? Home Learning, Parental Warmth, Class and Educational Outcomes." *Journal of Education Policy*, 30, 1: 21–38.

Hartocollis, Anemona. 2018, June 15. "Harvard Rated Asian-American Applicants Lower on Personality Traits, Suit Says." *New York Times*. Retrieved from www.nytimes.com.

Harvey, David. 2005. *A Brief History of Neoliberalism*. New York: Oxford University Press.

Hassrick, Elizabeth McGhee, Stephen W. Raudenbush, and Lisa Rosen. 2017. *The Ambitious Elementary School: Its Conception, Design, and Implications for Educational Equality*. Chicago: University of Chicago Press.

Hays, Sharon. 1996. *The Cultural Constructions of Motherhood*. New Haven, CT: Yale University Press.

Haytko, Diana L., and Julie Baker. 2004. "It's All at the Mall: Exploring Adolescent Girls' Experiences." *Journal of Retailing*, 80, 1: 67–83.

Heim, Joe. 2015, May 25. "Indian Americans Dominate the National Spelling Bee: Why Should They Take Abuse on Social Media for It?" *Washington Post*. Retrieved from www.washingtonpost.com.

Heinrich, Carolyn, Robert Meyer, and Greg Whitten. 2010. "Supplemental Education Services under No Child Left Behind: Who Signs Up, and What Do They Gain?" *Educational Evaluation and Policy Analysis*, 32, 2: 273–98.

Heitin, Liana. 2016, May 17. "Elite Math Competitions Struggle to Diversify Their Talent Pool." *Education Week*. Retrieved from www.edweek.org.

Henkin, Roxanne, Janis Harmon, Elizabeth Pate, Honor Moorman, Lisa Storm Fink, et al. 2008, March. "An Insider's Perspective on the National Spelling Bee: An Interview with James Maguire." *National Council of Teachers of English*. Retrieved from https://search.proquest.com.

Hexco. n.d. "How Do I Get Past the National Spelling Bee Written Round?" *Hexco*. Retrieved from www.hexco.com.

———. n.d. "Spelling Coach." *Hexco*. Retricved from www.hexco.com.

Heynen, Nik. 2007. *Neoliberal Environments: False Promises and Unnatural Consequences*. New York: Routledge.

Hijioka, Shihoko, and Joel Wong. 2012, May. "Suicide among Asian-Americans." *American Psychological Association*. Retrieved from www.apa.org.

Hills, Tynette W. 1987. "Hothousing Young Children: Implications for Early Childhood Policy and Practice." *ERIC Digests*. Retrieved from https://files.eric.ed.gov.

Hirschman, Charles, and Jennifer Lee. 2005. "Race and Ethnic Inequality in Educational Attainment in the United States." Pp. 107–38 in *Ethnicity and Causal Mechanisms*. Cambridge: Cambridge University Press.

Hirschman, Charles, and Morrison G. Wong. 1986. "The Extraordinary Educational Attainment of Asian-Americans: A Search for Historical Evidence and Explanations." *Social Forces*, 65, 1: 1–27.

History and Educational Models in Early Childhood Education. n.d. "Historical Foundations of Early Childhood Education." *History and Educational Models in Early Childhood Education*. Retrieved from http://earlychildhoodhistory.weebly.com.

Ho, Phoebe, Hyunjoon Park, and Grace Kao. 2018. "Racial and Ethnic Differences in Student Participation in Private Supplementary Education Activities." *Research in Social Stratification and Mobility*, 59: 46–59.

Hofferth, Sandra, and John Sandberg. 2001. "Changes in American Children's Time, 1981–1997." *Advances in Life Course Research*, 6: 193–229.

Holt, Nicholas L., Katherine A. Tamminen, Danielle E. Black, Zoe L. Sehn, and Michael P. Wall. 2008. "Parental Involvement in Competitive Youth Sport Settings." *Psychology of Sport & Exercise*, 9, 5: 663–85.

Honoré, Carl. 2010. *Under Pressure: Putting the Child Back in Childhood*. Toronto: Vintage.

Houlihan, Barrie, and Mick Green, eds. 2010. *Routledge Handbook of Sports Development*. New York: Routledge.

Huntsinger, Carol, Paul Jose, Fong-Ruey Liaw, and Wei-Di Ching. 1997. "Cultural Differences in Early Mathematics Learning: A Comparison of Euro-American, Chinese-American, and Taiwan-Chinese Families." *International Journal of Behavioral Development*, 21, 2: 371–88.

Hurrelmann, K. 1988. *Social Structure and Personality Development: The Individual as a Productive Processor of Reality*. New York: Cambridge University Press.

Hursh, David. 2007. "Assessing No Child Left Behind and the Rise of Neoliberal Education Policies." *American Educational Research Journal*, 44, 3: 493–518.

Hwang, Suein. 2005, November 19. "The New White Flight." *Wall Street Journal*. Retrieved from www.wsj.com.

Hyman, Vicki. 2013, March 31. "The Know Where It's At: Indian-Americans Rule at National Geographic Bee." *NJ.com*. Retrieved from www.nj.com.

Imoagene, Onoso. 2017. *Beyond Expectations: Second-Generation Nigerians in the United States and Britain*. University of California Press.

India Herald. 2017, August 23. "North South Foundation in Houston Successfully Conducts 25th National Finals." *India Herald*. Retrieved from www.india-herald.com.

Irwin, Sarah, and Sharon Ellcy. 2011. "Concerted Cultivation? Parenting Values, Education and Class Diversity." *Sociology*, 45, 3: 480–95.

———. 2013. "Parents' Hopes and Expectations for Their Children's Future Occupations." *Sociological Review*, 61, 1: 111–30.

Ispa-Landa, Simone, and Jordan Conwell. 2015. "'Once You Go to a White School, You Kind of Adapt': Black Adolescents and the Racial Classification of Schools." *Sociology of Education*, 88, 1: 1–19.

Italie, Leanne. 2011, June 15. "New Parenting Guide Offers the Art of Safe Roughhousing." *St. Louis Post-Dispatch*. Retrieved from www.stltoday.com.

Iyer, Deepa. 2015. *We Too Sing America: South Asian, Arab, Muslim, and Sikh Immigrants Shape Our Multiracial Future*. New York: New Press.

Iyer, Ram. n.d. *Geography Bee Coaching by Ram Iyer*. Retrieved from www .geographybee-coaching.com.

Jambunathan, Saigeetha, and Kenneth Counselman. 2002. "Parenting Attitudes of Asian Indian Mothers Living in the United States and in India." *Early Child Development and Care*, 172, 6: 657–62.

Janetsky, Megan. 2018, September 19. "'It Runs in Her Culture': Spelling Bees Transforming One Navajo Community." *Arizona Republic*. Retrieved from www .azcentral.com.

Jaschik, Scott. 2017, August 7. "The Numbers and the Arguments on Asian Admissions." *Inside Higher Ed*. Retrieved from www.insidehighered.com.

Jenks, Chris. 2005. *Childhood: Critical Concepts in Sociology*. New York: Routledge.

Jetten, J., F. Mols, N. Healy, and R. Spears. 2017. "'Fear of Falling': Economic Instability Enhances Collective Angst among Societies' Wealthy Class." *Journal of Social Issues*, 73, 1: 61–79.

Jimenez, Tomas. 2017. *The Other Side of Assimilation: How Immigrants Are Changing American Life*. Berkeley: University of California Press.

Jordan, Miriam. 2016, April 7. "Demand for H1-B Skilled-Worker Visas Forces Agency into Lottery." *Wall Street Journal*. Retrieved from www.wsj.com.

Journell, Wayne. 2010. "The Influence of High-Stakes Testing on High School Teachers' Willingness to Incorporate Current Political Events into the Curriculum." *High School Journal*, 93, 3: 111–25.

Kadvany, Elena. 2015, February 6. "Palo Alto High Schools Take Action to Ease Student Stress." *Palo Alto Online*. Retrieved from www.paloaltoonline.com.

Kalleberg, Arne. 2009. "Precarious Work, Insecure Workers: Employment Relations in Transition." *American Sociological Review*, 74, 1: 1–22.

Kao, Grace. 2000. "Group Images and Possible Selves among Adolescents: Linking Stereotypes to Expectations by Race and Ethnicity." *Sociological Forum*, 15, 3: 407–30.

———. 2004. "Parental Influences on the Educational Outcomes of Immigrant Youth." *International Migration Review*, 38, 2: 427–49.

Kao, Grace, and Martin Tienda. 1995. "Optimism and Achievement: The Educational Performance of Immigrant Youth." Pp. 331–43 in *The New Immigration: An Interdisciplinary Reader*, edited by Carola Suarez-Orozco, Marcelo Suarez-Orozco, and Desiree Baolian Qin-Hilliard. New York: Routledge.

Karlson, K. B. 2015. "Expectations on Track? High School Tracking and Adolescent Educational Expectations." *Social Forces*, 94, 1: 115–41.

Kasinitz, Philip. 2016. "Explaining Asian American Achievement." *Ethnic and Racial Studies*, 39, 13: 2391–97.

Kasinitz, Philip, John Mollenkopf, Mary Waters, and Jennifer Holdaway. 2008. *Inheriting the City: The Children of Immigrants Come of Age*. Cambridge, MA: Harvard University Press.

Katz, Brigit. 2017, April 5. "The National Spelling Bee Adjusts Its Rules to Prevent Ties." *Smithsonian Magazine*. Retrieved from www.smithsonianmag.com.

Kaufman, Jason, and Jay Gabler. 2004. "Cultural Capital and the Extracurricular Activities of Girls and Boys in the College Attainment Process." *Poetics*, 32, 2: 145–68.

Kefalas, M. 2003. *Working-Class Heroes: Protecting Home, Community, and Nation in a Chicago Neighborhood*. Berkeley: University of California Press.

Keisch, Deborah M., and Tim Scott. 2015. "US Education Reform and the Maintenance of White Supremacy through Structural Violence." *Landscapes of Violence*, 3, 3: 6.

Kendall, Lori. 1999. "Nerd Nation: Images of Nerds in US Popular Culture." *International Journal of Cultural Studies*, 2, 2: 260–83.

———. 2011. "'White and Nerdy': Computers, Race, and the Nerd Stereotype." *Journal of Popular Culture*, 44, 3: 505–24.

Khan, Salman. 2012. *The One World Schoolhouse: Education Reimagined*. New York: Twelve.

Khan, Shamus. 2011. *Privilege: The Making of an Adolescent Elite at St. Paul's School*. Princeton, NJ: Princeton University Press.

Kibria, Nazli. 2002. *Becoming Asian American: Second-Generation Chinese and Korean American Identities*. Baltimore, MD: Johns Hopkins University Press.

Kim, Claire Jean. 1999. "The Racial Triangulation of Asian Americans." *Politics & Society*, 27, 1: 105–38.

Kim, Ryan. 2001, June 7. "Asian Teen Mothers a Quiet State Crisis / Problem Will Be Addressed in Oakland Tonight." *SFGate*. Retrieved from www.sfgate.com.

Kim, S. Y., Y. Wang, D. Orozco-Lapray, Y. Shen, and M. Murtuza. 2013. "Does 'Tiger Parenting' Exist? Parenting Profiles of Chinese Americans and Adolescent Developmental Outcomes." *Asian American Journal of Psychology*, 4, 7–18.

Kimball, Miles, Smith, Noah, and Quartz. 2013, October 28. "The Myth of 'I'm Bad at Math.'" *Atlantic*. Retrieved from www.theatlantic.com.

King, Jamilah. 2013, September 6. "Asian Americans Students Still Face Bullying in New York City Schools." *Colorlines*. Retrieved from. www.colorlines.com.

Kinney, David. 1993. "From Nerds to Normals: The Recovery of Identity among Adolescents from Middle School to High School." *Sociology of Education*, 66, 1: 21–40.

Korean-American Scientists and Engineers Association. 2019. "National Math & Science Competition 2019." *Korean-American Scientists and Engineers Association*. Retrieved from www.nmsc.ksea.org.

Koshy, Susan. 2013. "Neoliberal Family Matters." *American Literary History*, 25, 2: 344–80.

Kozol, Jonathan. 1991. *Savage Inequalities: Children in America's Schools*. New York: Baker & Taylor.

Kremer-Sadlik, T., C. Izquierdo, and M. Fatigante. 2010. "Making Meaning of Everyday Practices: Parents' Attitudes toward Children's Extracurricular Activities in the United States and in Italy." *Anthropology & Education Quarterly*, 41, 1: 35–54.

Kulkarni, Pramod. 2017, August 18. "Houston Hosts North South Foundation's 25th Anniversary of Academic Contests." *Indo American News*. Retrieved from www.indoamerican-news.com.

Kumon. 2015a, January 5. "Entrepreneur Magazine Ranks Kumon No. 1 Education Franchise for 14th Consecutive Year." *Kumon*. Retrieved from www.kumon.com.

Kumon. 2015b, December 9. "Kumon Surpasses Student Enrollment Milestones Nationwide." *Kumon.* Retrieved from www.kumonfranchise.com.

Kumon. 2014. "Fostering Academically Advanced Students in Kumon." *Kumon.* Retrieved from www.kumon.com.

Kumon. 2017. "Investment Fees." *Kumon Franchise.* Retrieved from www .kumonfranchise.com.

Kusow, Abdi. 2004. "Contesting Stigma: On Goffman's Assumptions of Normative Order." *Symbolic Interaction*, 27, 2: 179.

Lacy, Karyn. 2007. *Blue-Chip Black Race: Class, and Status in the New Black Middle Class.* Berkeley: University of California Press.

Lambert, Diana. 2018, May 21. "Tests Got You Stressed? Try 'Primal Screaming.'" *Sacramento Bee.* Retrieved from www.sacbee.com.

Lamont, Michèle. 1992. *Money, Morals, and Manners: The Culture of the French and the American Upper-Middle Class.* Chicago: University of Chicago Press.

———. 2000. *The Dignity of Working Men: Morality and the Boundaries of Race, Class, and Immigration.* New York: Russell Sage Foundation.

Lamont, Michèle, and Christopher Bail. 2007. "Bridging Boundaries: The Equalization Strategies of Stigmatized Ethno-racial Groups Compared." *Harvard University Center for European Studies Working Paper Series #154.*

Lamont, Michèle, Graziella Moraes Silva, Jessica Welburn, Joshua Guetzkow, Nissim Mizrachi, Hanna Herzog, and Elisa Reis. 2016. *Getting Respect: Responding to Stigma and Discrimination in the United States, Brazil, and Israel.* Princeton, NJ: Princeton University Press.

Lan, Pei-Chia. 2018. *Raising Global Families: Parenting, Immigration, and Class in Taiwan and the US.* Palo Alto, CA: Stanford University Press.

Land, Stephanie. 2016, April 9. "Free-Range Parenting Is a Privilege for the Rich and White." *Medium.* Retrieved from https://medium.com.

Lareau, Annette. 2003. *Unequal Childhoods: Class, Race, and Family Life.* Berkeley: University of California Press.

Lareau, Annette, and Wesley Shumar. 1996. "The Problem of Individualism in Family-School Policies." *Sociology of Education*, 69: 24–39.

Lareau, Annette, and Erin McNamara Horvat. 1999. "Moments of Social Inclusion and Exclusion: Race, Class, and Cultural Capital in Family-School Relationships." *Sociology of Education*, 72, 1: 37–53.

Laughlin, Lynda. 2014, December. "A Child's Day: Living Arrangements, Nativity, and Family Transitions: 2011 (Selected Indicators of Child Well-Being)." *United States Census Bureau.* Retrieved from www.census.gov.

LeBel, Thomas. 2008. "Perceptions of and Responses to Stigma." *Sociology Compass*, 2, 2: 409–32.

Lebesco, Kathleen. 2011. "Neoliberalism, Public Health, and the Moral Perils of Fatness." *Critical Public Health*, 21, 2: 153–64.

Lee, Jennifer, and Min Zhou. 2015. *The Asian American Achievement Paradox.* New York: Russell Sage Foundation.

Lee, Jennifer C. 2013. "Employment and Earnings in High-Tech Ethnic Niches." *Social Forces*, 91, 3: 747–84.

Lee, Sharon. 2002. "Do Asian American Faculty Face a Glass Ceiling in Higher Education?" *American Educational Research Journal*, 39, 3: 695–724.

Lee, Stacey. 1994. "Behind the Model-Minority Stereotype: Voices of High- and Low-Achieving Asian American Students." *Anthropology & Education Quarterly*, 25, 4: 413–29.

———. 2009. *Unraveling the "Model Minority" Stereotype: Listening to Asian American Youth*. New York: Teachers College Press.

Lee, Sunmin, Hee-Soon Juon, Genevieve Martinez, Chiehwen E. Hsu, E. Stephanie Robinson, Julie Bawa, and Grace X. Ma. 2009. "Model Minority at Risk: Expressed Needs of Mental Health by Asian American Young Adults." *Journal of Community Health*, 34, 2: 144–52.

Lenz, Bob. 2016. "Project-Based Learning with an Equity Lens," *Education Week*, August 22. Retrieved from http://blogs.edweek.org.

Leong, Frederick T. L., and Mei Tang. 2016. "Career Barriers for Chinese Immigrants in the United States." *Career Development Quarterly*, 64, 3: 259–71.

Lessinger, Leon M. 1970. *Every Kid a Winner: Accountability in Education*. New York: Simon & Schuster.

Levey, Hilary. 2009. "Pageant Princesses and Math Whizzes: Understanding Children's Activities as a Form of Children's Work." *Childhood*, 16, 2: 195–212.

Levine, Sheen S., and Stark, David. 2015, December 9. "Diversity Makes You Brighter." *New York Times*. Retrieved from www.nytimes.com.

Lew, Jamie. 2006. *Asian Americans in Class: Charting the Achievement Gap among Korean American Youth*. New York: Teachers College Press.

Lewis, Amanda. 2003. *Race in the Schoolyard: Negotiating the Color Line in Classrooms and Communities*. New Brunswick, NJ: Rutgers University Press.

Lewis, Amanda, and Michelle J. Manno. 2011. "The Best Education for Some: Race and Schooling in the United States Today." Pp. 93–109 in *State of White Supremacy: Racism, Governance, and the United States*, edited by Moon-Kie Jung, Joao H. Costa Vargas, and Eduardo Bonilla-Silva. Stanford, CA: Stanford University Press.

Lewis-McCoy, R. L'Heurex. 2014. *Inequality in the Promised Land: Race, Resources, and Suburban Schooling*. Palo Alto, CA: Stanford University Press.

Li, Yan, Philip R. Costanzo, and Martha Putallaz. 2010. "Maternal Socialization Goals, Parenting Styles, and Social-Emotional Adjustment among Chinese and European American Young Adults: Testing a Mediation Model." *Journal of Genetic Psychology*, 171, 4: 330–62.

Lingard, Bob, Wayne Martino, and Goli Rezai-Rashti. 2013. "Testing Regimes, Accountabilities and Education Policy: Commensurate Global and National Developments." *Journal of Education Policy*, 28, 5: 539–56.

Link, Bruce, and Jo Phelan. 2001. "Conceptualizing Stigma." *Annual Review of Sociology*, 27, 1: 363–85.

Lite, Lori. 2014. *Stress Free Kids: A Parent's Guide to Helping Build Self-Esteem, Manage Stress, and Reduce Anxiety in Children*. United States: Adams Media.

LIVE Kelly and Ryan. 2018, May 18. "Kelly & Ryan Have a Rematch with MATHCOUNTS Winner Luke Robitaille." *YouTube*. Retrieved from www.youtube.com.

Long, Marilee, Jocelyn Steinke, Brooks Applegate, Maria Knight Lapinski, Marne J. Johnson, and Sayani Ghosh. 2010. "Portrayals of Male and Female Scientists in Television Programs Popular among Middle School-Age Children." *Science Communication*, 32, 3: 356–82.

Lorenzo, May Kwan, Abbie Frost, and Helen Reinherz. 2000. "Social and Emotional Functioning of Older Asian American Adolescents." *Child and Adolescent Social Work Journal*, 17, 4: 289–304.

Louie, Vivian. 2004. *Compelled to Excel: Immigration, Education, and Opportunity among Chinese Americans*. Stanford, CA: Stanford University Press.

Loveless, Tom. 2017, March 22. "Brown Center Report on American Education: Survey of Foreign Exchange Students." *Brookings Institution*. Retrieved from www .brookings.edu.

Loveless, Tom, Steve Farkas, and Ann Duffett. 2008, June 18. "High-Achieving Students in the Era of NCLB." *Thomas B. Fordham Institute*. Retrieved from https:// edex.s3-us-west-2.amazonaws.com.

Lowe, Lisa. 1996. *Immigrant Acts: On Asian American Cultural Politics*. Durham, NC: Duke University Press.

Lung-Amam, Willow. 2017. *Trespassers? Asian Americans and the Battle for Suburbia*. Berkeley: University of California Press.

Luthar, Suniya, Samuel H. Barkin, and Elizabeth J. Crossman. 2013. "'I Can, Therefore I Must': Fragility in the Upper-Middle Classes." *Development and Psychopathology*, 25, 4: 1529–49.

Luthar, Suniya, and Bronwyn Becker. 2002. "Privileged but Pressured? A Study of Affluent Youth." *Child Development*, 73, 5: 1593–610.

Lythcott-Haims, Julie. 2015. *How to Raise an Adult: Break Free of the Overparenting Trap and Prepare Your Kid for Success*. New York: Henry Holt.

MacPherson, Robert. 2015, May 27. "Racist Trolling Casts Pall over US Spelling Bee." *Yahoo*. Retrieved from www.yahoo.com.

Maguire, James. 2006. *American Bee: The National Spelling Bee and the Culture of Word Nerds*. New York: Rodale.

Maira, Sunaina. 2002. *Desis in the House: Indian American Youth Culture in NYC*. New York: Temple University Press.

Mandell, Nina. 2016, June 15. "Dez Bryant Meets the Spelling Bee Champion Who Threw Up His 'X' Celebration." *USA Today*. Retrieved from www.usatoday .com.

Manor-Bullock, Rochelle, Christine Look, and David N. Dixon. 1995. "Is Giftedness Socially Stigmatizing? The Impact of High Achievement on Social Interactions." *Journal for the Education of the Gifted*, 18, 3: 319–38.

Martin, Danny Bernard. 2009. "Researching Race in Mathematics Education." *Teachers College Record*, 111, 2: 295–338.

Massachusetts Society of Professional Engineers. 2015, January 24. "MATHCOUNTS Program Has Double-Digit Growth; Volunteers Wanted at Chapter Competitions in Late JAN/Early FEB." *Massachusetts Society of Professional Engineers*. Retrieved from www.mspe.com.

MasterClass. "Private Equity Investing in For-Profit Education Companies." *MasterClass*. Retrieved from www.capitolroundtable.com.

MATHCOUNTS Foundation. 2012, February 17. "MATHCOUNTS Competition Series—2011 Raytheon MATHCOUNTS National Competition." *YouTube*. Retrieved from www.youtube.com.

Mathew, Biju. 2008. *Taxi! Cabs and Capitalism in New York City*. Ithaca, NY: Cornell University Press.

Mathews, Jay. 2000, December 5. "Teaching beyond the Middle." *Washington Post.* Retrieved from www.washingtonpost.com.

Mathnasium. 2016, June 16. "National PTA Expands STEM Initiative with New Collaboration with Mathnasium." *Mathnasium.* Retrieved from www.mathnasium.com.

Mau, Wei-Cheng. 1997. "Parental Influences on the High School Students' Academic Achievement: A Comparison of Asian Immigrants, Asian Americans, and White Americans." *Psychology in the Schools,* 34, 3: 267–77.

Maynard, Nathan, and Brad Weinstein. 2019. *Hacking School Discipline: 9 Ways to Create a Culture of Empathy and Responsibility Using Restorative Justice.* Highland Heights, OH: Times 10.

McArthur, Rachel. 2011, September 21. "Out of Many, One: Spelling Bees and the United States National Spelling Bee." *English Languages: History, Diaspora, Culture,* 2.

McCarty, Teresa. 2002. *A Place to be Navajo: Rough Rock and the Struggle for Self-Determination in Indigenous Schooling.* New York: Routledge.

McHale, Susan M., Ann C. Crouter, and Corinna J. Tucker. 2001. "Free-Time Activities in Middle Childhood: Links with Adjustment in Early Adolescence." *Child Development,* 72, 6: 1764–78.

McNeal, R. B., Jr. 1998. "High School Extracurricular Activities: Closed Structures and Stratifying Patterns of Participation." *Journal of Educational Research,* 91, 3: 183–91.

Media Matters Staff. 2019, June 6. "Tucker Carlson Guest: If White Privilege Explained Everything, Please Tell Me How 7 Out of 8 of the Recent National Spelling Bee Champions Were Indian-Americans." *Media Matters.* Retrieved from www.mediamatters.org.

Mehta, Jal. 2013. *The Allure of Order: High Hopes, Dashed Expectations, and the Troubled Quest to Remake American Schooling.* New York: Oxford University Press.

Messner, Michael, and Michela Musto. 2016. "Introduction: Kids and Sport." Pp. 1–19 in *Child's Play: Sport in Kids' Worlds,* edited by Michael Messner and Michela Musto. Minneapolis: University of Minnesota Press.

Milner, M. 2013. *Freaks, Geeks, and Cool Kids.* New York: Routledge.

Minero, Emelina. 2018, April 19. "Schools Struggle to Support LGBTQ Students." *Edutopia.* Retrieved from www.edutopia.com.

Mizrachi, Nissim, and Adane Zawdu. 2012. "Between Global Racial and Bounded Identity: Choice of Destigmatization Strategies among Ethiopian Jews in Israel." *Ethnic and Racial Studies,* 35, 3: 436–52.

Modica, Marianne. 2015. "Unpacking the 'Colorblind Approach': Accusations of Racism at a Friendly, Mixed-Race School." *Race Ethnicity and Education* 18, 3: 396–418.

Moll, Luis, and Richard Ruiz. 2008. "The Schooling of Latino Children." Pp. 362–74 in *Latinos: Remaking America,* edited by Marcelo M. Suárez-Orozco and Mariela Páez. Berkeley: University of California Press.

Molnar, Alex. 2006. "The Commercial Transformation of Public Education." *Journal of Education Policy,* 21, 5: 621–40.

Molnar, Michele. 2013, August 20. "Tutoring Firms Hit Hard by NCLB Waivers." *Education Week.* Retrieved from www.edweek.org.

Moretti, Enrico. 2012. *The New Geography of Jobs*. Boston: Houghton Mifflin Harcourt.

Mori, Izumi. 2013. "Supplementary Education in the United States: Policy Context, Characteristics, and Challenges." Pp. 191–207 in *Out of the Shadows: The Global Intensification of Supplementary Education*, edited by J. Aurini, S. Davies, and J. Dierkes. Bingley, UK: Emerald Group.

Mori, Izumi, and David Baker. 2010. "The Origin of Universal Shadow Education: What the Supplemental Education Phenomenon Tells Us about the Postmodern Institution of Education." *Asia Pacific Education Review*, 11, 1: 36–48.

Moss, Emily. 2014, October 24. "Controversy Arises over Russian Math at North." *Newtonite*. Retrieved from www.thenewtonite.com.

MSN. 2015, May 30. "Hear the Theory Why Certain Kids Win the Spelling Bee." *MSN*. Retrieved from www.msn.com.

Muñoz, Marco, Allison Potter, and Steven Ross. 2008. "Supplemental Educational Services as a Consequence of the NCLB Legislation: Evaluating Its Impact on Student Achievement in a Large Urban District." *Journal of Education for Students Placed at Risk*, 13, 1: 1–25.

Najar, Nida. 2011, October 13. "Squeezed Out in India, Students Turn to U.S." *New York Times*. Retrieved from www.nytimes.com.

Nakamura, Lisa. 2009. "Don't Hate the Player, Hate the Game: The Racialization of Labor in World of Warcraft." *Critical Studies in Media Communication*, 26, 2: 128–44.

Namkung, Victoria. 2004. "Reinventing the Wheel: Import Car Racing in Southern California." Pp. 159–76 in *Asian American Youth: Culture, Identity, and Ethnicity*, edited by Jennifer Lee and Min Zhou. New York: Routledge.

National Center for Education Statistics. 2009, May 28. "The Condition of Education 2009." *National Center for Education Statistics*. Retrieved from https://nced.ed.gov.

National Post. 2016, June 27. "The Dark Side of Being a 'Tiger Mom': Perfectionist Parenting Style May Be Detrimental to Your Child, Study Says." *National Post*. Retrieved from www.nationalpost.com.

National Research Council; Division of Behavioral and Social Sciences and Education; Board on Children, Youth, and Families; Committee on Increasing High School Students' Engagement Motivation to Learn; and Institute of Medicine. 2004. *Engaging Schools: Fostering High School Students' Motivation to Learn*. Washington, DC: National Academies Press.

NBC News. 2014, February 11. "Teens More Stressed-Out Than Adults, Survey Shows." *NBC News*. Retrieved from www.nbcnews.com.

Neckerman, Kathryn M., Prudence Carter, and Jennifer Lee. 1999. "Segmented Assimilation and Minority Cultures of Mobility." *Ethnic and Racial Studies*, 22, 6: 945–65.

Nelson, Margaret. 2010. *Parenting Out of Control: Anxious Parents in Uncertain Times*. New York: New York University Press.

New Jersey Department of Education. 2012. "Understanding Your Annual Progress Targets." *New Jersey Department of Education*. Retrieved from www.state.nj.us.

New York City Department of Education. 2002. "Lesbian, Gay, Bisexual, and Transgender Support." *New York City Department of Education*. Retrieved from www.schools.nyc.gov.

New York Times. 1990. "Probing School Success of Asian Americans." *New York Times*. Retrieved from www.nytimes.com.

New York Times Editorial Board. 2015, December 31. "Reducing the Stresses Students Face." *New York Times*. Retrieved from www.nytimes.com.

Newman, Katherine. 1999. *No Shame in My Game: The Working Poor in the Inner City*. New York: Knopf Books, Russell Sage Foundation.

Newman, Tony. 2000. "Workers and Helpers: Perspectives on Children's Labour 1899–1999." *British Journal of Social Work*, 30, 3: 323–38.

Newsweek Staff. 2006, September 10. "The New First Grade: Too Much Too Soon." *Newsweek*. Retrieved from www.newsweek.com.

Ng, Wendy. 2002. *Japanese American Internment during World War II: A History and Reference Guide*. Westport, CT: Greenwood.

Nimetz, Lloyd. 2017. August 24. "The 'Asian Tax' in College Admissions." *Medium*. Retrieved from www.medium.com.

Noguchi, Sharon. 2016, April 9. "Schools Target Asian Parental Expectations." *Mercury News*. Retrieved from www.mercurynews.com.

North South Foundation. n.d. "Coaching." *North South Foundation*. Retrieved from www.northsouth.org.

Nuckols, Ben. 2016, May 27. "National Spelling Bee Ends in Its Unlikeliest Tie to Date." *AP News*. Retrieved from www.apnews.com.

———. 2018, May 31. "Elite 8: National Spelling Bee Too Easy for Octet of Champs." *AP News*. Retrieved from www.apnews.com.

Oakes, Jeannie. 1985. *Keeping Track: How Schools Structure Inequality*. New Haven, CT: Yale University Press.

———. 1987. "Tracking in Secondary Schools: A Contextual Perspective." *Educational Psychologist*, 22, 2: 129–53.

Ochoa, Gilda. 2013. *Academic Profiling: Latinos, Asian Americans, and the Achievement Gap*. Minneapolis: University of Minnesota Press.

Odenbring, Ylva. 2016. "Childhood, Free Time and Everyday Lives: Comparing Children's Views in Sweden and the United States." *Early Child Development and Care*, 1–9.

Ogbu, John. 2003. *Black American Students in an Affluent Suburb: A Study of Academic Disengagement*. New York: Routledge.

Okazaki, Sumie, and Noriel Lim. 2011. "Academic and Educational Achievement among Asian American Children and Youth." *Asian American and Pacific Islander Children and Mental Health*, 1: 143–68.

Okihiro, Gary. 1994. *Margins and Mainstreams: Asians in American History and Culture*. Seattle: University of Washington Press.

Omi, Michael, and Howard Winant. 1994. *Racial Formation in the United States: From the 1960s to the 1990s*. New York: Routledge.

Onoso, Imoagene. *Beyond Expectations: Second-Generation Nigerians in the United States and Britain*. Berkeley: University of California Press, 2017.

Overman, Stephenie. n.d. "Fighting the Stress of Teaching to the Test." *National Education Association*. Retrieved from www.nea.org.

Owens, Ann. 2016. "Inequality in Children's Contexts: Income Segregation of Households with and without Children." *American Sociological Review*, 81, 3: 549–74.

Pandya, Sameer. 2017. "Freaks and Geeks: On the Provisional Citizenship of Indian American Spelling Bee Winners." *Journal of Asian American Studies*, 20, 2: 245–63.

Park, Clara, and Marilyn Mei-Ying Chi. 1999. *Asian American Education: Prospects and Challenges*. Westport, CT: Bergin & Garvey.

Park, Hyunjoon, Claudia Buchmann, Jaesung Choi, and Joseph J. Merry. 2016. "Learning beyond the School Walls: Trends and Implications." *Annual Review of Sociology*, 42, 1: 231–52.

Park, Hyunjoon, Soo-yong Byun, and Kyung-keun Kim. 2011. "Parental Involvement and Students' Cognitive Outcomes in Korea: Focusing on Private Tutoring." *Sociology of Education*, 84, 1: 3–22.

Park, Julie J. 2018. *Race on Campus: Debunking Myths with Data*. Cambridge, MA: Harvard Education Press.

Park, Julie, and Amy Liu. 2016. "Interest Convergence or Divergence? A Critical Race Analysis of Asian Americans, Meritocracy, and Critical Mass in the Affirmative Action Debate." *Journal of Higher Education*, 85, 1: 36–64.

Parmar, Parminder, Sara Harkness, and Charles M. Super. 2004. "Asian and Euro-American Parents' Ethnotheories of Play and Learning: Effects on Preschool Children's Home Routines and School Behaviour." *International Journal of Behavioral Development*, 28, 2: 97–104.

Pascoe, C. J. 2007. *Dude, You're a Fag: Masculinity and Sexuality in High School*. Berkeley: University of California Press.

Patel, Jyoti. 2014. "The Patel Spelling Prep Master Wordlist—Volume 1." *Amazon*. Retrieved from www.amazon.com.

Paul, Annie Murphy. 2011, January 20. "Tiger Moms: Is Tough Parenting Really the Answer?" *Time*. Retrieved from www.time.com.

Payne, Melissa. 2015, May 29. "LeBron James's Biggest Fan Co-wins Scripps National Spelling Bee." *Washington Post*. Retrieved from www.washingtonpost.com.

Pearce, Richard. 2006. "Effects of Cultural and Social Structural Factors on the Achievement of White and Chinese American Students at School Transition Points." *American Educational Research Journal*, 43, 1: 75–101.

Peng, Samuel S., and Deeann Wright. 1994. "Explanation of Academic Achievement of Asian American Students." *Journal of Educational Research*, 87, 6: 346–52.

Perrier, Maud. 2013. "Middle-Class Mothers' Moralities and 'Concerted Cultivation': Class Others, Ambivalence and Excess." *Sociology*, 47, 4: 655–70.

Pew Research Center. 2015, December 17. "Parenting in America." Pew Social Trends. Retrieved from www.pewsocialtrends.org/2015/12/17/1-the-american-family-today/.

Phelan, Patricia., Hanh Cao Yu, and Ann Locke Davidson. 1994. "Navigating the Psychosocial Pressures of Adolescence: The Voices and Experiences of High School Youth." *American Educational Research Journal*, 31, 2: 415–47.

Pizmony-Levy, Oren. 2019. "Opinion: The Opt Out Movement Is Gaining Ground, Quietly." *Hechinger Report*. Accessed June 12, 2019. Retrieved from https://hechingerreport.org.

Plain Dealer. 2003, December 7. "Are Asian American Kids Smarter Than Everyone Else?" *Plain Dealer, Sunday Magazine*.

Platt, Anthony. 1977. *The Child Savers: The Invention of Delinquency*. Chicago: University of Chicago Press.

Pong, Suet-ling, Lingxin Hao, and Erica Gardner. 2005. "The Roles of Parenting Styles and Social Capital in the School Performance of Immigrant Asian and Hispanic Adolescents." *Social Science Quarterly*, 86, 4: 928–50.

Poon, OiYan. 2014. "'The Land of Opportunity Doesn't Apply to Everyone': The Immigrant Experience, Race, and Asian American Career Choices." *Journal of College Student Development*, 55, 6: 499–514.

Poros, Martisa V. 2010. *Modern Migrations: Gujarati Indian Networks in NewYork and London*. Stanford, CA: Stanford University Press.

Portes, Alejandro, Patricia Fernandez-Kelly, and William Haller. 2005. "Segmented Assimilation on the Ground: The New Second Generation in Early Adulthood." *Ethnic and Racial Studies*, 28, 6: 1000–1040.

Portes, Alejandro, and Ruben G. Rumbaut. 2001. *Legacies: The Story of the Immigrant Second Generation*. Berkeley: University of California Press.

———. 2006. *Immigrant America: A Portrait*. Berkeley: University of California Press.

Portes, Alejandro, and Min Zhou. 1993. "The New Second Generation: Segmented Assimilation and Its Variants." *Annals of the American Academy of Political and Social Science*, 530: 74–96.

Poth, Rachelle Dene. 2019. *The Future Is Now: Looking Back to Move Ahead*. Edu-Gladiators LLC.

Price-Mitchell, Marilyn. 2019, August 14. "Children and Families Thrive When Communities Care." *Roots for Action*. Retrieved from www.rootsofaction.com.

Pugh, Allison. 2009. *Longing and Belonging: Parents, Children, and Consumer Culture*. Berkeley: University of California Press.

Purkayastha, Bandana. 2005. *Negotiating Ethnicity: Second-Generation South Asian Americans Traverse a Transnational World*. New Brunswick, NJ: Rutgers University Press.

Putnam, Robert D. 2015. *Our Kids: The American Dream in Crisis*. New York: Simon & Schuster.

Qiao, George. 2017. "Why Are Asian American Kids Killing Themselves?" October 8. Retrieved from https://planamag.com.

Qin, Desiree Baolian, Niobe Way, and Meenal Rana. 2008. "The 'Model Minority' and Their Discontent: Examining Peer Discrimination and Harassment of Chinese American Immigrant Youth." *New Directions for Child and Adolescent Development*, 121, 27–42.

Quail, Christine. 2011. "Nerds, Geeks and the Hip/Square Dialectic in Contemporary Television." *Television & New Media*, 12, 5: 460–82.

Quindlen, Anna. 1987, February 22. "The Drive to Excel." *NewYork Times*. Retrieved from www.nytimes.com.

Radford, Jynnah. 2019, June 3. "Key Findings about U.S. Immigrants." *Pew Research Center*. Retrieved from www.pewresearch.org.

Raj, Anita, and Jay G. Silverman. 2007. "Domestic Violence Help-Seeking Behaviors of South Asian Battered Women Residing in the United States." *International Review of Victimology*, 14, 1: 143–70.

Raleigh, Elizabeth, and Grace Kao. 2010. "Do Immigrant Minority Parents Have More Consistent College Aspirations for Their Children?" *Social Science Quarterly*, 91, 4: 1083–102.

Ramakrishnan, Karthick, and Janelle Wong. 2018, June 18. "Survey Roundup: Asian American Attitudes on Affirmative Action." *AAPI Data*. Retrieved from www .aapidata.com.

Ramakrishnan, Karthick, Janelle Wong, Jennifer Lee, and Taeku Lee. 2017, May 16. "2016 Post-election National Asian American Survey." *National Asian American Survey*. Retrieved from www.naasurvey.com.

Ravitch, Diane. 1990. "Multiculturalism: E Pluribus Plures." *American Scholar*, 59, 3: 337–54.

———. 2017, July 13. "Bill Gates: Selling Bad Advice to the Public Schools." *Daily Beast*. Retrieved from www.thedailybeast.com.

Read, Allen Walker. 1941. "The Spelling Bee: A Linguistic Institution of the American Folk." *PMLA: Publications of the Modern Language Association of America*, 56, 2: 495–512.

Read, Jason. 2009. "A Genealogy of Homo-economicus: Neoliberalism and the Production of Subjectivity." *Foucault Studies*, 6: 25–36.

Reddy, Chandan. 2011. *Freedom with Violence: Race, Sexuality, and the US State*. Durham, NC: Duke University Press.

Rega, Sam, and Chris Weller. 2018. *Breaking the Bee*. United States: Exit Zero Productions.

Rios, Victor. 2011. *Punished: Policing the Lives of Black and Latino Boys*. New York: New York University Press.

Ripp, Pernille. 2014. *Empowered Schools, Empowered Students: Creating Connected and Invested Learners*. New York: SAGE.

Ritzer, George. 1983. "The 'McDonaldization' of Society." *Journal of American Culture*, 6, 1: 100–107.

Roach, Andrew T., and Jennifer L. Frank. 2008. "Large-Scale Assessment, Rationality, and Scientific Management." *Journal of Applied School Psychology*, 23, 2: 7–25.

Roediger, David. 2017. *Class, Race, and Marxism*. New York: Verso.

Rosenberg. Merri. 2004, April 18. "When Homework Takes Over." *New York Times*. Retrieved from www.nytimes.com.

Rosenbloom, Susan Rakosi, and Niobe Way. 2004. "Experiences of Discrimination among African American, Asian American, and Latino Adolescents in an Urban High School." *Youth & Society*, 35, 4: 420–51.

Rosenfeld, Alvin, and Nicole Wise. 2010. *The Over-Scheduled Child: Avoiding the Hyper-Parenting Trap*. New York: St. Martin's Griffin.

Rosier, Katherine, and William A. Corsaro. 1993. "Competent Parents, Complex Lives: Managing Parenthood in Poverty." *Journal of Contemporary Ethnography*, 22, 2: 171–204.

Rosin, Hanna. 2015, December. "The Silicon Valley Suicides." *Atlantic*. Retrieved from www.theatlantic.com.

Ryan, Julia. 2013, December 3. "American Schools vs. the World: Expensive, Unequal, Bad at Math." *Atlantic*. Retrieved from www.theatlantic.com.

Ryback, David. 2006. "Self-Determination and the Neurology of Mindfulness." *Journal of Humanistic Psychology*, 46, 4: 474–93.

Sakamoto, Arthur, Isao Takei, and Hyeyoung Woo. 2011. "Socioeconomic Differentials among Single-Race and Multi-race Japanese Americans." *Ethnic and Racial Studies*, 34, 9: 1445–65.

———. 2012. "The Myth of the Model Minority Myth." *Sociological Spectrum*, 32, 4: 309–21.

SAMPAN. 2018, May 30. "Mayor, School Committee Chairperson and Superintendent Honor 36 Valedictorians from the Boston Public Schools Class of 2018." *SAMPAN*. Retrieved from https://sampan.org.

Sanchez, Claudio. 2016, April 17. "Why Gifted Latinos Are Often Overlooked and Underserved." *NPR*. Retrieved from www.npr.org.

Sandberg, John F., and Sandra L. Hofferth. 2001. "Changes in Children's Time with Parents: United States, 1981–1997." *Demography*, 38, 3: 423–36.

Sandlin, Jennifer A., and Julie Garlen Maudlin. 2015. "Disney's Pedagogies of Pleasure and the Eternal Recurrence of Whiteness." *Journal of Consumer Culture*, 17, 2: 397–412.

Saran, Rupam. 2015. *Navigating Model Minority Stereotypes: Asian Indian Youth in South Asian Diaspora*. New York: Routledge.

Saraswathy, M. 2014, June 4. "Liberal Arts Education Expands Presence in India." *Business Standard*. Retrieved from www.business-standard.com.

Sattin-Bajaj, Carolyn, and Allison Roda. 2018. "Opportunity Hoarding in School Choice Contexts: The Role of Policy Design in Promoting Middle-Class Parents' Exclusionary Behaviors." *Educational Policy*. https://doi.org/10.1177/0895904818802106.

Saturdays with Stuti. 2016, January 31. "Dictionary Words Part VI." *Saturdays with Stuti*. Retrieved from https://spellingmantra.com.

Sayer, Liana C., Suzanne M. Bianchi, and John P. Robinson. 2004. "Are Parents Investing Less in Children? Trends in Mothers' and Fathers' Time with Children." *American Journal of Sociology*, 110, 1: 1–43.

Schlee, Bethanne M., Ann K. Mullis, and Michael Shriner. 2009. "Parents Social and Resource Capital: Predictors of Academic Achievement during Early Childhood." *Children and Youth Services Review*, 31, 2: 227–34.

Schneider, Barbara, and Yongsook Lee. 1990. "A Model for Academic Success: The School and Home Environment of East Asian Students." *Anthropology & Education Quarterly*, 21, 4: 358–77.

Schudson, Michael. 1989. "How Culture Works." *Theory and Society*, 18, 218(2): 153–80.

Schwartz, Katrina. 2014, May 6. "How Are Teachers and Students Using Khan Academy?" *KQED*. Retrieved from www.kqed.org.

Scripps. n.d. "Frequently Asked Questions." *Scripps National Spelling Bee*. Retrieved from https://spellingbee.com.

———. n.d. "International Spellers." *Scripps National Spelling Bee*. Retrieved from https://spellingbee.com.

———. n.d. "RSVBee." *Scripps National Spelling Bee*. Retrieved from https://spellingbee.com.

———. n.d. "The Scripps National Spelling Bee Experience." *Scripps National Spelling Bee*. Retrieved from https://spellingbee.com.

———. n.d. "Scripps National Spelling Bee Introduces Changes and New Opportunities through RSVBee." *Scripps*. Retrieved from www.scripps.com.

Segool, N. K., J. S. Carlson, A. N. Goforth, N. Von Der Embse, and J. A. Barterian. 2013. "Heightened Test Anxiety among Young Children: Elementary School Students' Anxious Responses to High-Stakes Testing." *Psychology in the Schools*, 50, 5: 489–99.

Seigel, Jerrold. 2005. *The Idea of the Self: Thought and Experience in Western Europe since the Seventeenth Century*. Cambridge: Cambridge University Press.

Senior, Jennifer. 2014. *All Joy and No Fun: The Paradox of Modern Parenthood*. New York: HarperCollins.

Shah, Nayan. 2012. *Stranger Intimacy: Contesting Race, Sexuality and the Law in the North American West*. Berkeley: University of California Press.

Shankar, Shalini. 2016, June 1. "Is the Spelling Bee Success of Indian-Americans a Legacy of British Colonialism?" *Conversation*. Retrieved from www.theconversation.com.

———. 2019. *Beeline: What Spelling Bees Reveal about Generation Z's New Path to Success*. New York: Basic Books.

Shapira, Ian. 2017, May 30. "The National Spelling Bee's New Normal: $200-an-Hour Teen Spelling Coaches." *Washington Post*. Retrieved from www.washingtonpost.com.

Sharma, Suruchi. 2012, June 18. "90 Percenters Get Cornell, Ivy League, but Not DU." *Times of India*. Retrieved from www.timesofindia.indiatimes.com.

Shell, Adam. 2017, September 5. "Why Families Stretch Their Budgets for High-Priced Youth Sports." *USA Today*. Retrieved from www.usatoday.com.

Sherman, Rachel. 2017. "Conflicted Cultivation: Parenting, Privilege, and Moral Worth in Wealthy New York Families." *American Journal of Cultural Sociology*, 5, 1: 1–33.

Shrake, Eunai. 2010. "Cram Schools." Pp. 211–15 in *Encyclopedia of Asian American Issues Today*, edited by Edith Wen-Chu Chen and Grace Yoo. Santa Barbara, CA: ABC-CLIO.

Sikh Coalition. 2014. "'Go Home Terrorist': A Report on Bullying against Sikh American School Children." *Sikh Coalition*. Retrieved from. https://sikhcoalition.org.

Sinha, Mrinalini. 1995. *Colonial Masculinity: The "Manly Englishman" and the "Effeminate Bengali" in the Late Nineteenth Century*. Manchester, UK: Manchester University Press.

Siu, Sau-Fong. 1996. "Asian American Students at Risk." *CRESPAR Report*, no. 8. Baltimore, MD: Center for Research on the Education of Students Placed at Risk; Johns Hopkins University; Howard University.

Skenazy, Leonore. 2009. *Free-Range Kids: Giving Our Children the Freedom We Had*. San Francisco: Jossey-Bass.

Skoll Foundation. n.d. "Khan Academy." *Skoll Foundation*. Retrieved from http://skoll.org.

Slater, Graham B. 2015. "Education as Recovery: Neoliberalism, School Reform, and the Politics of Crisis." *Journal of Education Policy*, 30, 1: 1–20.

Slivka, Kevin. 2011. "Art, Craft, and Assimilation: Curriculum for Native Students during the Boarding School Era." *Studies in Art Education*, 52, 3: 225–42.

Small, Mario L. 2002. "Culture, Cohorts, and Social Organization Theory: Understanding Local Participation in a Latino Housing Project." *American Journal of Sociology*, 108, 1: 1–54.

Smith, Jill M., and Ken Chih-Yan Sun. 2016. "Privileged American Families and Independent Academic Consultants They Employ." *Sociological Forum*, 31, 1: 159–80.

Smith, Stephen. 2013, June 20. "Children of 'Tiger Parents' Develop More Aggression and Depression, Research Shows." *CBS News*. Retrieved from www.cbsnews.com.

Smith, Tovia. 2012, May 29. "Why Indian-Americans Reign as Spelling Bee Champs." *NPR*. Retrieved from www.npr.org.

———. 2019, May 13. "Felicity Huffman, in Tears, Pleads Guilty in College Bribery Scandal." *NPR*. Retrieved from www.npr.org.

Smyth, Ciara. 2016. "Getting Ahead in the Preschool Years: An Analysis of a Preschool Enrichment and Entertainment Market." *Sociology*, 50, 4: 731–47.

Solomona, R. Patrick, John P. Portelli, Beverly-Jean Daniel, and Arlene Campbell. 2005. "Discourse of Denial: How White Teacher Candidates Construct Race, Racism and 'White Privilege.'" *Race Ethnicity and Education*, 8, 2: 147–69.

Southgate, Darby. 2013. "Family Capital: A Determinant of Supplementary Education in 17 Nations." Pp. 245–58 in *Out of the Shadows: The Global Intensification of Supplementary Education*, edited by J. Aurini, S. Davies, and J. Dierkes. Bingley, UK: Emerald Group.

Spencer, Kyle. 2013, April 2. "Centers See New Faces Seeking Test Prep." *New York Times*. Retrieved from www.nytimes.com.

———. 2015, December 25. "New Jersey School District Eases Pressure on Students, Baring an Ethnic Divide." *New York Times*. Retrieved from www.nytimes.com.

———. 2017, April 5. "It Takes a Suburb: A Town Struggles to Ease Student Stress." *New York Times*. Retrieved from www.nytimes.com.

Spencer, Renée, Jill Walsh, Belle Liang, Angela M. Desilva Mousseau, and Terese J. Lund. 2018. "Having It All? A Qualitative Examination of Affluent Adolescent Girls' Perceptions of Stress and Their Quests for Success." *Journal of Adolescent Research*, 33, 1: 3–33.

Spring, Joel. 2016. *Deculturalization and the Struggle for Equality: A Brief History of the Education of Dominated Cultures in the United States*. New York: Routledge.

Squires, Peter, and John Lea. 2012. *Criminalisation and Advanced Marginality: Critically Exploring the Work of Loïc Wacquant*. Chicago: Policy Press.

Staiger, Annegret. 2004. "Whiteness as Giftedness: Racial Formation at an Urban High School." *Social Problems*, 51, 2: 161–81.

Steele, Claude, and Joshua Aronson. 1995. "Stereotype Threat and the Intellectual Test Performance of African Americans." *Journal of Personality and Social Psychology*, 69, 5: 797–811.

Stephens, Sharon. 1995. *Children and the Politics of Culture*. Princeton, NJ: Princeton University Press.

Stephenson, Hank. 2017, April 27. "House Republican Leader: Teachers Get Second Jobs to Buy Boats, Enjoy Finer Things in Life." *Arizona Capitol Times*. Retrieved from www.azcapitoltimes.com.

Stevens, Lisa Patel. 2009. "Maps to Interrupt a Pathology: Immigrant Populations and Education." *Critical Inquiry in Language Studies*, 6, 1–2: 1–14.

Stevens, William, James Macaulay, and William Haig Miller. 1873. *The Leisure Hour: An Illustrated Magazine for Home Reading*. London: Religious Tract Society.

Stevenson, D. L., and D. P. Baker. 1992. "Shadow Education and Allocation in Formal Schooling: Transition to University in Japan." *American Journal of Sociology*, 97, 6: 1639–57.

Stewart, Nichole Helene. 2007. "No Child Left Behind's Supplemental Educational Services: A Case Study of Participant Experiences in an Urban Afterschool

Program in the District of Columbia." PhD diss., University of Maryland, College Park.

Strauss, Valerie. 2013a, January 9. "Education Reform as a Business." *Washington Post*. Retrieved from www.washingtonpost.com.

———. 2013b, February 21. "U.S. Teachers' Job Satisfaction Craters—Report." *Washington Post*. Retrieved from www.washingtonpost.com.

———. 2013c, July 17. "A Former Teach for America Manager Speaks Out." *Washington Post*. Retrieved from www.washingtonpost.com.

———. 2014, June 10. "Gates Foundation Backs Two-Year Delay in Linking Common Core Test Scores to Teacher Evaluation, Student Promotion." *Washington Post*. Retrieved from www.washingtonpost.com.

———. 2015, January 3. "That Surprising Thing Bill Gates Said." *Washington Post*. Retrieved from www.washingtonpost.com.

———. 2016, June 2. "Gates Foundation Chief Admits Common Core Mistakes." *Washington Post*. Retrieved from www.washingtonpost.com.

Su, Lac. 2011, January 20. "'Tiger Mothers' Leave Lifelong Scars." *CNN*. Retrieved from www.cnn.com.

Suárez-Orozco, Carola, and Marcelo M. Suárez-Orozco. 1995. *Transformations: Immigration, Family Life, and Achievement Motivation among Latino Adolescents*. Palo Alto, CA: Stanford University Press.

Subramanian, Ajantha. 2000. "Indians in North Carolina: Race, Class, and Culture in the Making of Immigrant Identity." *Comparative Studies of South Asia, Africa and the Middle East*, 20, 1 105–14.

Sue, Stanley, and Sumie Okazaki. 1990. "Asian-American Educational Achievements: A Phenomenon in Search of an Explanation." *American Psychologist*, 45, 8: 913.

Suratt, Julie. 2017, August 27. "In Praise of Mediocre Kids." *Boston Magazine*. Retrieved from www.bostonmagazine.com.

Swalwell, K. 2013. "'With Great Power Comes Great Responsibility': Privileged Students' Conceptions of Justice-Oriented Citizenship." *Democracy and Education*, 21, 1: 1–11.

Swartz, Teresa, Alex Manning, and Lisa Gulya. 2016. "What Parents and Kids Think of Extracurricular Activities: Varying Motivations, Understandings, and Experiences." Presentation at the 2016 Annual Conference of the Midwest Sociological Society, Chicago.

Swiatek, Mary Ann. 2001. "Social Coping among Gifted High School Students and Its Relationship to Self-Concept." *Journal of Youth and Adolescence*, 30, 1: 19–39.

Sy, Susan, and John Schulenberg. 2005. "Parent Beliefs and Children's Achievement Trajectories during the Transition to School in Asian American and European American Families." *International Journal of Behavioral Development*, 29, 6: 505–15.

Takaki, Ronald. 1989. *Strangers from a Different Shore: A History of Asian Americans*. New York: Penguin Books.

Takanishi, Ruby. 1978. "Childhood as a Social Issue: Historical Roots of Contemporary Child Advocacy Movements." *Journal of Social Issues*, 34, 2: 8–28.

Takei, Isao, and Arthur Sakamoto. 2008. "Do College-Educated, Native-Born Asian Americans Face a Glass Ceiling in Obtaining Managerial Authority?" *Asian American Policy Review*, 17: 73–85.

———. 2011. "Poverty among Asian Americans in the 21st Century." *Sociological Perspectives*, 54, 2: 251–76.

Taylor, Kate, and Motoko Rich. 2015, April 20. "Teachers' Unions Fight Standardized Testing, and Find Diverse Allies." *New York Times*. Retrieved from www.nytimes.com.

Teranishi, Robert. 2010. *Asians in the Ivory Tower: Dilemmas of Racial Inequality in American Higher Education*. New York: Teachers College Press.

Thangaraj, Stanley I. 2015. *Desi Hoop Dreams: Pickup Basketball and the Making of Asian American Masculinity*. New York: New York University Press.

———. 2015. "They Said 'Go Back to Afghanistan': South Asian American Basketball Culture and Challenging the 'Terrorist' Stereotype." *Amerasia Journal*, 41, 2: 25–46.

Thomas, William I., and Florian Znainiecki. 1918. *The Polish Peasant in Europe and America*. Boston: Gorham Press.

Thorne, Barrie. 2004. "The Crisis of Care." Pp. 165–78 in *Work-Family Challenges for Low-Income Parents and Their Children*, edited by Ann C. Crouter and Alan Booth. New York: Routledge.

Tierney, John. 2012, October 13. "AP Classes Are a Scam." *Atlantic*. Retrieved from www.theatlantic.com.

Tocci, Jason. 2009. "Geek Cultures: Media and Identity in the Digital Age." PhD diss., University of Pennsylvania.

Tran, Van C., and Nicol M. Valdez. 2017. "Second-Generation Decline or Advantage? Latino Assimilation in the Aftermath of the Great Recession." *International Migration Review*, 51, 1: 155–90.

Trask, Haunani Kay. 1991. "Lovely Hula Hands: Corporate Tourism and the Prostitution of Hawaiian Culture." *Contours (Bangkok)*, 5, 1: 8–14.

Trei, Lisa. 2005, April 20. "Study: Student Success Linked to Certification." *Stanford News*. Retrieved from www.news.stanford.edu.

TV by the Numbers. 2012, June 1. "2012 Scripps National Spelling Bee Final Is Most-View Ever on Cable Television." *TV by the Numbers*. Retrieved from https://tvbythenumbers.zap2it.com.

———. 2014, May 30. "Thursday Cable Ratings: NBA Conference Finals Win Night, 'Pawn Stars,' 'Loiter Squad,' 'The Challenge,' & More." *TV by the Numbers*. Retrieved from http://tvbythenumbers.zap2it.com.

Tyler, D. 1993. "Making Better Children." Pp. 35–60 in *Child and Citizen: Genealogies of Schooling and Subjectivity*. Brisbane: Griffith University Press.

US Census Bureau. n.d. "US Census Bureau, 2010–2014 American Community Survey 5-Year Estimates." *United States Census Bureau*. Retrieved from www.census.gov.

———. n.d. "US Census Bureau: State and County QuickFacts. Data Derived from Population Estimates, American Community Survey, Census of Population and Housing, State and County Housing Unit Estimates, County Business Patterns, Nonemployer Statistics, Economic Census, Survey of Business Owners, Building Permits." *United States Census Bureau*. Retrieved from www.census.gov.

———. 2014, December 9. "Nearly 6 Out of 10 Children Participate in Extracurricular Activities, Census Bureau Reports." *United States Census Bureau*. Retrieved from www.census.gov.

US Department of Education. 2012, September 7. "U.S. Secretary of Education Arne Duncan Recognizes 269 Schools as 2012 National Blue Ribbon Schools." *US Department of Education*. Retrieved from www.ed.gov.

———. 2013. "Choices for Parents." February 2. *US Department of Education*. Retrieved from www.ed.gov.

UT Dallas. 2018, September 24. "Scholar Offers Words of Wisdom in Mentoring Aspiring Spelling Champs." *UT Dallas*. Retrieved from www.utdallas.edu.

Vaisey, S. 2010. "What People Want: Rethinking Poverty, Culture, and Educational Attainment." *ANNALS of the American Academy of Political and Social Science*, 629, 1: 75–101.

Vallejo, Jody Agius. 2012. *Barrios to Burbs: The Making of the Mexican American Middle Class*. Stanford, CA: Stanford University Press.

Vargas, João H. Costa. 2018. *The Denial of Antiblackness: Multiracial Redemption and Black Suffering*. Minneapolis: University of Minnesota Press.

Verma, Suman, and Joyeeta Gupta. 1990. "Some Aspects of High Academic Stress and Symptoms." *Journal of Personality and Clinical Studies*, 6, 1: 7–12.

Vimeo. 2016. "Sylvan Learning of Savannah—'Mom Understands.'" *Vimeo*. Retrieved from www.vimeo.vom.

Vincent, Carol, and Stephen Ball. 2007. "'Making Up' the Middle-Class Child: Families, Activities and Class Dispositions." *Sociology*, 41, 6: 1061–77.

Vincent, Carol, and Claire Maxwell. 2016. "Parenting Priorities and Pressures: Furthering Understanding of 'Concerted Cultivation.'" *Discourse: Studies in the Cultural Politics of Education*, 37, 2: 269–81.

Vincent, Carol, Nicola Rollock, Stephen Ball, and David Gillborn. 2013. "Raising Middle-Class Black Children: Parenting Priorities, Actions and Strategies." *Sociology*, 47, 3: 427–42.

Wagner, Barry M., Robert E. Cole, and Paul Schwartzman. 1995. "Psychosocial Correlates of Suicide Attempts among Junior and Senior High School Youth." *American Association of Suicidology*, 25, 3: 358–72.

Waldinger, Roger, and Cynthia Feliciano. 2010. "Will the New Second Generation Experience 'Downward Assimilation'? Segmented Assimilation Re-assessed." *Ethnic and Racial Studies*, 27, 3: 376–402.

Walker, Stephen P. 2010. "Child Accounting and 'the Handling of Human Souls.'" *Accounting, Organizations and Society*, 35, 6: 628–57.

Wallace, Kelly. 2015, April 24. "Parents All over U.S. 'Opting Out' of Standardized Student Testing." *CNN*. Retrieved from www.cnn.com.

Warikoo, Natasha Kumar. 2011. *Balancing Acts: Youth Culture in the Global City*. Berkeley: University of California Press.

Washbrook, Elizabeth, Jane Waldfogel, Bruce Badbury, Miles Corak, and Ali Akbar Ghanghro. 2012. "The Development of Young Children of Immigrants in Australia, Canada, the United Kingdom and the United States." *Child Development*, 83, 5: 1591–607.

Washington, Robert E., and David Karen. 2001. "Sport and Society." *Annual Review of Sociology*, 27: 187–212.

Waters, M. 1999. *Black Identities*. Cambridge, MA: Harvard University Press.

Weeks, Kathi. 2011. *The Problem with Work: Feminism, Marxism, Antiwork Politics, and Postwork Imaginaries*. Durham, NC: Duke University Press.

Weiss, Heather, Priscilla Little, Suzanne Bouffard, Sarah Deschenes, and Helen Janc Malone. 2009. "Strengthen What Happens outside School to Improve What Happens Inside." *Phi Delta Kappan*, 90, 8: 592–96.

Whang, Patricia, and Gregory Hancock. 1994. "Motivation and Mathematics Achievement: Comparisons between Asian-American and Non-Asian Students." *Contemporary Educational Psychology*, 19, 3: 302–22.

Wiley, Terrence G. 2000. "Continuity and Change in the Function of Language Ideologies in the United States." Pp. 67–85 in *Ideology, Politics and Language Policies: Focus on English*, edited by Thomas Ricento. Amsterdam: John Benjamins.

Williams, Christine. 2006. *Inside Toyland: Working, Shopping, and Social Inequality*. Berkeley: University of California Press.

Wilson, Ernest J. 2008. "Hard Power, Soft Power, Smart Power." *ANNALS of the American Academy of Political and Social Science*, 616, 1: 110–24.

Wimmer, Andreas. 2008. "The Making and Unmaking of Ethnic Boundaries: A Multilevel Process Theory." *American Journal of Sociology*, 113, 4: 970–1022.

Wolk, Martin. 2005, August 4. "Tutoring Firms Stand to Gain from Ailing Schools." *NBC News*. Retrieved from www.nbcnews.com.

Wong, Alia. 2015, December. "The Bloated Rhetoric of No Child Left Behind's Demise." *Atlantic*. Retrieved from www.theatlantic.com.

Woo, S. B. 2012. "Discrimination Is Obvious." *New York Times*, December 19, 2012. Retrieved from www.nytimes.com.

Wood, Jennifer M. 2018, May 31. "25 Facts about the Scripps National Spelling Bee." *Mental Floss*. Retrieved from http://mentalfloss.com.

Woodard, Diann. 2013, August 6. "The Corporate Takeover of Public Education." *Huffington Post*. Retrieved from www.huffpost.com.

Woodland, Malcolm. 2008. "Whatcha Doin' after School? A Review of the Literature on the Influence of After-School Programs on Young Black Males." *Urban Education*, 43, 5: 537–60.

Wrigley, Julia, and Martin Carnoy. 1986. "Schooling and Work in the Democratic State." *Contemporary Sociology*, 15, 2: 248–49.

Wu, Chunxia, and Ruth Chao. 2011. "Intergenerational Cultural Dissonance in Parent-Adolescent Relationships among Chinese and European Americans." *Developmental Psychology*, 47, 2: 493–508.

Wu, Frank. 2003. *Yellow: Race in America beyond Black and White*. New York: Basic Books.

Wu, Shan. 2018, October 23. "Asian-Americans Should Be Angry about Allegations against Harvard." *CNN*. Retrieved from www.cnn.com.

Wun, Connie. 2016. "Unaccounted Foundations: Black Girls, Anti-Black Racism, and Punishment in Schools." *Critical Sociology* 42, 4–5: 737–50.

Xie, Yu, and Kimberly Goyette. 2003. "Social Mobility and the Educational Choices of Asian Americans." *Social Science Research*, 32, 3: 467–98.

Yeh, Christine, and Mayuko Inose. 2002. "Difficulties and Coping Strategies of Chinese, Japanese, and Korean Immigrant Students." *Adolescence*, 37, 145: 69.

Yi, Joseph. 2013. "Tiger Moms and Liberal Elephants: Private, Supplemental Education among Korean-Americans." *Society*, 50, 2: 190–95.

Yoshikawa, Hirokazu, Rashmita Mistry, and Yijie Wang. 2016. "Advancing Methods in Research on Asian American Children and Youth." *Child Development*, 87, 4: 1033–50.

Young, Bryan-Mitchell. 2014. "Frag: An Ethnographic Examination of Computer Gaming Culture and Identity at LAN Parties." PhD diss., Indiana University.

Zernike, Kate. 2011, May 13. "Fast-Tracking to Kindergarten." *New York Times*. Retrieved from www.nytimes.com.

Zhou, M., and C. Bankston. 1998. *Growing Up American: How Vietnamese Children Adapt to Life in the United States.* New York: Russell Sage Foundation.

Zhou, Min, and Susan Kim. 2006. "Community Forces, Social Capital, and Educational Achievement: The Case of Supplementary Education in the Chinese and Korean Immigrant Communities." *Harvard Educational Review*, 76, 1: 1–29.

Zhou, Min, and Xi-Yuan Li. 2003. "Ethnic Language Schools and the Development of Supplementary Education in the Immigrant Chinese Community in the United States." *New Directions for Student Leadership*, 2003, 100: 57–73.

Zhou, Qing, Nancy Eisenberg, Yun Wang, and Mark Reiser. 2004. "Chinese Children's Effortful Control and Dispositional Anger/Frustration: Relations to Parenting Styles and Children's Social Functioning." *Developmental Psychology*, 40, 3: 352–66.

Zong, Jie, and Jeanne Batalova. 2017, August 31. "Indian Immigrants in the United States." *Migration Policy Institute*. Retrieved from www.migrationpolicy.org.

# INDEX

academic bullying, 24–28, 44, 56, 89
academic competitions, 1–4, 7, 257; as "brain sports," 244–46; cost of, 201; friendship and, 221–25; negative effects of, 211–13. *See also* math competitions; spelling bees
academics: cultural meanings of, 126–27; as deprioritized by educators, 9; as deprioritized by schools, 141–43; as deprioritized by whites, 168–69, 212; hiding of achievements, 241, 248, 254; as prioritized by Asian Americans, 26–27, 100, 118, 131, 133, 168, 252; stigma of, 241–44
administrators, 46, 52, 265, 270, 271
affirmative action, 112–14, 293n31, 294nn35–36
African Americans, 154, 185–87, 252, 270, 294n52; immigrant, 295n19; school culture and, 237, 264, 271, 298n25; spelling bees and, 228, 297–98n4; sports and, 102, 231; stereotypes of, 3, 37, 44, 53–54, 258, 268
alcohol use, 31, 127, 132
antiblackness, 54, 154, 185–87, 268, 296n30
AP classes, 45, 98, 146, 159
Art of Problem Solving, 6, 69–70, 292n100
Asian Americans: competition success, 3–4, 6; as "model minority," 3, 103, 172–73, 255, 270–71, 285n30; praise of, by whites, 168, 262–63; racialization of, 14; seen as foreigners, 180, 228, 229, 232, 254, 262; seen as threat, 38; values and, 127–29, 133. *See also* Chinese Americans; Indian Americans; Korean Americans

assimilation, 14, 47, 57, 263; dangers of, 143, 144–45; downward, 152–55, 186, 268; fear of, 152–55; resistance to, 100, 124, 131, 169, 170, 243, 258, 268, 290n84; schools and, 264; spelling bees and, 248
authoritative parenting, 43

Barth, Frederick, 150–51
*Battle Hymn of the Tiger Mother* (Chua), 11, 150
belonging, 122, 241, 247, 267
Bill and Melinda Gates Foundation, 60–61, 148
binary: academics/sports, 104, 142, 171–72, 233–34; American/foreign, 231; proper/improper behavior, 255; respect/criticism, 229; safety/risk, 95, 126, 193, 258
biopolitics, 48, 293n18
body schema, 104
Bourdieu, Pierre, 184
boys, 230–31; academic stigma and, 241; sports and, 244; violence and, 129. *See also* masculinity
"brain sports," 244–46
*Breaking the Bee* (Rega and Weller), 84, 193
bullying, 54–55, 232, 235; academic, 24–28, 44, 56, 89
burnout, 22, 32, 101, 116, 213
buxiban spaces, 5

career capital, 109–10, 115
character building, 138–41, 145
charter schools, 59, 62, 266, 286n5
childhood, 50, 181; children's reflections on, 205; ideals of, 261; meaning of, 9, 67; "taking back" of, 9, 47, 88, 285n59

lives of, 205; societal pressure on, 218, 232–33; sports and, 244; values and, 128. *See also* femininity

hagwons, 5, 115, 151
helicopter parenting, 23, 99, 261, 285n59
"hidden curriculum," 44, 264
high-performing students, 62–66, 70–71, 73, 143; peer reactions to, 235
homework, 25, 72, 163–64; limiting of, 265; as too easy, 143, 159
"hothousing," 11
human capital, 67, 68, 69; hyper education as developing, 112, 141, 152, 212, 262; need for, 100, 124, 268; reliance on, 108, 109; values and, 168
humanism, 39–40, 118, 164–68, 178
hyper education: alternatives to, 264–67; competitiveness and, 95–96, 257; as concerted cultivation, 15–16, 184, 259; coolness and, 254; criticism of, 287n12; defense of, 215; definition of, 7–8; as fitting current trends, 66, 258–60; as foreign, 9, 14, 150–52, 257; identity and, 192, 269; implications of, 11–12; as institutional practice, 13–14; morals and, 15–16, 126, 155, 185–87, 252, 258, 268–69; motivations for, 10–11, 14–16, 108, 115, 183–87, 215–21, 267, 269–70; negative consequences of, 25, 241, 270; nonacademic benefits of, 246–47; as normal, 225–26; symbolism of, 181–83; as threat, 9

"immigrant mentality," 173, 175, 183
immigrants, 10, 55–56, 172–73; assimilation and, 47; background of, 6, 116–17; education levels of, 103, 116; narrative of, 247, 253; as pragmatic, 136; resentment toward, 228; scholarship on, 267; white, generations of, 175, 176, 181–83; white identification with, 173–75, 187
India, 10, 252–53; career options in, 118; education in, 63, 93–95, 98, 118, 290n84, 294nn41–42; history of, 103; sports in, 103, 104

Indian Americans: competitiveness of, 14–15, 85, 94–95, 97–99, 106, 124; confusion and, 213–14; ethnic connections and, 224; as hiding ethnicity, 243; as "model minority," 253; pride in heritage, 253; as pushing children, 178–79; racist criticism of, 227–28; seen as foreigners, 247; spelling bees and, 3, 41, 81, 84–85, 121–22, 292n106, 298n5; stereotypes of, 88
indigenous peoples, 266
inequality: academic, 45, 64; class, 64, 163, 260; economic, 67, 84, 261; educational, 8–9, 65–66, 75–76, 257–58; racial, 269
international schools, 63, 159–60, 168

Junior Kumon, 6, 70

keeping up, 9, 24, 27–28, 39, 115, 118
Khan, Salman, 61–62, 148, 288n27
Khan Academy, 61, 288n27
Kimble, Paige, 84, 298n5
kindergarten, 30, 96
Korean Americans, 3–4, 5, 115, 151; parenting styles, 43
Kumon, 4, 69–70, 72, 74, 210

Latinxs, 154, 264, 270; school culture and, 237, 271, 298n25; stereotypes of, 3, 44
learning centers, 4, 7, 59, 69–77, 97, 140, 257, 285n26; business model, 74–76; classroom learning and, 32; franchises, 74–76; pedagogical model, 76–77; as private school proxies, 157; school performance and, 163–64. *See also* math centers
LGBTQ students, 31, 54–55
liberalism, 69–70
lived hybridity, 299n37

mainstream media, 72, 216, 254, 271; Asian American depictions in, 16, 229–31; pressure from, 235; spelling bees and, 80, 290n80, 291n90. *See also* ESPN
masculinity, 103, 230–31, 299nn37–38

## ABOUT THE AUTHOR

**Pawan Dhingra** is a professor at Amherst College and a multiple award-winning author. He also is a former museum curator at the Smithsonian Institution. His work has been profiled and published in various outlets, including the *New York Times*, National Public Radio, the *Guardian*, *Colorlines*, *Times of India*, and more. He has held tenured positions at Tufts University and Oberlin College.

Made in United States
North Haven, CT
25 August 2022

23232596R00211